# HEALING

## *Thoughts*

quotes, poems and musings

by Ryan Puusaari

# DEDICATION

# WELCOME

If you're holding this book, it's a small miracle. *Healing Thoughts* is a testament to defiance, a work that, by all accounts, shouldn't exist.

From the outset, the odds were stacked against it.

Born from a journey marked by setbacks and disbelief, this book is a celebration of perseverance.

I'm Ryan Puusaari, stepping out from the shadows as your ally on a journey filled with introspection and humble wisdom, traversing the complex maze that is life.

My path to becoming a writer was twisted, looping like a pretzel.

I've always had my struggles, both socially and professionally. I've dealt with childhood trauma, anxiety, and depression. I failed Grade 12 English. I've been fired from jobs, I watched a business I built from the ground up crumble to nothing, I owned a home, twice, and then lost everything, twice, winding up homeless.

Yet, here we are—I stand before you, book in hand.

Surprise! Defying rigid expectations and well-worn paths, I've made it.

This book is not your average self-help manual.

It's a revolt.

A daring venture into the dark to snatch hope from the jaws of despair.

This book originated from a flurry of daily texts sent to an amazing community eager for a dose of hope each day.[1] Over the years, these messages have built a robust foundation of inspiration and resilience.

Initially, the goal was simply to gather my favorite quotes into one place, but the project quickly grew into something more significant and meaningful.

This book has become a rich blend of motivational messages and deep poetic thoughts. Each page crafted to not only provide comfort but also to fortify and elevate the spirit.

## Now, pause for a moment.

Do you sense the book's weight in your hands?

That feeling of the cover's texture, the excitement for the anticipation of the words inside—it's all part of our plot.

Feel the pages beneath your fingers, the crisp sound they produce as you flip them. Each word, each line is an act of rebellion against the monochrome backdrop of conformity.

Imagine a world where every *no* is a stepping-stone, every rejection a redirection.

That's the world this book has navigated.

It's not just a collection of pages; it's a symbol of resilience.

Against the backdrop of doubt, your hands now cradle a story that refused to be silenced.

I invite you to share your thoughts on this unexpected journey.

Your review is more than just feedback; it's a ray of hope for others who seek comfort in these words. It's a reminder that the underdog story isn't just a trope—it's a reality for those who dare to dream.

---

1. If you wish to connect with like-minded individuals, or if you're simply curious to learn more, you're invited to join our community. Visit RyanPuusaari.com to connect and discover how you can be part of this thriving group that finds joy and support in our shared daily messages.

As a self-published author, I'm plunging headfirst into the deep, sometimes daunting sea of storytelling. Please, help me disturb the waters, create ripples, and perhaps, just perhaps, *even create a wave.*

If a flicker of recognition lights up within you, if you find yourself nodding in silent agreement, or if the words within this book ignite joy in anyway, *why keep it to yourself?*

Your review isn't merely feedback; it's a signal, lighting up the night sky, guiding others on their own quests for meaning and healing.

Thank you for joining this adventure, for unraveling the essence of my story, and for considering the idea of leaving your own, distinctive mark by leaving a review at the retailer of your choice.

## Your voice, your viewpoint, is invaluable.

Together, we're not just leafing through a set of pages; we're beginning on a journey of growth, rebellion, and the hint of hope for brighter days just over the horizon.

*See you on the inside.*

# Word on the Street

"I don't know if you get these texts.

I'm too old and out of the loop to figure out websites and whatever you said we needed to do to let you know what these texts mean to us. So I'll say it here, knowing you probably won't even see it. But I'll have said it.

They saved my life.

They save my life every day. Every fcking day. Thank you."

_ele_

"Thank you!!! love the positivity you spread!
The world needs people like you more than ever!!"

*"It's crazy how you know exactly what I'm thinking about when you send these texts."*

"Btw. Thank you for these. Every day..I know u may not understand... but most the time they come at the perfect time."

*"maybe all I needed to make it one more day... thank you"*

"I really needed this right now.
Thank you. you just saved my life I'm serious"

*"Thank you!!! I love the positivity you spread! The world needs people like you more than ever!!"*

"You're an amazing person! Thank you for texting me everyday Ryan!! Makes me realize I can make it everyday and that means so much to me—thank you"

*"You enlighten my soul everyday just being you, your journey really hits a special place with me!! You have made me realize I can do this, it won't be easy, but i can do it. Thank you for each and everything you do Ryan i really do appreciate you"*

"I want to thank you from the bottom of my heart Ryan for these daily text messages. You have absolutely no idea how much they have meant to me and how much they have helped me. Even on my darkest day I smile when they come through."

*"Thank you. These messages have been life saving in such a dark place."*

"I appreciate you and your daily texts more then I can even put into words. Some days I feel invisible as a single mother with two jobs ad then I get your messages and I smile."

*"Honestly, these little daily messages are something I look forward to. I know it can be difficult if you're not feeling amazing yourself, so I want to let you know that I am grateful to share spins with you on this planet."*

"You give hope in a world that has given up on hope."

**"The curious paradox is that when I accept myself just as I am, then I can change."**

—Carl R. Rogers, On Becoming a Person (1961)

Embrace your hot mess and watch it transform into a masterpiece. Acceptance is the first step to fabulousness!

# CONTENTS

# Purpose and Expectations

## A Glimpse into Healing Thoughts

W ELCOME TO *HEALING THOUGHTS*. This is more than a book. It's a journey in words. A blend of experiences, emotions, and insights. Crafted to comfort and guide.

It connects you with your inner world. An exploration of finding yourself.

## Purpose of This Book

This book shares the beginning of my story—from deep despair to healing. It turns tough challenges into strength and wisdom.

### Here's what it offers:

- **Comfort:** Words that will touch your heart—bringing understanding in hard times.

- **Healing Inspiration:** My story serving as a reflection for anyone healing from their past.

- **Self-Discovery:** The opportunity to explore your own story—understanding your darkness and your light.

- **Connection:** It highlights our shared human experiences and connection.

## What to Expect

Inside *Healing Thoughts* you'll find:

- **Personal Stories:** Insights into my own life. From initial childhood struggles to finding my path after hitting rock bottom.

- **Inspirational Quotes:** Powerful quotes from my daily text's community.[1] Each comes with reflections for deeper insight.

- **Community Voices:** Stories from our daily text community—showcasing diverse journeys of healing.

- **Practical Guidance:** Insights for coping and growing—please note though: this is a companion for your journey, not a therapy replacement.

*Healing Thoughts* invites you on an adventure.

It's about overcoming your struggles and finding your light. It connects you with others on similar paths.

Within these pages, you will find words that resonate and inspire.

Welcome this journey of healing and self-discovery.

**Open your heart and mind.**

Let *Healing Thoughts* guide you to inner peace and renewed strength.

---

1. Ryan shares daily messages of hope and healing with a community across the USA and Canada, offering inspiration and support through each text. To discover more about this heartfelt service, explore RyanPuusaari.com.

# INTRODUCTION

Alone in my car, homeless, I managed to stumble upon a spark of hope. In these moments of introspection, I laid the groundwork for *Healing Thoughts*—a journey that transformed me from a state of despair to becoming a symbol of determination for many.

This story isn't about my personal growth—it is about the connections we all share and the indomitable spirit within each of us. This book is a testament to transitioning from feelings of isolation to standing united as a community bonded in solidarity.

*It signifies stepping out of darkness and into the brightness of unity.*

I am so happy that you found these pages.

There is a surreal sense of excitement in the air as I think about our two souls being able to connect through time and space, no matter where you are or even when you are. There is such satisfaction in knowing that our paths can cross through the power of the written word.

As I try to imagine the hands these pages will find themselves in, it almost feels magical. The realization that we can share this moment—just me and you.

But before we get too intimate here, I should properly introduce myself—

Hi. I'm Ryan Puusaari.

This book is more than my story. It's an exploration of healing, hope, and growth for every person who finds comfort in my texts.

*It's our shared story, a blend of all our voices.*

My life was tough—a broken home, childhood neglect, drug addition, poverty and countless betrayals. The breaking point was an affair that shattered my heart. It left me homeless and alone in my car. There, under the moon, I released my frustrations into my journal. Each word was a step toward healing.

Within those pages, I found strength I didn't know I had.

The daily text community[1] was conceived on those lonely nights.

Inspired by my once-busy phone, now in a constant state of silence, I began to ask myself...

*"Why do I even have this thing?"*

I knew there must be others out there who felt the same way.

Knowing the comfort a simple message could bring, I wanted to reach out to them.

So, I began sending daily messages.

They were filled with hope and empathy. Each message was a light in the darkness—an offer of comfort and understanding.

*The responses were incredible!*

Every reply showed our shared struggles, our search for meaning, and our need for connection. People from all walks of life responded, sharing their stories and finding hope in my words.

---

1. Ryan sends out daily text messages filled with hope and healing to a community across Canada and the USA. To learn more about this inspiring service, visit RyanPuusaari.com.

What began as a thought quickly turned into a community. We became a family, not through blood but through healing and sharing.

This book is more than just quotes—it's a Pandora's box of possibilities.

One where we explore life's ups and downs, the lessons learned along the way, and offer support for those going through challenging times.

The first ten chapters act as a brief introduction to my story.

They cover my initial struggles during childhood, my awakening in my mid-30s after my life fell apart, and how this book came to be. You'll read about how and why I started a daily text community, ventured onto TikTok, and began creating journals.

This isn't just a chronicle of some life events.

*This is about change.*

**It shows how we can grow and rise once we genuinely decide to.**

Where my story ends, the heart of the book begins.

The following twenty chapters bring you quotes, reflections, and thoughtful questions.

These aren't just simple messages. These are deep thoughts that have significantly moved people in our community. They've sparked reflection and helped us to understand ourselves better.

Each one is a guide and a reminder. We're all in this together.

As you read through these pages, remember that you're not alone. You are part of a community that cares.

*That understands.*

We're all searching for acceptance.

*Healing Thoughts* is more than words. It's your companion in tough times.

It's hope for when you're feeling down.

*This book shows that there's a promise of light and comfort even in the darkness.*

# In the Beginning

## Early Life and Background

"The ache for home lives in all of us, the safe place where we can go as we are and not be questioned."
—Maya Angelou, All God's Children Need Traveling Shoes (1986)

I WAS BORN INTO a world that was far different from the carefree childhoods we often imagine. My earliest memories revolve around living in a small apartment dominated by my father's absent presence. His focus was divided between work and alcohol, leading to an unreliable demeanor.

The environment I grew up in was more about-facing challenges than enjoying life.

Being an only child left me feeling isolated within the walls of our home.[1] The air was filled with a heaviness from words unspoken. What should have been a cheerful household, instead became an observer of my father's frustrations and the silence that followed his outbursts. The walls, adorned with his tobacco stains alongside my unwel-

---

1. Being an only child or experiencing isolation in childhood can have long-term effects on social development and mental health. See: Polit, D. F., & Falbo, T. (1987). Only children and personality development: A quantitative review. *Journal of Marriage and the Family*, 49(2), 309-325.

comed crayon drawings, reflected this neglect—representing the solitude and unease that characterized my days.

Tension lingered, constantly casting an unpleasant atmosphere over every corner of our home. It affected me deeply, reminding me to tread lightly at all times. I would move cautiously, pretending that I was a ninja or cat, gliding silently through our apartment with precision. This wasn't merely a child at play; it had become my way of self-preservation—a desperate attempt to avoid disrupting the fragile peace that hung precariously in the balance.[2]

**"Loneliness and the feeling of being unwanted is the most terrible poverty."**
- Mother Teresa, Nobel Peace Prize Acceptance Speech, 1979

Loneliness became a companion never far from my side.[3]

The quietness in our apartment wasn't the comforting kind; it felt like an emptiness, lacking connection and warmth. The dining table, meant for family gatherings, instead highlighted our disconnection.[4] I often dined alone—my dad, would be occasionally present there but lost in his own troubles.

At night, the house took on a different persona. The shadows stretched longer and darker, reflecting the loneliness I experienced. My tiny room, with one small window nestled in a corner, became my sanctuary. Surrounded by books and drawings, I found refuge in my imagination—creating worlds and sketching visions of a future for my father and I that was far different than our current reality.

---

2. Emotional neglect in childhood can lead to difficulties in forming secure attachments and managing emotions in adulthood. See: Webb, N. B. (2007). *The impact of trauma on child development.* In N. B. Webb (Ed.), *Working with traumatized youth in child welfare* (pp. 21-36). Guilford Press.

3. The lack of family connection and warmth can contribute to feelings of loneliness and emotional distress. See: Repetti, R. L., Taylor, S. E., & Seeman, T. E. (2002). Risky families: Family social environments and the mental and physical health of offspring. *Psychological Bulletin*, 128(2), 330-366.

4. Children of alcoholics often face unique challenges, including an increased risk of developing emotional problems and substance abuse issues later in life. See: Kelley, M. L., & Fals-Stewart, W. (2002). Children of alcoholics: The impact of parental substance abuse on psychosocial development. *Substance Use & Misuse*, 37(11), 1429-1448.

These activities weren't simple pastimes, they were my escape—a place where I felt secure.[5]

## A World Beyond the Walls

My school, supposed to be a place of fun and learning—quickly turned out to be another environment I didn't feel safe in.

At the age of six, a time when I should have been enjoying first-grade adventures—I instead found myself face-to-face with some pretty nasty bullying from my fellow classmates.[6]

The classroom, which at first felt lively, decorated with bright posters and cheerful alphabet displays, now felt cold and unwelcoming. The neatly arranged desks only emphasized the loneliness I felt. Instead of the joyous atmosphere it should have had, school filled me with fear. The playground, meant for fun under the sun, only brought me worry and dread.

Every school day seemed more like a challenge than an escape from home. In place of playful yelling and laughter, I faced mean comments and teasing from the other children. The bullying at school added to the struggles I faced at home, making me feel vulnerable wherever I went.[7]

Then came the day that changed everything for me—confirming all my fears in a single moment.

---

5. For children facing adversity, imagination and creative activities can serve as important coping mechanisms. See: Singer, J. L., & Singer, D. G. (1990). The house of make-believe: Children's play and the developing imagination. Harvard University Press.

6. Bullying in early childhood can have significant impacts on mental health and social development. See: Arseneault, L., Bowes, L., & Shakoor, S. (2010). Bullying victimization in youths and mental health problems: 'Much ado about nothing'? *Psychological Medicine*, 40(5), 717-729.

7. The cumulative effect of bullying and home stress can exacerbate feelings of vulnerability and anxiety in children. See: Lereya, S. T., Copeland, W. E., Costello, E. J., & Wolke, D. (2015). Adult mental health consequences of peer bullying and maltreatment in childhood: Two cohorts in two countries. *The Lancet Psychiatry*, 2(6), 524-531.

## The Day That Solidified My Reclusiveness

**"Trauma creates change you don't choose. Healing is about creating change you do choose."**
—Michelle Rosenthal, Heal Your PTSD (2015)

The school bell rang, signaling the arrival of Halloween festivities. Laughter echoed through the halls as children in costumes paraded around, bringing an air of excitement. The walls decorated with hand-crafted pumpkins and ghosts added to the atmosphere.

Dressed in a devilish costume sporting a red cape, horns and a plastic pitchfork, I joined in the fun alongside my peers.

The schoolyard transformed into a sea of colors as superheroes and monsters came to life through the lens of childhood imagination. The scent of candy danced through the air, mingling with the sounds of laughter that hinted at a day filled with amusement.

However, among the cheerfulness a dark undercurrent was beginning to rise to the surface.

As I walked through the schoolyard, my eyes made contact with a familiar group—the tormentors who had been making my school days unbearable. Their faces light up with excitement when they saw me, but it was not the kind that matched the days energy—there was a malevolent gleam that flickered in their eyes as they fixed their gaze on me with predatory intent.[8]

A shiver ran down my spine as they stepped towards me, overshadowing the jovial sounds around us. Tension hung heavy in the air, intensifying my escalating anxiety and causing the decorations to blend into a blur as my heart began to pound erratically. Paralyzed

---

8. The anticipation of bullying can trigger a physiological stress response, heightening anxiety and fear. See: Vaillancourt, T., Hymel, S., & McDougall, P. (2013). The biological underpinnings of peer victimization: Understanding why and how the effects of bullying can last a lifetime. *Theory into Practice*, 52(4), 241-248.

by fear and the feeling of vulnerability, what started as a day brimming with excitement morphed into one fraught with apprehension in a matter of seconds.

As they approached me, reality sank in.

I found myself in a situation that was a far cry from the normally playful tricks and treats of Halloween. I was on the brink of a sentencing without trail that would forever test my beliefs about relationships and trust.

Then without warning, one of the boys clenched his hand.

Time seemed to slow down as his fist came towards me—each millisecond feeling like an eternity. Then the punch landed. The impact was jarring. The pain that followed matched the hostility in his eyes.

My body surrendered to the force of the blow, and I collapsed to the ground.

The world spun around me as I tried to make sense of what had transpired. While lying there shook and hurt, they continued their assault.

A storm of kicks descended upon me.

Their laughter was icy and heartless. The pain was excruciating.

But it was the sense of helplessness in that moment that truly shook me.

This wasn't a game; it had turned into a violent ordeal—a stark lesson in the cruelty lurking within others.[9]

Then, in a final act of horror, one of the boys grabbed my plastic pitchfork from the ground. Our gazes met briefly as he lifted the pitchfork above his head. In that instant, a sinister darkness manifested before me—seemingly transcending our years. A wicked grin spread across his face as he brought down the pitchfork, striking my eye with precision. My sight blurred into swirling shades of red and black, a pool of blood forming around me. Shock and disbelief washed over me as I struggled to comprehend the horror. My reality had become a nightmare—one I couldn't escape from. Desperate cries for help pierced the air as fear gripped my heart with the thought of losing my sight.

---

9. Experiences of physical assault can have profound psychological effects, including the development of post-traumatic stress disorder (PTSD). See: Kilpatrick, D. G., Saunders, B. E., & Smith, D. W. (2003). Youth victimization: Prevalence and implications. *NIJ Research in Brief*. National Institute of Justice.

This harrowing moment shattered my world violently, leaving me feeling exposed and defenseless. It drove me deeper into isolation, constructing walls around my soul to shield myself from pain.[10]

From that day on, opening up to others would forever be a chore—entering my life would no longer be an easy task.

I transformed myself into a figure cloaked in an aura of unapproachability, masking my vulnerabilities in a desperate attempt to protect myself from further suffering.[11]

## The Formation of Shadows

My early years were quite challenging. Those experiences, filled with obstacles, deeply influenced me. There are so many more I could share but that's not the point of this book. You can always read more in my newsletter, at *HealingThoughts.com*.

> **"We cannot change anything unless we accept it. Condemnation does not liberate, it oppresses."**
> -Carl Jung, Modern Man in Search of a Soul (1933)

Reflecting on the past, I now realize how I used defense mechanisms such as repression, denial, and projection to shield myself from pain.[12] However, this approach also led to

---

10. The experience of trauma can lead to social withdrawal and isolation as a coping mechanism. See: Charuvastra, A., & Cloitre, M. (2008). Social bonds and posttraumatic stress disorder. *Annual Review of Psychology*, 59, 301-328.

11. Traumatic experiences can result in changes to one's sense of self and interpersonal relationships. See: Herman, J. L. (1992). *Trauma and recovery*. Basic Books.

12. Defense mechanisms are psychological strategies used to protect oneself from anxiety or unacceptable thoughts and feelings. See: Cramer, P. (2000). Defense mechanisms in psychology today. *American Psychologist*, 55(6), 637-646.

shadows masking my emotions. These unresolved shadows impacted my relationships and decisions, often resulting in difficulties and self-destructive behavior.[13]

The neighborhood where I spent my childhood played a role in shaping who I am.

It was a place where the harsh realities of life were starkly evident. Showing vulnerability was considered a weakness, so I learned to conceal my feelings and put on a façade to blend in. This became my survival strategy within the street culture.[14]

It influenced my inner world as well. Juggling between staying true to myself and meeting others' expectations proved challenging.[15]

These childhood issues persisted unnoticed, causing me to repeat patterns throughout my life. It wasn't until my mid-thirties, when my life fell apart, leaving me homeless, that I finally woke up to these tendencies. It was then, that all of my pain and problems would be abruptly forced to the surface—leaving me with no choice but to face these long-ignored emotional challenges.[16]

---

13. Unresolved emotional issues, or "shadows," can lead to difficulties in relationships and decision-making. See: Jung, C. G. (1951). *Aion: Researches into the Phenomenology of the Self*. Princeton University Press.

14. The environment and culture of one's childhood neighborhood can have a significant impact on their development and coping strategies. See: Leventhal, T., & Brooks-Gunn, J. (2000). The neighborhoods they live in: The effects of neighborhood residence on child and adolescent outcomes. *Psychological Bulletin*, 126(2), 309-337.

15. The struggle to balance authenticity with societal expectations can be a source of internal conflict. See: Higgins, E. T. (1987). Self-discrepancy: A theory relating self and affect. *Psychological Review*, 94(3), 319-340.

16. Hitting "rock bottom" can often serve as a catalyst for confronting and addressing long-standing emotional issues. See: Dodes, L. M., & Khantzian, E. J. (2004). Using the concept of the "near miss" in understanding the process of hitting bottom and seeking help for addiction. *Journal of Psychoactive Drugs*, 36(1), 49-55.

# Blessings in Disguise

## Echoes of a Shattered Love

**"The hottest love has the coldest end."**
—Socrates, Lives of Eminent Philosophers (translated 1925)

I N MY MID-THIRTIES, EVERYTHING took a turn. Love seemed to slip, and betrayal entered the picture. The youthful, care-free love of my days began to dim as the routines of life consumed us.

The weight of our duties became burdensome.[1]

My spouse and I, who had once crafted a life overflowing with aspirations and joy, gradually drifted apart. We became strangers sharing the same space. The intimacy that used to permeate our home now lingered as a distant memory, leaving behind an unsettling void where our connection once thrived.[2] The laughter that used to echo within its walls had vanished, replaced by a silence that mirrored the growing chasm between us. Each room,

---

1. The accumulation of routine responsibilities can lead to a sense of burden and strain in relationships. See: Doss, B. D., Rhoades, G. K., Stanley, S. M., & Markman, H. J. (2009). The effect of the transition to parenthood on relationship quality: An 8-year prospective study. *Journal of Personality and Social Psychology*, 96(3), 601-619.

2. Gradual emotional detachment in a relationship can lead to feelings of alienation and loneliness. See: Weiss, R. S. (1973). Loneliness: The experience of emotional and social isolation. MIT Press.

once alive with our affection, now felt desolate, its walls reflecting the harsh realities of our circumstances.[3]

The atmosphere was heavy with unspoken words and unmet needs.

That period in my life, proved challenging, ultimately signaling the conclusion of our marriage.[4]

## In the Aftermath of Loss

After my divorce, I found myself standing alone in the quiet of what used to be our home. The stillness weighed heavily on me, serving as a reminder of my family's downfall. The cheerful hallways now only haunted with memories, each room's emptiness reflecting my sense of isolation.[5]

*My heart ached with sorrow.*

Feeling empty and alone, I sought comfort in cannabis.[6] It became my way of escaping the reality that surrounded me. The temporary numbness offered relief from the constant ache that dwelled in my heart.

During this period of sadness, where each day blurred into the next and hope seemed distant, something unexpected occurred—an old friend reentered my life. She brought a glimmer of possibility—a chance for something new after the divorce. Being with her

---

3. The loss of laughter and joy in a household can be indicative of underlying relational issues. See: Gottman, J. M., & Levenson, R. W. (1992). Marital processes predictive of later dissolution: Behavior, physiology, and health. *Journal of Personality and Social Psychology*, 63(2), 221-233.

4. Unaddressed emotional needs and lack of communication can contribute to the dissolution of a marriage. See: Amato, P. R., & Previti, D. (2003). People's reasons for divorcing: Gender, social class, the life course, and adjustment. *Journal of Family Issues*, 24(5), 602-626.

5. The silence and emptiness of a once-shared home can amplify feelings of loneliness and loss after a divorce. See: Kposowa, A. J. (2000). Marital status and suicide in the National Longitudinal Mortality Study. *Journal of Epidemiology & Community Health*, 54(4), 254-261.

6. Cannabis is often used as a coping mechanism for emotional pain, providing temporary relief from distressing feelings. See: Hyman, S. M., & Sinha, R. (2009). Stress-related factors in cannabis use and misuse: Implications for prevention and treatment. *Journal of Substance Abuse Treatment*, 36(4), 400-413.

filled the void left by my failed marriage. Her words and laughter seemed to alleviate my pain, providing a sense of comfort and understanding.

It felt like I had found someone to lean on—who saw me for who I really was, not just the broken person I had become.[7]

## The Illusion of a New Beginning

Our love story began with joy and excitement. We appeared to be a perfect match.

> **"The greatest deception men suffer is from their own opinions."**
> —Leonardo da Vinci, Thoughts on Art and Life (1906)

She showered me with constant affection, making me feel like the most important person in her world. Her words touched my heart in ways I had never experienced before, making me believe I was her everything—her sun, moon, and stars. During those moments, every action of hers seemed to resonate within me, drawing me closer to her. Her presence captivated me and convinced me that this bond was the epitome of love.

However, as our relationship progressed and I moved in with her, things took a turn. The endearing displays of affection started becoming suffocating and controlling. The overwhelming love and attention that initially made me feel cherished now felt like a constraint; freedom gave way to dependence. What was once a connection gradually transformed into something I didn't recognize from those happy early days.

Beneath the surface, a darker truth lurked.

She was not only manipulating me, but my friends and family as well. With a sweet smile and gentle words, she began to damage my reputation, planting seeds of doubt amongst

---

7. Finding someone who understands and accepts you can be crucial for emotional recovery and rebuilding one's sense of self after a significant loss. See: Bowlby, J. (1980). *Attachment and loss: Vol. 3. Loss: Sadness and depression.* Basic Books.

my peers. This cunning tactic isolated me, ensuring that my loyalty remained with her and her alone.[8]

This toxic shift resembled falling into an illusion of affection—a trap disguised as love.[9]

**"In the end, we will remember not the words of our enemies, but the silence of our friends."**
—Martin Luther King Jr., often attributed to King

My attempt to heal from the pain of shattered dreams and to mend my broken heart was fruitless. Instead of finding comfort, I found myself entangled in a relationship that slowly led to my downfall. The woman who once symbolized hope for me gradually transformed into a controlling figure, leaving me dependent, and under her influence.[10]

By this point my radar was on full alert. I could see the writing on the wall with the control tactics and was looking for anything suspicious when a darker truth came out. The sudden end to text conversations upon my arrival in the room and the discovery of an email account linked to dating sites shattered the illusion of what I believed was genuine.[11]

It was a shocking truth that pierced right through my heart and into my soul.

I descended into a rabbit hole of betrayal and sorrow. I found myself alone, engulfed in bitterness and disillusionment. Everything I thought I had grasped about love crumbled,

---

8. Manipulative behaviors in relationships can lead to isolation and control, damaging one's social support network. See: Stark, E. (2007). *Coercive Control: How Men Entrap Women in Personal Life.* Oxford University Press.

9. The concept of an "illusion of affection" refers to a situation where perceived love is actually a form of manipulation or control. See: Simon, G. K. (1996). *In Sheep's Clothing: Understanding and Dealing with Manipulative People.* A. J. Christopher & Company.

10. The gradual realization of manipulation and control in a relationship can be a painful and disillusioning experience. See: Forward, S., & Frazier, D. (1997). *Emotional Blackmail: When the People in Your Life Use Fear, Obligation, and Guilt to Manipulate You.* HarperCollins.

11. Discovering deceit or infidelity can be a turning point in recognizing the true nature of a relationship. See: Shackelford, T. K., & Buss, D. M. (1997). Cues to infidelity. *Personality and Social Psychology Bulletin*, 23(10), 1034-1045.

leaving me homeless in my car with nothing but shattered aspirations and unfulfilled promises.[12]

## Solitude in the City

As I sat behind the wheel of my car, the silence felt deafening, starkly contrasting the once lively conversations that normally filled the air. My vehicle, which used to be a symbol of our shared adventures together, now only mirrored my despair. The empty passenger seat, once her place, was now a constant reminder of her betrayal.

Night after night, I slept in my car—alone in a world that felt both huge and suffocatingly small. Parked beneath a city streetlamp, my car became my refuge, a temporary escape from the painful reality I was forced to confront.

Peering through the windshield, the familiar streets and structures seemed foreign, belonging to a different chapter of life. The engine's hum and the wipers' rhythmic swish, once a backdrop to our laughter, now underscored my contemplations.[13]

The affair that plunged me into this darkness was a blur of deceit, a blow that shattered my existence. The person I trusted, with whom I shared my dreams and aspirations with, had betrayed that trust, leaving behind a trail of wreckage. Amid these shattered promises, I grappled with an overwhelming sense of emptiness.

*The betrayal felt like a funeral for that one last part of me that had still clung onto the hope of finding love unconditionally.*[14]

---

12. The aftermath of a manipulative and controlling relationship can leave one feeling betrayed, disillusioned, and alone. See: Herman, J. L. (1992). *Trauma and Recovery: The Aftermath of Violence--From Domestic Abuse to Political Terror*. Basic Books.

13. Familiar environments can take on a different meaning and evoke a sense of alienation after a significant life event. See: Fullilove, M. T. (1996). Psychiatric implications of displacement: Contributions from the psychology of place. *American Journal of Psychiatry*, 153(12), 1516-1523.

14. The experience of betrayal can feel like a loss of a part of oneself and the death of cherished hopes. See: Gobodo-Madikizela, P. (2018). *A Human Being Died That Night: A South African Story of Forgiveness*. Houghton Mifflin Harcourt.

This bond was more than a relationship; it had become a piece of my identity. I had opened up to her in ways I had never opened up to anyone before. I shared my deepest aspirations and fears, only to have that trust shattered—those dreams and anxieties used against me in malicious attacks of manipulation. It wasn't just a relationship that ended; it was a part of me that was lost.[15]

However, deep within, this situation had awakened something—*and it was screaming to be recognized, listened to, and understood.*[16]

---

15. Sharing one's deepest self in a relationship only to be betrayed can result in a profound sense of loss and identity crisis. See: Erikson, E. H. (1959). *Identity and the Life Cycle.* International Universities Press.

16. Traumatic experiences can trigger a process of self-discovery and transformation. See: Tedeschi, R. G., & Calhoun, L. G. (2004). Posttraumatic growth: Conceptual foundations and empirical evidence. *Psychological Inquiry,* 15(1), 1-18.

# Vulnerability Ventures

## Reflections of a Shattered Heart

**"Sometimes good things fall apart so better things can fall together."**

—Marilyn Monroe, often attributed to Monroe

A FTER MY RELATIONSHIP ENDED, it felt as if my heart had shattered like a mirror, each fragment serving as a reminder of what was once whole. These scattered pieces within me resembled a dismantled puzzle reflecting back a mix of emotions—love twisted into pain, trust eroded into doubt, and dreams warped into haunting realities. It was almost like I could feel these sharp pieces inside me, mirroring the turmoil of emotions I was going through.[1]

As I sifted through these shards, memories of our time resurfaced, now tainted with betrayal. Some things became more apparent, while others remained enigmatic. Joyful moments now carried a tinge. A gentle touch that once brought comfort now evoked a

---

1. The physical sensation of emotional pain is a phenomenon known as psychosomatic pain, where psychological distress manifests as physical discomfort. See: Lumley, M. A., Cohen, J. L., Borszcz, G. S., Cano, A., Radcliffe, A. M., Porter, L. S., Schubiner, H., & Keefe, F. J. (2011). Pain and emotion: A biopsychosocial review of recent research. *Journal of Clinical Psychology*, 67(9), 942-968.

chill down my spine. The shared smiles and affectionate laughter we once shared, now seemed like scenes from an old movie where I was just a naive participant.[2]

## Anxiety Made Me Its Bitch

During all the chaos of my life post-breakup, anxiety—an old constant friend of mine, transformed into something much more menacing than its usual self. It had always lingered in the background as a voice in my mind. But now it loomed larger and more foreboding than ever before.

It felt as though the earth had suddenly cracked open, releasing a haunting manifestation of my deepest fears.[3]

> **"Anxiety is the dizziness of freedom."**
> —Søren Kierkegaard, The Concept of Anxiety (1844)

This fresh wave of anxiety was all-encompassing.

The atmosphere seemed denser, saturated with a sense of dread that made each step feel laborious, almost like I was trudging through mud. Familiar surroundings now appeared alien and unwelcoming, as if this ominous force had seeped into every corner of my world.[4]

---

2. The process of revisiting memories after a betrayal can alter one's perception of past events, casting them in a different light and revealing previously unnoticed aspects. See: Baumeister, R. F., & Newman, L. S. (1994). How stories make sense of personal experiences: Motives that shape autobiographical narratives. *Personality and Social Psychology Bulletin*, 20(6), 676-690.

3. The intensification of anxiety can be triggered by significant life events, leading to a heightened state of alertness and fear. See: Andrews, G., & Slade, T. (2002). Agoraphobia without a history of panic disorder may be part of the panic disorder syndrome. *Journal of Nervous and Mental Disease*, 190(9), 624-630.

4. Anxiety can alter one's perception of their environment, making familiar settings feel unfamiliar and threatening. See: Bar-Haim, Y., Lamy, D., Pergamin, L., Bakermans-Kranenburg, M. J., & van IJzendoorn, M. H. (2007). Threat-related attentional bias in anxious and nonanxious individuals: A meta-analytic study. *Psychological Bulletin*, 133(1), 1-24.

This wasn't just a quiet, annoying feeling anymore. My anxiety had become a dominating force, a loud noise in my head—a mix of fears and doubts that overpowered all my other thoughts.

Anxiety held me captive, asserting its control over me. It reduced me to its mercy. My heart would race without cause, its beats matching the pace of my thoughts. I would find myself breathing rapidly and shallowly as if my lungs were becoming smaller and smaller. Tears would well up in my eyes.[5] Anxious thoughts filled my head with lies and overreactions, making me see the future in the darkest way possible, distorting my perception of reality. Every opportunity appeared to be overshadowed by impending doom.[6]

I remained on edge constantly, easily startled, feeling like a marionette manipulated by my fear.[7]

## Night After Night

Night after night, my sleep was disrupted by anxiety, leaving me feeling restless. I would toss and turn, waking up in a puddle of sweat. My mind flooded with traumatic thoughts.[8]

**"Sleep is often the first casualty of our anxieties and stresses."**
—Arianna Huffington, The Sleep Revolution (2016)

---

5. Physical symptoms of anxiety, such as increased heart rate and shallow breathing, are common manifestations of the body's fight-or-flight response. See: Thayer, J. F., Åhs, F., Fredrikson, M., Sollers III, J. J., & Wager, T. D. (2012). A meta-analysis of heart rate variability and neuroimaging studies: Implications for heart rate variability as a marker of stress and health. *Neuroscience & Biobehavioral Reviews*, 36(2), 747-756.

6. Anxiety can lead to cognitive distortions, causing individuals to perceive situations more negatively than they are. See: Beck, A. T., Emery, G., & Greenberg, R. L. (2005). *Anxiety disorders and phobias: A cognitive perspective*. Basic Books.

7. Heightened anxiety can result in increased sensitivity to stimuli and a feeling of being constantly on edge. See: Grillon, C. (2002). Startle reactivity and anxiety disorders: Aversive conditioning, context, and neurobiology. *Biological Psychiatry*, 52(10), 958-975.

8. Anxiety can significantly disrupt sleep patterns, leading to restlessness and night sweats. See: Staner, L. (2003). Sleep and anxiety disorders. *Dialogues in Clinical Neuroscience*, 5(3), 249-258.

Instead of feeling refreshed, I would wake up engulfed in a sense of dread. It felt like a weight holding me down in bed, making it difficult to muster the strength to get up. The morning light, a symbol of fresh beginnings, now seemed to cast shadows that played tricks on my anxious mind. Each day began with this heavy sensation, like a cloud hanging over me, casting a darkness over everything.[9]

Engaging in conversations became increasingly challenging as each word struggled to pass the lump in my throat. Even simple statements felt arduous to articulate. My steady voice now stumbled, reflecting the inner pain I was experiencing. It felt as though I was under scrutiny, sensing everyone's eyes on me and envisioning their judgments.[10]

## Panic Attacks

Frequent and intense panic attacks suddenly became a regular occurrence in my life, catching me off guard—consuming me with an overwhelming fear. Each attack hit me like waves, flooding me with a rush that seemed to strip away all my sense of control.[11]

During these moments of distress, shapes and sounds would blend together into a haze. Everything around me would blur into a swirl of colors as if I was on a scary carnival ride that wouldn't stop. The thumping of my heartbeat reverberated loudly in my ears, and I felt detached as if I was observing from afar, to powerless to intervene. The air felt too thick to breathe, as if I was trying to breathe through a cloth. The ground seemed shaky,

9. Morning anxiety is a common phenomenon, where individuals wake up feeling an overwhelming sense of dread or unease. See: Zisook, S., & Rush, A. J. (1990). Prolonged reactions to a traumatic event: Toward an understanding of early and late onset anxiety and depression. *Journal of Affective Disorders*, 19(2), 93-102.

10. Anxiety can affect speech, leading to difficulty in articulating words and a sense of being judged by others. See: Levinson, C. A., Rodebaugh, T. L., Shumaker, E. A., Menatti, A. R., Weeks, J. W., Heimberg, R. G., & Brown, P. J. (2015). Perception matters for clinical perfectionism and social anxiety. *Journal of Anxiety Disorders*, 29, 61-71.

11. Panic attacks are characterized by sudden and intense periods of fear or discomfort, often accompanied by physical symptoms such as heart palpitations and shortness of breath. See: American Psychiatric Association. (2013). *Diagnostic and Statistical Manual of Mental Disorders* (5th ed.). DSM-5.

feeling as though it might open up and swallow me at any moment.[12] This overwhelming anxiety consumed my thoughts entirely, leaving behind nothing but fear and uncertainty.

I found myself trapped in a cycle of recurring questions:

*"How did this come to be?"—"Why can't I put an end to it?"—"Where should I even begin?"*

The sense of betrayal that shattered my heart also ignited a storm of anxiety within me that tore through every fiber of my being. These incessant inquiries continued to race through my mind as I tried to make sense of all the chaos, leaving me feeling utterly helpless.[13]

*"Is this the normal?"—"How does one rebuild after experiencing such a betrayal?"*

The future ahead seemed daunting, surrounded by chaos and destruction.

## Finding Refuge in Nature and Words

During these times, I unexpectedly discovered a type of therapy in two things: nature's presence and my journal's inviting pages. Nature, in its untouched form, became my escape. Its natural beauty resonated with my soul. The sounds of nature seemed to empathize with my pain, offering words of comfort that soothed me.[14]

**"Everyone must take time to sit and watch the leaves turn."**
—Elizabeth Lawrence

---

12. During a panic attack, individuals may experience derealization (feeling detached from one's surroundings) and depersonalization (feeling detached from oneself). See: Baker, D., Hunter, E., Lawrence, E., Medford, N., Patel, M., Senior, C., Sierra, M., Lambert, M. V., Phillips, M. L., & David, A. S. (2003). Depersonalisation disorder: Clinical features of 204 cases. *The British Journal of Psychiatry*, 182(5), 428-433.

13. The aftermath of betrayal can trigger a cycle of rumination and anxiety, making it difficult to find a sense of closure or direction. See: Cann, A., Norman, M. A., Welbourne, J. L., & Calhoun, L. G. (2008). Attachment styles, conflict styles and humour styles: Interrelationships and associations with relationship satisfaction. *European Journal of Personality*, 22(2), 131-146.

14. The healing power of nature is well-documented in research, showing its positive effects on mental well-being. See: Kaplan, R., & Kaplan, S. (1989). *The Experience of Nature: A Psychological Perspective*. Cambridge University Press.

I felt a connection to everything around me.

The rustling leaves offered words of encouragement, sharing tales of perseverance and change. The gentle flow of a stream symbolized the passage of time and the promise of new beginnings. The soft breeze seemed to understand my pain, easing my burdens and granting me peace from the storm within.[15]

Every encounter with nature brought healing.

Walking beneath the canopy of trees felt like I was stepping into a green cathedral, with the branches forming a shelter, keeping me away from the world's harsh judgments. The earthy scent of the forest grounded me, bringing tranquility to my being.[16] The various shades of green, from lime to emerald, delighted my senses and lifted me up from sorrow. Sunlight filtering through the leaves created a mesmerizing play of light and shadow on the forest floor.[17]

*In these moments, surrounded by nature's beauty, I found peace.*

It was a rare, quiet break that let me breathe, think, and experience life without the burden of my worries.

## The Therapy of Storytelling

My journal, always with me, documented these brief peaceful moments. Its pages, filled with my hurried thoughts and reflections from my time outdoors, became a record of my

---

15. The calming effect of a gentle breeze is an example of how natural elements can provide comfort and relief from emotional pain. See: Ulrich, R. S. (1984). View through a window may influence recovery from surgery. *Science,* 224(4647), 420-421.

16. The scent of the forest, known as 'phytoncides,' has been shown to have calming effects and reduce stress. See: Li, Q. (2010). Effect of forest bathing trips on human immune function. *Environmental Health and Preventive Medicine,* 15(1), 9-17.

17. The interplay of light and shadow in natural settings can create a visually soothing environment, enhancing the sense of peace. See: Joye, Y., & van den Berg, A. (2011). Is love for green in our genes? A critical analysis of evolutionary assumptions in restorative environments research. *Urban Forestry & Urban Greening,* 10(4), 261-268.

healing path. They were a safe place for my soul, where I could freely express my fears, hopes, and sadness without worry of being judged.[18]

This journal absorbed all my emotions—the anger, the hurts, and the aspirations. It captured my experiences through hard times in written form. Filled with confessions, it stood as a testament to my quest for self-understanding.

It was not just ink on paper but a reflection of my inner-self.

> **"The best way out is always through."**
> —Robert Frost, A Servant to Servants (1914)

Keeping track of my struggles offered me moments of clarity. Each time I penned down my feelings, it felt like a moment of peace amid the chaos of my life.[19]

While immersing myself in nature and pouring out thoughts in my journal brought comfort, I soon realized these were temporary solutions to some deeper-seeded issues. While they provided relief from the grips of anxiety, they did not address its core.

I needed more than another place to hide—I needed something that could not only soothe but also fight against these crushing feelings.[20]

## Confronting Anxiety

---

18. Journaling provides a therapeutic outlet for self-expression and emotional processing. See: Pennebaker, J. W. (1997). Writing about emotional experiences as a therapeutic process. *Psychological Science*, 8(3), 162-166.

19. Writing down one's struggles can provide moments of clarity and help in organizing thoughts. See: Baikie, K. A., & Wilhelm, K. (2005). Emotional and physical health benefits of expressive writing. *Advances in Psychiatric Treatment*, 11(5), 338-346.

20. Temporary coping mechanisms may provide relief but may not address the underlying issues of anxiety. See: Hayes, S. C., Strosahl, K. D., & Wilson, K. G. (2012). *Acceptance and Commitment Therapy: The Process and Practice of Mindful Change* (2nd ed.). Guilford Press.

In a moment of clarity, an idea struck me that was bold, perhaps even daring. I decided to take on anxiety in the bustling arena of TikTok.[21] It seemed like an odd choice for someone grappling with these feelings perhaps.

**"When we are no longer able to change a situation, we are challenged to change ourselves."**
—Viktor E. Frankl, Man's Search for Meaning (1946)

Why would I, someone with deep-seated social anxieties, willingly choose to expose myself in such a public and unpredictable space? It's an environment where judgments come swiftly and can be harsh, where individuals may harbor unkindness behind the shield of anonymity. Yet I viewed this platform's openness and wide reach as an opportunity for a confrontation with my fears.

The decision to utilize TikTok was a leap into unknown territory pushing against my very nature. There was no room for hiding. By baring my story and authentic self without filters, I was stepping out of my comfort zone and directly confronting my anxiety.[22]

Each video and post acted as a step into new territory.

Every time I was about to post, I felt a wave of fear. It was like standing on the edge of a cliff, heart racing, filled with doubts.

My journey on TikTok resembled that of a rollercoaster ride. At times, I experienced the exhilaration of sharing my story; at other times, I felt incredibly exposed, with each share unveiling a piece of myself. The platform amplified every aspect of my journey and every emotion I felt. Each view and comment seemed like a glimpse into my world.

Nevertheless, despite its intimidating nature, sharing ultimately brought liberation. It served to release the burdens I had carried for so long. Every TikTok video provided a

---

21. Explore the diverse content created by Ryan, who started on TikTok and now engages audiences on all major social media platforms. For official profiles and more, visit RyanPuusaari.com.

22. Stepping out of one's comfort zone is a crucial aspect of personal growth and confronting anxiety. See: Kashdan, T. B., & McKnight, P. E. (2013). Commitment to a purpose in life: An antidote to the suffering by individuals with social anxiety disorder. *Emotion*, 13(6), 1150-1159.

window into my soul, showcasing myself without any pretense. There were no façades in front of the camera— just the truth of who I was and what I was going through.[23]

This work of baring my soul to the world was rife with highs and lows. Each post represented a venture into uncertainty—a showdown with my fears.

> **"You may not control all the events that happen to you, but you can decide not to be reduced by them."**
> —Maya Angelou, to My Daughter (2009)

As I continued to open up about my challenges and the steps I took to recovery, I discovered a sense of empowerment. With each video I shared, I felt like I was dismantling the barriers of my anxiety.

In the act of being raw and vulnerable, I unearthed a new strength. Utilizing TikTok as a platform became a tool in my battle against anxiety—a means to confront and chip away at the shadows that had loomed over me for so long. It showcased the significance of being open and the significant impact of sharing one's truth regardless of how daunting it may appear.[24]

## Tracing Back the Roots

Opening up on TikTok meant peeling back the layers of my past—where each video revealed more about the origins of my anxiety.

---

23. Sharing personal stories on social media can provide a sense of liberation and catharsis. See: Pennebaker, J. W., & Seagal, J. D. (1999). Forming a story: The health benefits of narrative. *Journal of Clinical Psychology*, 55(10), 1243-1254.

24. Utilizing social media as a tool for confronting anxiety highlights the importance of openness and sharing one's truth in the healing process. See: Grieve, R., Indian, M., Witteveen, K., Anne Tolan, G., & Marrington, J. (2013). Face-to-face or Facebook: Can social connectedness be derived online? *Computers in Human Behavior*, 29(3), 604-609.

**"Owning our story and loving ourselves through that process is the bravest thing that we will ever do."**
—Brené Brown, The Gifts of Imperfection (2010)

The initial root traced back to recollections of my father, whose life was marred by alcoholism.[25] Each memory evoked the scent of alcohol and the unpredictability of his demeanor. His struggle with alcohol cast a lingering shadow over my childhood, creating a sense of unease. I recounted nights with tension, his footsteps signaling another evening lost to addiction, as well as the bewilderment and helplessness that engulfed a child living within such an environment.

A significant source of my anxiety stemmed from the bullying I endured during my school days. I recounted the words, physical threats and constant social rejection. The bullying didn't just harm me physically; it also eroded my self-esteem, digging a well of self-doubt and unease. Each memory felt like stepping onto a battlefield, reawakening the feelings of vulnerability and fear that had left scars on my psyche.[26]

I also talked about the crime in my neighborhood, painting a picture of an environment that shaped my early views of safety and trust. I shared stories of dark experiences and the constant vigilance that is needed in such a place. These circumstances made me see threats everywhere, making anxiety a constant companion for survival.[27]

The hardest part to share was the betrayal in my relationship. This wasn't just about revisiting events, but facing the emotions they stirred up within me. I spoke about the trust-shattered aspirations and deep grief and disillusionment that ensued. This betrayal

---

25. The impact of parental alcoholism on children's mental health and development is well-documented. See: Barnard, M., & McKeganey, N. (2004). The impact of parental problem drug use on children: What is the problem and what can be done to help? *Addiction*, 99(5), 552-559.

26. The long-term effects of bullying on mental health and self-esteem are significant. See: Arseneault, L., Bowes, L., & Shakoor, S. (2010). Bullying victimization in youths and mental health problems: 'Much ado about nothing'? *Psychological Medicine*, 40(5), 717-729.

27. Exposure to crime and violence in one's neighborhood can contribute to the development of anxiety and a heightened sense of vigilance. See: Foster, H., & Brooks-Gunn, J. (2009). Neighborhood, family and individual influences on school physical victimization. *Journal of Youth and Adolescence*, 38(9), 1181-1191.

wasn't just a personal tragedy; it was what made me deeply reevaluate my views on love, trust, and relationships.[28]

Each story shared openly marked a step toward unravelling the complexities of my anxiety. Acknowledging and discussing these experiences, I worked to comprehend myself. This wasn't about sharing with others; it was about reclaiming my story and transforming my past from a source of hurt into a pillar of resilience and self-awareness.

Opening up about my struggles on TikTok felt like shedding layers of protection, leaving me emotionally drained. However, the sense of relief that followed each disclosure was profound and liberating. Each experience I confronted and disclosed felt like releasing a burden from my shoulders, bringing not just comfort but a growing feeling of freedom and empowerment.[29]

I realized that managing my anxiety wasn't about conquering a battle; it was about learning to work through, sit with and understand the emotions it stirred within me. It involved acknowledging its presence, accepting it, but refusing to let it dictate my life.

> **"You don't have to control your thoughts. You just have to stop letting them control you."**
> —Dan Millman, Way of the Peaceful Warrior (1980)

I began to understand that it wasn't about overcoming anxiety or waiting for it to disappear; it was about adapting to live with it—to find joy within the chaos of my struggles. This wasn't simply coping; it was about reshaping how I interacted with my anxiety and discovering a path that allowed me to regain command over my life.

---

28. The emotional impact of betrayal in intimate relationships can lead to a reevaluation of one's views on trust and relationships. See: Leary, M. R., & Springer, C. (2001). Hurt feelings: The neglected emotion. In R. M. Kowalski (Ed.), *Behaving badly: Aversive behaviors in interpersonal relationships* (pp. 151-175). American Psychological Association.

29. Disclosing personal experiences, especially on a public platform like TikTok, can lead to emotional vulnerability but also a sense of liberation. See: Pennebaker, J. W. (1997). Writing about emotional experiences as a therapeutic process. *Psychological Science*, 8(3), 162-166.

## The Power of Shared Vulnerability

Each video I created and shared felt like progress in my confrontation with anxiety. Making these videos expressing my thoughts openly felt like gearing up for a battle. The camera captured all my emotions, every trembling voice, moments of uncertainty, and bravery.

Sharing each video felt like aiming at anxiety with an arrow. Bringing me closer to conquering the fears that haunted me.

Behind the scenes, these moments were filled with nervousness and vulnerability. Before each video went live, I experienced a mix of emotions—my heart would race and my palms would sweat at the fear of criticism or being misunderstood. I'd often sit there with my finger just hoovering over the post button, paralyzed by the concern of being too open, yet filled with hope that my message would resonate with others.

Despite these fears, there was a sense of achievement with each upload. They stood as a declaration that I was no longer allowing my anxieties to dictate my actions. Within this journey, I discovered the power of sharing my struggles—*turning vulnerabilities into acts of defiance against forces that sought to keep me concealed within the fake illusions of comfort.*

> **"Our wounds are often the openings into the best and most beautiful part of us."**
> —David Richo,The Five Things We Cannot Change (2005)

As time went on in my TikTok journey, something amazing and unexpected started to happen. I began receiving messages from people who had quietly watched and connected with my stories.

> "I just wanted to say thanks for posting your videos. I have a lot going on and dealing with anxiety and depression doesn't help. You have made statements in your videos that I have been trying to explain for so long. As bad as it sounds it makes it easier knowing someone out there kinda gets what I'm going through. Even though I know I don't know you and most likely never will; Your videos help. Please don't stop posting."

These messages were digital high-fives, coming from people I never met but who were with me on my journey all along. My unfiltered and transparent account had transcended confines, touching lives in ways I hadn't envisioned possible. Each message served as a reminder that others bore the same burdens I did.[30]

"Hey Ryan, I saw your videos on tiktok, and I had to interact!
I feel like I know what you are talking, because I feel it, but I can't talk or write about it. I attended a therapy and I believe I am doing better, but still dealing with the ptsd which I have developed from a burnout but watching your videos gives me hope! Thanks."

## A Community Strengthened

Each time I got a new message, it felt like a light cutting through the haze, showing how much my shared experiences mattered. The platform, which started as a way for me to heal, became a guiding light for others facing their own tough times. It was like my fight against anxiety and fear was helping others find their way.

These conversations were more than just talking; they were like bridges over the loneliness that often comes with mental health issues. Every comment and heartfelt message added to a big picture of our shared human experiences, full of struggles, bouncing back, and persevering.

Whenever someone said that my honest sharing had saved their life, I felt a mix of disbelief and humility. It was hard to believe that my story, with its ups and downs, could mean so much to someone else. Reading these messages, where strangers shared how my journey gave them hope in their dark times, was overwhelming.

---

30. Receiving messages of support and shared experiences can provide comfort and a sense of community for individuals sharing their struggles on social media. See: Naslund, J. A., Aschbrenner, K. A., Marsch, L. A., & Bartels, S. J. (2016). The future of mental health care: Peer-to-peer support and social media. *Epidemiology and Psychiatric Sciences*, 25(2), 113-122.

*Could my tough path have actually helped light up someone else's way or even changed their direction?* This introspective thought was both humbling and amazing. It showed how powerful it is to share your deepest fears and weaknesses. Each message reminded me of the strong connections we make through our shared human experiences, connections we might never fully understand.

Reading these messages of thanks sparked a significant change in me. I could see things more clearly and understand more than I did before. My experiment on TikTok, which began as a way to fight my anxiety, had turned into something much bigger. It was no longer just my fight but a group effort.[31]

This wasn't just a change in how I saw things; it was a whole new direction for my purpose on the platform. What started as a way for me to face my fears and heal was now growing into a broader mission. My TikTok, where I shared my deepest struggles, was becoming a safe space for others dealing with mental health issues.

The significant impact of my openness drove this change.

People weren't just hearing my stories; they were connecting with them. The platform became a place where people could find comfort, knowing they weren't alone in their struggles.

**"Sharing our stories is one of the most powerful ways we have to remind each other that we're not alone in our struggles and that there's hope."**
—Lori Gottlieb, Maybe You Should Talk to Someone (2019)

Every video and story I shared was now part of a bigger human story.

My TikTok was turning into a community space, a place for understanding, empathy, and connection. My posts' real, unedited honesty encouraged others to share their struggles and find strength in our shared experiences.

This transformation was both humbling and empowering. It showed that when shared, our personal stories can go beyond our lives and touch others deeply. My TikTok, once

---

31. Engaging with a social media community can lead to a shift in perspective and a sense of collective effort in addressing mental health challenges. See: Rains, S. A., Brunner, S. R., & Oman, K. (2021). Self-disclosure and social media: Motivations, mechanisms, and psychological well-being. *Current Opinion in Psychology*, 39, 22-27.

a personal battleground, had become a symbol of hope and understanding, a sign of the power of being vulnerable and the strength that comes from our shared human connections.

Looking back on this now, I can see how my understanding of mental health has grown. What started as a personal search for healing became a group mission, creating a platform powered by our shared stories. My experiences, once just mine, now deeply resonated with others, creating a space where individual stories blended into a collective force of resilience and support.

This amazing change went beyond social media.

As the community grew, so too did the need for more caring guidance. This led to a daily text messaging service, a natural online extension of the community spirit. This service was a bridge, bringing me closer to the community that was starting to take flight.[32]

---

32. Expanding the reach of a social media community through additional platforms like text messaging services can enhance the sense of connection and support. See: Naslund, J. A., Aschbrenner, K. A., Marsch, L. A., & Bartels, S. J. (2016). The future of mental health care: Peer-to-peer support and social media. *Epidemiology and Psychiatric Sciences*, 25(2), 113-122.

# Desolation to Hope

## Dawn of a New Chapter

A S THE FIRST RAYS of the morning sun broke through the thin, small apartment curtains, I seemed—for a moment—to be basking in something warm and still so fresh it almost felt unreal. It had been a few months since I'd hauled myself back up from rock bottom on the homeless front. Now, here in this unpretentious little space that was my very own, there was a sense of peace that had been missing from my life for so long. It was a simple apartment, leaving just enough space for essentials. Yet, every bit in that space—from the second-hand couch to the little table by the window—said something about me and my strength, about how far I'd come.[1]

However, at times, a sense of isolation still lingered in my apartment.

> "Loneliness adds beauty to life. It puts a special burn on sunsets and makes night air smell better."
>
> —Henry Rollins, Solipsist (1998)

---

1. The transformation of living spaces can symbolize personal growth and resilience, reflecting the journey from adversity to stability. See: Mallett, S. (2004). Understanding home: A critical review of the literature. *The Sociological Review*, 52(1), 62-89.

One particular evening, that feeling of solitude became overwhelming. The familiar walls seemed distant. I sank into the couch, searching for a comfort that proved elusive.

My eyes drifted to my phone, its gentle glow triggering memories of when my car served as both a refuge and a confinement, each detail etched vividly in my mind—inside that car, my breath would fog up the windows, blending the outside world into a blur of neon lights and shadows. The cold would seep in, chilling every nook and cranny, turning the steering wheel icy to the touch. Now, sitting in my apartment with a sense of stability, memories from those challenging times came rushing back. The quiet surroundings of my apartment transported me right back to those solitary nights spent in my car.

Despite the growing online community, the silence of my phone emphasized the feeling of loneliness within me. It was during those moments in my car that I had an idea but not the means to see it through—a concept waiting to bloom—but now, in a slightly better financial place, I decided it was time to carry out this vision. These memories, clear and unforgettable, were more than just reminders of the past; they lit a fire of purpose within me.

## The Birth of a Community

The thought was simple; to send out daily text messages that could truly resonate with people, messages brimming with empathy and compassion.[2] As I began to write that inaugural message, I was both excited and nervous. The sensation of my fingertips tapping on the sleek phone felt simultaneously familiar yet foreign, as though each touch was adding a new line to a story in the lives of those I'd never meet.

Upon sending out that maiden message, my apartment seemed to grow a little quieter, as if anticipating something remarkable. Before long, responses began trickling in—each one like a small wave reaching back to me from the big ocean I had reached out to. The usual muted buzz of my phone transformed into a symphony of connections.

---

2. The creation of an online community through text messaging can provide a sense of belonging and support for individuals seeking solace and inspiration. See: Pfeil, U., & Zaphiris, P. (2007). Patterns of empathy in online communication. In *Proceedings of the SIGCHI conference on Human factors in computing systems* (pp. 919-928). ACM.

Each gentle vibration played an appealing tune, disrupting the usual quietness around me with soft sounds of optimism. The glow from my phone's screen illuminated the dimly lit room, casting playful shadows on the walls. It felt as though the room was slowly coming alive with each new message, dispelling the previous sense of solitude.

The lingering aroma of my morning coffee intertwined with this newfound sense of purpose, creating a space that felt both reassuring and invigorating.

With each incoming reply, the sounds of connection grew louder, each notification reinforcing the bond we were forming through shared experiences. A cool morning breeze from the open window brushed against my skin, offering a refreshing contrast to the warmth blossoming in my heart. It served as a gentle reminder of the world beyond, now intricately connected to me through the invisible threads of digital communication.

> **"Invisible threads are the strongest ties."**
> —Friedrich Nietzsche, Thus Spoke Zarathustra (1891)

In my modest apartment, accompanied by the distant hum of city noises, the act of typing out messages gave rise to a sense of community. It was a community that transcended physical boundaries, extending into the vast online realm and uniting individuals seeking solace and inspiration amidst darkness. It marked the beginning of a journey, not only for me but for all those who sought comfort in our shared conversations. A road to healing, forging connections and rediscovering ourselves.

## A New Chapter: The Power of Routine

My apartment was more than just four walls—it was where I felt most at peace. Every morning, I settled into a routine as comfortable and familiar as breathing. Texting friends became a staple of my day. As I sat at my wooden table, the morning sun would cast beautiful patterns across the floor, its light offering me comfort and a quiet moment to reflect.

Tapping away on my phone was like a calming ritual. In the morning's soft light, my phone screen seemed like a blank canvas ready for my thoughts. In this quiet time of introspection and sharing, I turned my feelings into messages, creating connections and finding parts of myself in the process. Writing wasn't just about putting words down; it was a journey of healing and discovering myself anew.

> **"Writing is a form of therapy; sometimes I wonder how all those who do not write, compose or paint can manage to escape the madness, melancholia, the panic and fear which is inherent in a human situation."**
> —Graham Greene, The Times (London, 18 January 1977)

Lost in my thoughts, I would stroll down memory lane, reminiscing about joy and sorrow, lessons learned, and personal growth. Writing these messages helped me piece together fragments of myself that had been concealed or abandoned.[3] The warmth emanating from the community cut through my solitude like sunlight piercing through clouds. Each expression of gratitude and every shared story resonated deeply with me, reinforcing the significance of my actions.

My routine may have seemed simple on the surface, but it held meaning.[4]

This daily ritual, to the sounds of a waking city and the tranquility of my space, highlighted the power of words and connection. It reminded me that even in solitude, we can touch lives and bridge distances—one message, one day, one thought at a time.

## Invisible Strings

Fast-forward a year, and I was now leading a growing community that inspired thousands, my life finally getting back on track with purpose and meaning. On the outside, I looked like a symbol of hope and strength, my posts and messages guiding those lost in their own

---

3. Reflecting on past experiences through writing can aid in piecing together one's identity. See: McAdams, D. P. (2001). The psychology of life stories. *Review of General Psychology*, 5(2), 100-122.

4. The significance of daily rituals in creating a sense of purpose and connection is underscored. See: Csikszentmihalyi, M. (1990). *Flow: The Psychology of Optimal Experience*. Harper & Row

struggles. However, internally, a separate undercurrent existed—a hidden presence that came and went on its own. It was a part of me yet still felt detached, like a misaligned shadow.[5]

This hidden force, sneaky like a predator, always showed up at the worst times. I could sense its presence like an abrupt drop in the temperature, a shift that sent tingles down my spine. Just as I would be on the brink of celebrating a triumph, or reveling in the accomplishment, it would cast a lengthy, somber shadow over my thoughts. *This darkness wasn't merely an absence of light; it was active and transformative—converting happiness into uncertainty and confidence into a swamp of anxious inquiries. The sweet taste of success would often turn sour, as if this part of me was set on ruining the celebration of my achievements.*[6] It was really good at overreacting, making every small problem seem like a huge mountain. Even the tiniest mistake, a simple slip-up, would suddenly feel overwhelming, casting a heavy cloud over my whole mood.

> **"Our deepest fear is not that we are inadequate. Our deepest fear is that we are powerful beyond measure. It is our light, not our darkness, that most frightens us."**
> —Marianne Williamson, A Return to Love (1992)

At times, I felt a force pushing me towards self-sabotage, filling my mind with subtle uncertainties and worries that made me question my worthiness of success and happiness. I recognized this inner presence as an unexplored facet of myself. It was like a shadow from someone just out of view, a shape suggested but never fully seen. The more I tried to grasp it, the more elusive it became, residing in the obscure corners of my psyche where fears and doubts dwell like mysterious creatures in the depths of a murky pond.[7]

---

5. The coexistence of hope and resilience with an underlying sense of unease illustrates the multifaceted nature of emotional experiences. See: Lazarus, R. S. (1993). *From psychological stress to the emotions: A history of changing outlooks.* Annual Review of Psychology, 44, 1-21.

6. The transformation of positive emotions into uncertainty and self-doubt highlights the influence of internal conflicts on personal well-being. See: Leary, M. R., & Tangney, J. P. (Eds.). (2012). *Handbook of self and identity.* Guilford Press.

7. The recognition of an unexplored facet of oneself and the challenges of grappling with internal fears and doubts are explored. See: Jung, C. G. (1957). *The Undiscovered Self.* Routledge & Kegan Paul.

# Behind the Veil

## The Elusive Sensation of Aspiration

L ET'S TRAVEL BACK A bit for added context—as I entered into my early twenties, it felt like I was beginning on the grand adventure of life, filled with a burning passion to improve my family's financial future. Growing up in an environment filled with poverty and struggle, I was overflowing with ideas of a better life.

I began attending various seminars, where I unearthed something extraordinary—a significant thirst for knowledge as vast as the starlit sky. This quest for enlightenment surpassed the fleeting allure of wealth and material possessions, it marked the commencement of an educational journey that would come to sculpt my identity.

But under all these dreams, there was always this annoying, lingering feeling, like a chilly breeze in a room that's supposed to be warm. This indescribable feeling was tricky to nail down, like trying to catch smoke with your hands.[1]

**"There is no end to education. It is not that you read a book, pass an examination, and finish with education. The whole of life, from**

---

1. The experience of growing up in poverty can instill a strong desire for a better future, but it may also be accompanied by an underlying sense of unease. See: Duncan, G. J., & Brooks-Gunn, J. (Eds.). (1997). *Consequences of growing up poor*. Russell Sage Foundation.

**the moment you are born to the moment you die, is a process of learning."**

—Jiddu Krishnamurti, Life Ahead (1963)

Over the years, I have accumulated a pretty impressive collection of books, each one unveiling secrets from diverse fields of knowledge. I found both comfort and excitement in the quiet company of written ideas and thoughts. Gradually, I curated my own personal library, with each book being a symbol of my relentless quest for understanding. With every page turned, I began constructing a pathway from my humble present to a future illuminated by comprehension. Books became my haven, a place where my curious mind could quench its thirst.

Yet during this perpetual exploration—I couldn't shake off a feeling of dissatisfaction—a sense that no matter how much I learned, it was never enough. Despite being surrounded by an abundance of knowledge, there lingered an elusive gap; a subtle indication that something crucial remained elusive. It felt like I was collecting pieces of a huge puzzle, but the picture they were supposed to create was still unclear.

I was living a paradox—always learning, yet somehow not able to turn all that knowledge into real change.[2] That was until years later, when my world got rocked by the betrayal and infidelity after the collapse of my marriage, that I would finally wake up to these tendencies.

## Heartbreak and Discovery

As I sat there, grappling with the aftermath of betrayal and my persistent worries, I found myself in the shadowy corners of my room where time appeared to slow down, allowing me moments for reflection and healing. While the world outside hurried on, internally, I was consumed by my own thoughts. It was in these instances that I stumbled upon Dr. Nicole LePera's Instagram profile. Her insightful posts that linked our present challenges with our past deeply resonated with me. Every word felt like it was speaking right to me.

---

2. The paradox of always learning but not achieving desired change highlights the challenges of applying knowledge to real-life situations. See: Argyris, C., & Schön, D. A. (1974). *Theory in practice: Increasing professional effectiveness.* Jossey-Bass

Her book, *"How to Do the Work,"* captivated me like a moth drawn to a soft, radiant glow. Holding the book gave off a sense of warmth and solace, almost as if it possessed life itself—extending comfort and empathy towards me.

Every time I turned a page, I felt like I was moving deeper into a world of understanding and acceptance, accompanied by the gentle rustle of paper serving as a soothing backdrop to my exploration. Her words were like a nod to the steps I had taken and the long path still ahead. They felt like a reassuring hand on my shoulder, a comforting presence of validation in my solo journey.[3]

> **"The journey to self-healing begins with self-observation. Observing our thoughts, feelings, and behaviors without judgment allows us to gain insight into our patterns and conditioning."**
> —Dr. Nicole LePera, How to Do the Work (2021)

Within her wise words, I stumbled upon a concept new to me—*the shadow self.* This mention, subtle at first, sparked a curiosity in me. The term *shadow self* lingered in my thoughts, a haunting tune that refused to fade away. It stirred something within me, a blend of apprehension and an insatiable desire to explore this concealed aspect of myself.[4]

TikTok, aided by its clever algorithm, unexpectedly turned that spark into a flame, igniting my growing curiosity. A video on shadow work caught my attention, opening a pandoras box full of questions. My heart raced with anticipation and a hint of trepidation as I stepped into this uncharted territory. I found myself eagerly consuming one video after another, unable to tear my eyes away from the screen as new revelations dawned on me. With each fresh insight and perspective, it felt as though I was unearthing facets of myself that had been lying dormant since childhood. The shadow self, a part of me I had ignored or pushed away, started to reveal itself. It was a bit unsettling, but there was also a part of me that was thrilled about finally witnessing these hidden parts.

---

3. The act of reading and engaging with meaningful literature can provide a source of comfort and a catalyst for introspection, supporting the healing process. Reference: Nell, V. (1988). *Lost in a Book: The Psychology of Reading for Pleasure.* Yale University Press.

4. The concept of the hidden self highlights the importance of exploring the unconscious aspects of our psyche to achieve a deeper understanding of ourselves. Reference: Jung, C. G. (1958). *The Undiscovered Self.* Mentor.

As I sat there, my mind filled with various thoughts and emotions, I came to the realization that this was merely the beginning. I had started a journey into the deepest parts of my mind, which promised to be as tough as it was eye-opening.

**The road ahead was uncertain, but one thing was for sure:** I wasn't happy just living on the surface anymore. I was ready to go deep, to explore the hidden parts of my soul, and to find out what was underneath.[5]

A sense of awe mingled with trepidation washed over me—sending shivers down my spine.

*"What hidden facets of myself will I unearth?"*—I wondered, my heart racing with a blend of anxiety and anticipation.—*"How much about myself remains undiscovered?"*

## The Work Deepens

The moment I started to understand the idea of our subconscious motives—the powerful, often imperceptible influences shaping our words and deeds—was a significant revelation, altering my self-perception.[6] The concept of the shadow self helped me understand the foundation of human psychology. This revelation felt like the missing piece that countless seminars, podcasts and books had never fully explained to me before. It opened up new pathways for understanding the complex layers of the human psyche, making clear what had once been obscured through ignorance.

> **"The shadow is a moral problem that challenges the whole ego-personality, for no one can become conscious of the shadow without considerable moral effort. To become conscious of it involves recognizing the dark aspects of the personality as present and real."**
> —Carl Jung, Psychology and Religion (1958)

---

5. Embarking on a journey of self-discovery can be both challenging and enlightening, as it involves confronting and embracing the hidden facets of our being. Reference: Hillman, J. (1975). *Re-Visioning Psychology*. Harper & Row.

6. The subconscious mind plays a crucial role in shaping our thoughts, feelings, and behaviors, often operating below the level of conscious awareness. Reference: Freud, S. (1915). *The Unconscious*. SE, 14: 159-204.

As I got into the fascinating world of Jungian Philosophy, it opened up like an old scroll, showing me a complex network of archetypes, the symbols and collective unconsciousness.[7] Carl Jung's concept of the shadow self deeply enriched my personal growth, adding layers of depth and complexity to my understanding.

I also gained valuable insights from other notable thinkers. B.F. Skinner's theories on behavior and reinforcement provided a scientific basis for how our actions are influenced by rewards and punishments. Jean Piaget's stages of cognitive development showed how children build their understanding of the world, while Erik Erikson's psychosocial stages provided a lifespan view of human growth. Abraham Maslow's well-known hierarchy of needs highlighted the fundamental motivations driving human behavior, with a focus on achieving self-actualization. Carl Rogers' person-centered approach emphasized the importance of empathy and unconditional positive regard in personal development. Each thinker offered unique perspectives that helped me view the complexities of the human mind through various lenses.[8]

I started asking myself— *"How do these theories connect with my own life story? —What parts of myself are still hidden and waiting to be found?"*

The more I learned, the more I realized how much was still hidden in the dark.

Questions about the inaccessible corners of my consciousness arose— *What methods can I explore to uncover and understand the hidden aspects of my consciousness that remain in the shadows?—How do the buried parts of my psyche influence my thoughts, behaviors, and relationships without my conscious awareness?—In what ways can confronting and integrating my shadow self enhance my personal growth and self-awareness?*

With each new theory, each new insight, I was uncovering truths about myself that had been buried beneath years of life experiences and societal influences.

---

7. Jungian philosophy offers a comprehensive framework for understanding the human psyche, including the concepts of archetypes, the collective unconscious, and the shadow self. Reference: Jung, C. G. (1969). *Archetypes and the Collective Unconscious*. Princeton University Press.

8. Exploring various psychological theories, including behaviorism, developmental psychology, and humanistic psychology, provides a multi-faceted understanding of the human mind and behavior. Reference: Skinner, B. F. (1953). *Science and Human Behavior*. Macmillan; Piaget, J. (1952). *The Origins of Intelligence in Children*. International Universities Press; Erikson, E. H. (1950). *Childhood and Society*. W. W. Norton & Company; Maslow, A. H. (1943). A theory of human motivation. *Psychological Review*, 50(4), 370-396; Rogers, C. R. (1951). *Client-Centered Therapy: Its Current Practice, Implications, and Theory*. Houghton Mifflin.

This journey into self discovery wasn't just an academic pursuit; was a deeply personal. Each forward step brought a mix of anticipation and apprehension. The thrill of uncovering hidden aspects of myself often mingled with the discomfort of confronting parts I had long ignored. Despite the challenges, I persisted driven by a strong urge to comprehend, evolve and accept my truest self completely.[9]

## An Evolving Relationship

As time passed and weeks transitioned into months, I began to perceive my connection with my shadow in a new light. It felt as though I had acquired a newfound intuition, an ability to recognize this unseen companion. Its presence would manifest unexpectedly, resembling a reflection of my innermost thoughts, a gentle voice during the chaos of daily life.

**"Healing takes courage, and we all have courage, even if we have to dig a little to find it."**
—Tori Amos, Reader's Digest (2005)

Gradually, the shadow ceased to symbolize fear or linger as a foreboding entity on the fringes of my consciousness. Instead, it evolved into a guardian, a counselor, a source of wisdom. It transformed into a reflection revealing my deepest desires, buried sorrows and unaddressed fears. It became the voice of my silent contemplations, the resonance of my unspoken words.[10]

My familiar practice of journaling underwent a metamorphosis and assumed a new significance. What was once merely a means to chronicle daily occurrences now served

---

9. The process of self-discovery involves uncovering and integrating various aspects of the self, leading to a deeper understanding of one's identity and a more authentic way of living. Reference: Maslow, A. H. (1968). *Toward a Psychology of Being*. D. Van Nostrand Company.

10. The shadow self can serve as a source of insight and wisdom, guiding individuals toward a deeper understanding of their desires, fears, and unaddressed emotions. Reference: Jung, C. G. (1958). *The Undiscovered Self*. Mentor.

as a sanctuary for my shadow self. My journal transcended its role becoming a gateway to my subconscious.

I remember one night, under the soft light of my desk lamp, it seemed as though my pen possessed a will of its own. Words poured out onto the page. The shadows inside me manifested outwardly, revealing emotions and memories long kept hidden. With every pen stroke, my inner wounds and aspirations, fears and desires were laid bare, leading me deep within my psyche. It was almost as if the ink possessed a magical quality, unveiling the unseen parts of my inner self.

As I kept writing, a specific memory came to mind—a childhood experience where I felt completely unnoticed during a family gathering. As I put my thoughts into words, I realized how much that moment had instilled a feeling of not being good enough in me. Reflecting on it through writing, I started to see the links between that distant memory and my adult anxieties about rejection. This process of introspection and expression helped me confront that pain, grasp its roots and begin to release it.

My writing turned into a tool for unraveling the tangled emotions connected to my past, providing a way to address old hurts by acknowledging and accepting them. Revisiting my memories with pen in hand didn't just bring buried emotions to the surface; it showed me a route to reclaim parts of myself that I had unknowingly abandoned. By directly engaging with my past experiences, I found a way to forgive, grow and move forward with a better comprehension and affection for myself.

Every journal entry became a heartfelt conversation with my shadow self, a raw and empathetic exchange. It was a poignant exploration into uncharted territories of my being, an odyssey towards accepting and understanding all facets of myself.[11]

## Shadows Beyond the Self

As I continued to work with my shadows my awareness grew, it felt like a curtain had been pulled back, letting me see how the subconscious played a part in everyone's life. It was like

---

11. Engaging in reflective writing allows for a dialogue with the shadow self, providing a means to uncover and process hidden emotions, memories, and aspects of one's identity. Reference: Pennebaker, J. W., & Evans, J. F. (2014). *Expressive Writing: Words That Heal*. Idyll Arbor.

seeing a gentle dance in our daily lives, where everyone's happiness and sadness, victories and struggles, strengths and weaknesses were displayed in a ballet of light and dark.

I observed it in the sorrow etched on the face of a friend grappling with heartbreak. Their eyes concealing tears, their laughter tinged with fragility. Their smile appeared almost like a façade, barely masking the anguish lurking beneath. The anger of an embarrassed colleague was another easy one to spot. Clenched fists and forced smiles during meetings betraying simmering resentment and pent up frustration.[12] In contrast, witnessing the happiness of a child celebrating a small win—the pure joy, their eyes shining with delight—showed a lighter, happier side of their inner world. But it also prompted contemplation about the unseen fears and uncertainties that might be nestled within their youthful psyche. Then there was the grief of a stranger dealing with a loss. I observed it in the way they carried themselves, appearing burdened by an unseen weight with a slight hunch in their posture. Their sorrow was a silent companion, a constant reminder of their grief evident in the creases of their face and their cautious interactions with the world.[13]

Every emotion and every person revealed their hidden sides. It felt like each person was a canvas and their life stories painted a blend of brightness and darkness. This fusion of the visible and hidden created a portrait that was both captivating and poignant.

> **"There are moments when I wish I could roll back the clock and take all the sadness away, but I have the feeling that if I did, the joy would be gone as well."**
> —Nicholas Sparks, A Walk to Remember (1999)

As I continued to witness these shadows in others, I found myself contemplating my own.

*"How does my shadow appear to others?"* — *"What aspects of myself am I unintentionally revealing?"*

---

12. Emotional expressions, such as laughter or smiles, can sometimes mask underlying feelings of sorrow or anger, reflecting the complexity of human emotions. Reference: Ekman, P. (2003). *Emotions Revealed: Recognizing Faces and Feelings to Improve Communication and Emotional Life*. Times Books.

13. Grief and loss can manifest physically and emotionally, affecting an individual's posture, facial expressions, and interactions with others. Reference: Worden, J. W. (2009). *Grief Counseling and Grief Therapy: A Handbook for the Mental Health Practitioner*. Springer Publishing Company.

This fresh perspective wasn't just about observing others; it served as a mirror reflecting parts of myself that had gone unnoticed, urging me to acknowledge and comprehend them.[14]

This realization brought about both discomfort and insight. Every emotion and sensation seemed like a gentle nudge from my inner self, revealing deeper truths about who I am and what I have yet to confront. As I kept looking inward, I became more aware of the subtle signs of my inner world. For instance, my heart rate would slightly quicken during certain conversations or how I would avoid eye contact in moments of uncertainty. These signals were the language through which my inner self communicated via my physical and behavioral responses.[15]

> **"Until you make the unconscious conscious, it will direct your life and you will call it fate."**
> —Carl Jung, The Archetypes and the Collective Unconscious (1934)

With each observation, I came to realize that engaging with my shadow was not something to fear or evade but rather it was an opportunity to welcome as a powerful avenue for self-discovery and growth. It was a chance to dig deeper into my own mind, to find the hidden reasons and unresolved issues that influenced my thoughts and actions.

This new insight gave me a feeling of kindness, both for myself and others. I began perceiving people's actions and reactions with greater empathy, acknowledging that our shadows shape us in ways we may not entirely comprehend. This shift in perspective resulted in deeper connections and a heightened sense of belonging within the community around me.[16]

---

14. The process of observing others' behavior and reflecting on one's own can lead to increased self-awareness and understanding of unconscious aspects of the self. Reference: Jung, C. G. (1958). *The Undiscovered Self*. Mentor.

15. Physical and behavioral responses can provide valuable insights into our inner emotional states and the workings of our subconscious mind. Reference: Damasio, A. R. (1994). *Descartes' Error: Emotion, Reason, and the Human Brain*. G.P. Putnam's Sons.

16. A deeper understanding of one's own shadow can lead to greater empathy and compassion towards others, fostering deeper connections and a sense of community. Reference: Rogers, C. R. (1951). *Client-Centered Therapy: Its Current Practice, Implications, and Theory*. Houghton Mifflin.

## A Newfound Inspiration

As I laid in bed one night, with the room gently lit by moonlight, reflecting on the way shadow work had impacted my life, my thoughts drifted beyond my own experiences.

*"How can I help others see these hidden forces?"*—the question hanging in the air around me.

The silence felt like it was waiting for an answer that didn't manifest right away. But there was comfort in thinking about it, a feeling of meaning in trying to not just find my way but also light up these shadowy areas for others.

The thought of helping others become aware of the hidden aspects of themselves was challenging but incredibly motivating. I thought about sharing what I've learned and experienced, hoping to ignite a spark of understanding in those around me.

*"How can I use my own journey to guide others?"*—sensing the weight of responsibility and opportunity for profound connection on my shoulders.[17]

During that quiet night, I found a new sense of purpose.

My journey wasn't just about my own enlightenment; it was about lighting the way for others' self-discovery, helping them see what's hidden, and guiding them through their shadows to a deeper comprehension of themselves. As I began to drift off to sleep, I felt both humble and excited by the chance to impact others' lives, to assist them in exploring the unknown parts of their souls. I just needed to find the right avenue, something beyond just posting content.[18]

---

17. The process of self-reflection and contemplating how to share insights with others is an important aspect of personal growth and can lead to a sense of purpose. Reference: McAdams, D. P. (2001). *The Psychology of Life Stories*. Review of General Psychology, 5(2), 100-122.

18. The opportunity to positively impact the lives of others through guidance and mentorship brings a sense of humility and anticipation for those committed to personal development and helping others. Reference: Daloz, L. A. (2012). *Mentor: Guiding the Journey of Adult Learners*. Jossey-Bass.

# A World of Words

## The Transformative Role of My Journal

L OOKING BACK ON MY journey, the evolution of my relationship with my journal has been truly significant. Initially, it served as my private venting ground, a place where I poured out all my deepest sorrows, a silent companion during my toughest moments. As I explored deeper parts of myself, my journal changed with me.[1] Its pages saw the whole journey I was on, carefully noting all the different emotions and discoveries that shaped my path.

> **"The act of writing is the act of discovering what you believe."**
> —David Hare, The Paris Review, Issue 126 (1993)

Every entry acted as a snapshot, capturing the true essence of my experiences—the highs and lows, moments of happiness, times of sorrow, sudden realizations, and small steps forward. The journal was a loyal narrator, accurately capturing my life's story as it unfolded, with each word marking the ongoing progression of time and change.

---

1. The evolution of a journal alongside its writer reflects the dynamic nature of personal growth and self-discovery. Reference: Adams, K. (1990). *Journal to the Self: Twenty-Two Paths to Personal Growth*. Grand Central Publishing.

**"We write to taste life twice, in the moment and in retrospect."**

—Anaïs Nin, Diary of Anaïs Nin, Vol. 5 (1947)

Writing in my journal became a special ritual, a deep conversation with my unconscious self. In those quiet times with my pen, the journal helped guide me through my complicated thoughts and feelings. It gave me direction when I was lost, made things clear when I was confused, and offered insights when I reflected. The empty pages were like a map where I plotted my journey, describing my inner world with every word and line.[2]

At the same time, the journal acted as a a mirror, showing me my own soul's journey. It let me look straight into my inner self, facing truths that were sometimes hard to accept. In its pages, I could see my growth, the changes in my views, and how my understanding deepened. It was an honest mirror, showing me exactly who I was and who I was becoming.

**"Writing is a way of talking without being interrupted."**

—Jules Renard, Journal (1895)

With each new entry, the journal got thicker, becoming a physical symbol of my journey. It was like a living record, filled with the essence of my experiences. Flipping through its pages was like going through my life's timeline, with each page marking a significant moment. My journal wasn't just a collection of memories; it was an active part of my journey, a friend that witnessed my constant evolution.[3]

## Escaping into the Night

---

2. Journaling serves as a reflective practice, offering a space for introspection and self-guidance through the exploration of thoughts and feelings. Reference: Rainer, T. (2004). *The New Diary: How to Use a Journal for Self-Guidance and Expanded Creativity.* TarcherPerigee.

3. The physical growth of a journal over time symbolizes the writer's personal journey, serving as a tangible record of experiences and reflections. Reference: Grason, S. (2005). *Journalution: Journaling to Awaken Your Inner Voice, Heal Your Life, and Manifest Your Dreams.* New World Library.

One night, as I lay restless, my thoughts raced, and I felt an urge to escape my apartment. On impulse, I decided to go for a late-night drive, hoping the motion and cool air would clear my head.

I slipped into my car, its familiar scent a small comfort, as I drove into the night. The streets were empty, the world asleep—the engine's soft hum was calming. I drove without direction, letting the road lead me, until I reached a familiar spot from my homeless days. It was a secluded, quiet place, illuminated by a single streetlight. Parking under the flickering light, nostalgia and sadness washed over me. Everything outside was silent, with just the occasional rustling of leaves in the night breeze.[4]

Inside my car, thoughts weighed heavily. In that silence, I felt comfort and an eerie familiarity. This spot held memories of hardship and solitude, yet also a strange sense of security. Staring into the darkness under the weak glow of the streetlight, I wondered what had drawn me back here. My journey from homelessness to this moment was filled with many ups and downs. Beneath this streetlight, once a constant in my uncertain existence, I realized I was still seeking the same peace, understanding, and light in the darkness.

A cool breeze drifted in through a cracked window, bringing with it, scents from the outside world—a world that continued to move and change, just like I had. Alone under the streetlight, I grasped that this late-night drive was more than an escape; it was a confrontation with my past, its lingering shadows, and the fact that my quest for self-understanding and healing was still ongoing.[5]

In that dim, silent setting, an idea emerged.

My journal, filled with therapeutic prompts, had been a potent-force, guiding me through my mind's hidden recesses. I understood then that these prompts, which had helped me tremendously, could also offer that same hope and clarity to others.[6]

---

4. Revisiting places associated with past experiences, especially during times of solitude, can evoke a mix of nostalgia and sorrow, leading to introspection. Reference: Wildschut, T., Sedikides, C., Arndt, J., & Routledge, C. (2006). *Nostalgia: Content, triggers, functions.* Journal of Personality and Social Psychology, 91(5), 975-993.

5. Confronting past experiences and their lingering effects is a crucial step in the ongoing process of self-understanding and healing. Reference: Herman, J. L. (1997). *Trauma and Recovery: The Aftermath of Violence--From Domestic Abuse to Political Terror.* Basic Books.

6. The use of therapeutic prompts in journaling can serve as a valuable tool for navigating the complexities of the mind and can be shared to help others on their journey to self-discovery. Reference: Pennebaker, J. W., & Evans, J. F. (2014). *Expressive Writing: Words That Heal.* Idyll Arbor.

**"In the depth of winter, I finally learned that within me there lay an invincible summer."**

—Albert Camus, Return to Tipasa (1952)

This idea started as a small thought in the darkness of the night, but it quickly blossomed. I got to work right away, compiling a series of prompts, each meticulously designed to explore the subconscious, provoke thought and provide self-understanding.

I viewed these journals as companions on the path of self-discovery and healing, presenting daily questions that help people work through the intricate complexities of their emotions and experiences. Each prompt aimed to inspire introspection, unearth concealed emotions and aid individuals in gaining deeper self-awareness. Places where others could confront their hidden aspects, accept their vulnerabilities and revel in their personal growth.[7] I pictured people from diverse backgrounds exploring their own trials and triumphs finding comfort and wisdom within these pages.

As I sat beneath the flickering streetlight, this concept resonated with me.

It felt like a genuine calling, an opportunity to support those grappling with the same shadows that once consumed me. In that moment of darkness, the *365 Day Shadow Work Journals*[8] took shape—offering light and encouragement to those willing to explore their innermost depths. It was a way to pass on my insights and provide a structured yet flexible approach for self-exploration.

## The Global Impact of Shared Healing

---

7. The concept of using journals as a tool for self-exploration is supported by research in expressive writing and its therapeutic effects. Reference: Baikie, K. A., & Wilhelm, K. (2005). Emotional and physical health benefits of expressive writing. *Advances in Psychiatric Treatment*, 11(5), 338-346.

8. Discover the transformative journey of self-discovery with Ryan's 365-Day Shadow Work Journal series by visiting WoodIslandBooks.com.

The response to the *365-Day Shadow Work Journals* was beyond anything I could have imagined. The first book in the series resonated with people all over the world, and I started getting a flood of messages—each one sharing a tale.

"I wanted a shadow work journal that would whack me over the head and make me reevaluate my life in a meaningful way, and this does that. The questions are deep and thought provoking, and where I get a little intimidated by them, because of how personal they get, that's the point, right? I'll recommend this to others for sure."

-Goldenrose

These were not just comments; they offered insights into individual lives—accounts of challenges faced, epiphanies made, and victories achieved. They provided glimpses into the lives of individuals working on their own journey of self-discovery and healing.

First, I don't know Ryan Puusaari. I'm not a friend leaving a review. I wouldn't know Ryan in a line up of two next to Carl Jung. I wasn't given this book for free in exchange for a five star review. I'm giving it a five star review because it deserves one.

I was given this book as a gift. It's truly one of the best gifts I've ever been given. I stop writing and close this book and feel a little lighter. I feel like I've unraveled a part of me. I have clarity. I know why I've been doing this thing (like, say, not asking for help), why it's not benefitting me and how I can change it in the future.

A lot of the prompts are loaded questions and that's okay - that's why you're doing shadow work. To face all those loaded questions you've been avoiding your whole life. Some of the prompts and questions may seem very similar but they really aren't. They approach the same problem from a different perspective. It really teases out all of the feelings and issues you have about a certain topic. You really feel like you've gotten to the bottom of the issue.

If you're like me, you have a mountain of issues to deal with and you don't know how or where to begin. This book takes that mountain and breaks into small pebbles. Every day you pick up one of those pebbles and you look at it and think about how it doesn't serve you anymore and you throw it into a river and watch it wash downstream. The mountain is still there but today you got rid of one pebble. And day after day, you get rid of more pebbles and Mount Emotional Trauma gradually reduces in size. It becomes a hill. That's what this book does. It takes that mountain, breaks it into small pieces, and over time, it (and you) makes the mountain smaller until you can get over the hill.

So think of this book as the pick axe you need to tear that mountain down. You can't start chipping away on your own. This book is the tool that'll help you.

-Denise S.

When I read those messages, I was touched by their raw emotion and honesty. People shared how the journal prompts made them face parts of their subconscious they had previously ignored. They found comfort in penning their thoughts and the clarity from the well-crafted reflections and daily inquiries. For many, these journals became a daily ritual, offering a precious chance for genuine self-conversation.

Each message was proof of the transformative power of self-reflection and writing. They showed that simply writing down one's thoughts can untangle complex feelings and cultivate healing.

Stories of personal growth, overcoming internal battles highlighted our shared human experiences. These reactions did more than validate the impact of journaling; they were reminders of our collective humanity. They stressed that despite our varied backgrounds, cultures, or challenges, we all yearn for similar things—peace, understanding, and acceptance.

*Our diverse struggles are what bind us.*

# Deepening Dialogues

## The Evolution of a Healing Community

A s our community expanded, our casual conversations evolved into profound dialogues. People from around the world started asking for detailed stories about my life and how these influenced the ideas and advice I shared. Their inquiries became more intricate, showing they wanted not just advice, but a real, meaningful connection with the stories behind the process of healing.

This surge in interest from the community triggered a realization within me. There was a need for something bigger—a platform to support and grow this new level of interaction. That's when I came up with the idea for a weekly newsletter, a carefully put-together collection of thoughts, perspectives and stories from my personal journey. The goal of the newsletter would be to offer a more in-depth look into healing and personal development. It would serve as a space where I could candidly share aspects of my life—the challenges faced, the triumphs celebrated, and the lessons learned. Through this medium, I hoped to give a more impactful and relatable source of guidance for others on their self-discovery quest.

The newsletter wasn't going to be just a summary of my thoughts and experiences. I envisioned it as a mix of personal stories, philosophical reflections, and practical tips. All these elements would come together, providing a well-rounded view of the healing journey. It would be an extension of the community that grew from the daily text, TikTok and now the journals, continuing the discussions and connections that had started there.

## A New Foundation to Build On

During the summer of 2023, I launched the *Healing Thoughts Newsletter*, opening a new chapter for both myself and many others. This initiative quickly evolved from a concept into something bigger, becoming a source of hope and understanding for our expanding community.

Every edition of the newsletter was carefully crafted with the intention of resonating with readers on a personal level. The newsletter explored themes such as trauma, loneliness and the intricate interplay we have with our hidden selves. It served as a meeting ground where psychology intertwined with spirituality, mixing personal stories with universal truths.

> **"True community is not just about being geographically close to someone or part of the same social web network. It's about feeling connected and responsible for what happens."**
> —Yehuda Berg, The Power of Kabbalah (2004)

Over time, the *Healing Thoughts* community blossomed beautifully. Subscribers began to open up and share their own experiences, finding acceptance and validation in our shared stories. The newsletter transformed into a mirror reflecting our collective journey towards healing, uniting individuals from diverse backgrounds in realizing they were not alone in their challenges.

The heartfelt and inspiring responses from readers were both humbling and encouraging. Messages of gratitude, accounts of personal triumphs and expressions of newfound optimism poured in.

In this process, I too found further healing. Each issue of the *Healing Thoughts Newsletter* marked a step forward in my personal growth journey—a therapeutic practice of giving and contemplation. It evolved beyond being merely a chronicle of my experiences; it became a living entity shaped by every new narrative and insight shared by the community. It stood as a symbol to the strength of the human spirit, a reminder that even in our toughest times, we can find light, understanding, and a way to heal. We were all in this together, with each issue bringing us closer to a better understanding of ourselves and one another.

## Confronting Impostor Syndrome

Starting the *Healing Thoughts Newsletter* was a significant leap towards a long cherished aspiration. But underneath this new project, I grappled with insecurities and apprehensions. The persistent nagging of impostor syndrome echoed in my mind.[1]

*"Who am I, really?"*

Late at night, alone with my thoughts, these doubts would consume my mind.

*"Who would ever listen to you?"—"Why would anyone care about your story?"*

**"The cave you fear to enter holds the treasure you seek."**
—Joseph Campbell, often attributed to Campbell

Starting the newsletter felt like the natural progression, an extension of our community. Yet, for me, it held a deeper significance—it served as a shield, providing a sense of security against a more daunting aspiration, writing a book. The notion of pouring my emotions onto its pages was both my greatest desire and my greatest dread. It seemed like a distant dream meant for a version of myself from another timeline.[2]

In comparison, managing the newsletter appeared more approachable and less intimidating. It offered me the opportunity to engage, communicate and find my voice on my own terms, within boundaries that felt comforting. It became my subtle strategy to sidestep

---

1. Impostor syndrome is a common psychological phenomenon where individuals doubt their accomplishments and fear being exposed as a fraud. Reference: Clance, P. R., & Imes, S. A. (1978). The impostor phenomenon in high achieving women: Dynamics and therapeutic intervention. *Psychotherapy: Theory, Research & Practice*, 15(3), 241-247.

2. The fear of writing a book and exposing one's emotions is a common challenge for aspiring authors, often rooted in a fear of vulnerability and judgment. Reference: Kaufman, S. B., & Gregoire, C. (2015). *Wired to Create: Unraveling the Mysteries of the Creative Mind*. Penguin Books.

the leap into uncertainty and the overwhelming idea of unveiling my entire story to the world.

Each edition I crafted was a battle against my inner critic. While words flowed effortlessly, doubts crept in too.

*"Who am I to offer guidance?"—"You are just another broken, lost soul in this world"*

The irony wasn't lost on me—there I was, providing encouragement to others while grappling with feelings of self-worth. Nevertheless, as time progressed and the responses from our community grew more frequent and heartfelt, things began to shift. Every story shared and every piece of feedback received chipped away at the self-doubt within me. I came to understand that it wasn't about striving for perfection as a mentor; it was about authenticity, shared experiences and about the honest journey of healing.[3]

**"You are the only person who can use your ability. It is an awesome responsibility."**

—Zig Ziglar

The newsletter became my new battle ground, the next level where I confronted my own fears while assisting others in doing the same. It was during this period that I mustered the courage to face my greatest apprehension; *the sense of inadequacy, the feeling of not measuring up.*

I began to see that my chaotic upbringing had granted me a unique perspective that others could connect with. This marked a turning point for me. It empowered me to accept my story, find value in my challenges and realize that my loife could serve as inspiration for others.

What initially started as a sanctuary in the form of a newsletter evolved into the catalyst that propelled me towards embracing my ultimate challenge—penning a book.

---

3. Authenticity and shared experiences are key elements in providing meaningful guidance and support to others, especially when dealing with self-doubt and impostor syndrome. Reference: Brown, B. (2010). *The Gifts of Imperfection: Let Go of Who You Think You're Supposed to Be and Embrace Who You Are*. Hazelden Publishing.

# Planting Seeds

## Ascent into Clarity

"The creative process is a process of surrender, not control."
—Julia Cameron, The Artist's Way (1992)

T HE IDEA FOR THIS book, *Healing Thoughts*, hit me out of the blue on my yearly road trip with my son. We were going to hike to Mount Carleton in New Brunswick.

Back then, I was feeling really bogged down. Life's troubles were stacking up like huge mountains—money worries eating away at my peace of mind, nagging self-doubt, and a future that looked unclear. However, something changed inside me as I started climbing up that mountain.

Climbing up Mount Carleton was like a physical symbol of my inner battles. Each step was tough, weighed down by all my worries. But strangely, as I went higher, those worries started to feel lighter, almost as if the mountain was taking them away. The cool breeze against my skin was so refreshing, especially against the warmth of my effort. With every deep breath, I felt clearer, like I was breathing out my fears.

Mount Carleton, with its challenging trails cutting through the thick greenery and stunning views around each bend, was a tough climb but also a peaceful retreat. As I went up,

I was full of doubts—wondering if I was on the right track in life, if my work mattered. The financial debts I acquired from my divorce and separation felt like a heavy backpack that just wouldn't come off, reminding me of my burdens with every step. But the higher I got, the more amazing the views became, like opening up new ways of seeing things. The huge, beautiful landscape made my problems seem smaller, easier to handle.[1]

The idea sparked at the mountain's peak, where the world below seemed minuscule. In that instant, I grasped that I didn't need to pen an elaborate life story or probe deep into hidden realms. While those goals lingered, they still felt slightly out of reach.

For almost three years, I'd been sending out hope-filled text messages that resonated with many—*why not gather them in a book for the community to treasure?*

Fueled by a newfound strength and focus, I pictured a book overflowing with meaningful quotes, each shining with wisdom and comfort. This work, I hoped, would stand as a reminder, a tangible symbol to our shared healing journey.

## The Dormant Dream

Back home from the peaceful Mount Carleton, I was overflowing with ideas. My mind was alive with the thrill of creating as I started gathering quotes and thinking up cover designs for the book.

Every quote I picked was a special memory, a light of wisdom that had helped me and others in tough times. I worked excitedly on the cover, making it show the hope and healing I wanted to share. For a little while, the project was buzzing with potential, a real part of the clear purpose I felt on the mountain.

But as time went on and everyday life picked back up its fast pace, a familiar worry started to creep in. The lively energy that kicked off my creativity began to fade as old doubts

---

1. The experience of gaining new perspectives and feeling a sense of relief from burdens while ascending a mountain reflects the psychological benefits of nature exposure and physical challenges. Reference: Ulrich, R. S., Simons, R. F., Losito, B. D., Fiorito, E., Miles, M. A., & Zelson, M. (1991). Stress recovery during exposure to natural and urban environments. *Journal of Environmental Psychology*, 11(3), 201-230.

snuck back in. The project, which had been a bright spot of hope, a guiding light in the mist, started to get pushed aside, bit by bit.[2]

The everyday tasks, with their endless list of duties and must-dos, started to overwhelm the small, inspiring voice in my head. The doubts, which were once easy to ignore, became louder and more pressing. They made me question my skills, my purpose, and the worth of my work. The clear vision and sense of belonging I had felt on the mountain started to dissolve, covered by the usual worries and fears.

The bright energy I had while inf nature's grandeur started to fade under the stark light of real life. The project, once so clear and full of promise in my mind, now became inactive. It turned into a seed of potential buried under life's complicated layers, waiting for the right time to grow in the garden of forgotten dreams.

The book, which could have healed and inspired, was put on hold, a quiet sign of the battle between inspiration and the tough demands of real life. As I went through the ups and downs of everyday life, the dream of *Healing Thoughts* stayed just that—a dream, a faint glimmer in the back of my mind, waiting for the day it could really take root and flourish.

## A Conversation That Ignites Inspiration

It was a busy period at work. I had recently assumed a new leadership position, which, despite being significant, brought about its share of stress and obstacles.[3] The pressure was mounting, and I felt the need to ease the burden. Seeking an escape and fresh

---

2. The transition from creative enthusiasm to creeping doubts is a common challenge in the creative process, often influenced by the return to routine and external pressures. Reference: Sawyer, R. K. (2006). *Explaining Creativity: The Science of Human Innovation*. Oxford University Press.

3. The transition to a leadership role often brings a mix of stress and personal growth opportunities, as leaders navigate new responsibilities and challenges. Reference: Northouse, P. G. (2018). *Leadership: Theory and Practice*. Sage Publications.

perspective, I reached out to one of my closest friends for a heart-to-heart chat in a serene corner of a nearby park, away from the chaos of my professional life.[4]

As I opened up about my thoughts and challenges, I started to feel a weight lift off my shoulders. My friend attentively listened and provided not only comforting words but also insightful perspectives that allowed me to view things from a new angle. They highlighted my progress, the hurdles I had overcome and how each obstacle had contributed to my personal growth and knowledge. Their words calmed my anxious mind.[5]

During our conversation, I found myself filled with inspiration. The idea of writing a book, once just a distant aspiration, now appeared well within reach. My friend motivated me by highlighting how sharing my own experiences and insights could offer valuable support to others dealing with similar challenges, just like they had for her. That conversation marked a significant moment for me. I didn't just feel relieved; I felt a newfound sense of purpose.

The idea of translating my experiences, the lessons learned from my personal development and the guidance gained from leading others into a book became a goal brimming with optimism and determination. At that moment, I realized that this book would transcend being merely a collection of thoughts or my personal narrative. It would showcase the transformative power of introspection, the resilience of the human soul and how confronting your fears and anxieties can lead to lasting change.

## Committing to a Collective Healing Journey

Starting to work on this book marked the beginning of a new chapter in my life. It was time to bring a long-held aspiration to life. I aimed to document my healing journey

---

4. Seeking support and a fresh perspective from a trusted friend is a common coping strategy during stressful periods, providing emotional relief and valuable insights. Reference: Uchino, B. N. (2009). Understanding the links between social support and physical health: A lifespan perspective with emphasis on the separability of perceived and received support. *Perspectives on Psychological Science*, 4(3), 236-255.

5. Open communication with a supportive friend can provide comfort, reassurance, and new perspectives on personal challenges, contributing to stress relief and emotional well-being. Reference: Cohen, S., & Wills, T. A. (1985). Stress, social support, and the buffering hypothesis. *Psychological Bulletin*, 98(2), 310-357.

and support others on their paths. This project signified a dedication to my growth—an opportunity to connect with those seeking guidance.

**"Sometimes the smallest step in the right direction ends up being the biggest step of your life. Tiptoe if you must, but take the step."**
—Naeem Callaway

As I left the park's ambiance behind, a sense of purpose filled me with energy. I reached out to my community of readers. They were like family friends who had stood by me through life's challenges and triumphs. Their encouragement has always fueled my progress. Now, I was eager to hear their thoughts on my concept.

*"Hey everyone, I've been thinking about something, "* I typed out swiftly, expressing my ideas through the keyboard. *"How would you feel about me compiling the best quotes from these messages and putting them into a book? A compilation of our wisdom and lessons learned together."*

After sending the message, excitement and apprehension washed over me. This wasn't merely soliciting feedback; it was an invitation for them to join a cause—to spread hope and understanding in a new way.[6]

The responses came pouring in, filled with support, each expressing their confidence in me. *"What a fantastic idea!"* exclaimed one individual. *"Your insights have the potential to help people; a book is the ideal medium to spread them, "* remarked another.

The flood of feedback was genuinely affirming. Every encouraging message boosted my belief in the project. It wasn't about realizing my aspirations anymore; it had evolved into a shared objective, a collective desire to impart hope abroad.

Empowered by their encouragement, I felt prepared to take on this endeavor.

My narrative, intertwined with our gathered wisdom, would serve as the book's core. It would reflect our shared journey—not just my story but a tale that resonates with the essence of our community—a narrative embodying healing and growth.

---

6. The anticipation and excitement in sharing the book concept with the community highlight the significance of involving others in the creative process and the potential for collective impact. Reference: Amabile, T. M., & Kramer, S. J. (2011). *The Progress Principle: Using Small Wins to Ignite Joy, Engagement, and Creativity at Work.* Harvard Business Review Press.

## The All-Night Writing Binge

The enthusiasm from my friend, as well as my daily text group ignited a burst of creativity in me. As the evening transitioned into night, my mind buzzed with ideas. In the chaos of my study, where inspiration often stroke during late hours, I found comfort.[7]

Lost in writing, time slipped away. Every tap on the keyboard transformed my swirling thoughts into words. The computer screen turned into a canvas, capturing not only my reflections but also our community's shared experiences and struggles.

With each page filled, tales of resilience and progress emerged, drawing from my experience and our community members' valuable input. Remembering these moments and articulating thoughts lifted my mood.

> **"The discipline of creation, be it to paint, compose, write, is an effort towards wholeness."**
> —Madeleine L'Engle, Walking on Water (1980)

As the night wore on and the moon traversed the sky, the occasional flicker of a nearby candle added a touch of drama to my late-night writing session. Sustained by coffee, I persisted with unwavering determination. Each chapter celebrated our journey, making it feel like the spirit of our community was beside me.[8]

As dawn broke with its light peeking through, I leaned back, feeling a mix of exhaustion and satisfaction. The text on my computer screen was a mix of reflections and shared

---

7. The inspiration and solace found in a creative workspace reflect the importance of a conducive environment for creativity and writing. Reference: Csikszentmihalyi, M. (1996). *Creativity: Flow and the Psychology of Discovery and Invention*. Harper Perennial.

8. The act of writing and reflecting on personal experiences can lift mood and foster resilience, highlighting the therapeutic benefits of storytelling. Reference: Pals, J. L. (2006). Narrative identity processing of difficult life experiences: Pathways of personality development and positive self-transformation in adulthood. *Journal of Personality*, 74(4), 1079-1110.

aspirations. In the calmness of the morning, I realized that this piece was more than a resharing of past quotes—it symbolized our collective hopes and ambitions.

As the sunlight brightened my workspace, a feeling of achievement filled the air as I closed the lid of my laptop. What initially began as a response to the challenges of self-doubt and writer's block has transformed into something poised to touch and motivate even more individuals. With the manuscript beginning to take shape, I stood at the threshold of a new adventure, eager and prepared for whatever lay ahead, knowing that I had the support and encouragement of my daily text community to guide me through any future challenges.

**"There is no greater agony than bearing an untold story inside you."**
—Maya Angelou, I Know Why the Caged Bird Sings (1969)

For me, working on this book became a walk down memory lane, revisiting past moments. Every day, looked back on our text community discussions, where each message and quote held significance in my exploration, reflecting our shared experiences.

Selecting these quotes was a mix of excitement and emotional weight. Each quote captured a piece of my life story brimming with authenticity and vulnerability. They evoked memories of challenges faced with resilience and the glimmers of hope that fueled our conversations.

Writing this book was very therapeutic for me. It brought about a spectrum of emotions, as I retraced a path from pain and adversity to clarity and tranquility. The book challenges readers to begin on this healing adventure and provides insight into the process.

While putting together this collection, I intertwined my reflections with a tale that resonated with those who sought solace in my words. It felt as though they were beside me, influencing my writing. Each evening spent writing became a ritual to connect with my past and our collective stories.

During these writing sessions, when only the sound of typing filled the air, I felt deeply connected to my work.[9]

---

9. The deep connection felt during writing sessions highlights the introspective nature of the writing process and its role in self-exploration. Reference: Hunt, C. (2001). *Therapeutic Dimensions of Autobiography in Creative Writing*. Jessica Kingsley Publishers.

What started as a simple book of quotes gradually evolved. I began adding random musings and thoughts for motivation. During another writing phase, I decided to include my poetry alongside the quotes. This publication transcended being a compilation of quotes; it transformed into a chronicle of our shared challenges and triumphs, narrating a journey through despair, optimism, sorrow, and resilience.

## More Than a Collection

Reflecting upon the creation of *Healing Thoughts*, I view it as a pivotal moment in my life. This book transcends mere thoughts; it encapsulates a part of my essence, narrating the ebbs and flows of life.

It serves as a tribute to dedication, chronicling the hours spent in introspection and healing, seeking to unravel life's complexities. It stands as a testament to the power discovered in sharing our vulnerabilities. Every quote and page represents a milestone on my path, illustrating that confronting our fears and welcoming our obstacles leads to transformation.

> **"Books are mirrors: you only see in them what you already have inside you."**
> —Carlos Ruiz Zafón, The Shadow of the Wind (2001)

My aspirations for this book are abundant. Essentially, I desire it to serve as a companion, extending support and comfort to those navigating challenging times and reassuring them they are not alone.

I wish for it to offer hope and motivation, guiding readers through tranquil moments in life. Understanding that all life comprises both joy and trials—I endeavor to challenge perceptions surrounding well-being.

By sharing a small part of my story, I aim to create a space for conversations about mental and emotional well-being.

**"After nourishment, shelter and companionship, stories are the thing we need most in the world."**
—Philip Pullman, The Amber Spyglass (2000)

*Healing Thoughts* holds aspirations for me. It catalyzes reflection and healing, igniting a desire for introspection and progress. I aim for readers to find reflections of their own stories within its pages, acknowledging their strength and potential—motivating them to begin on their paths toward healing.

In my vision, *Healing Thoughts* transcends being just another book on your shelf collecting dust, and it instead becomes a trusted companion that aids you in your day-to-day life.

# Lasting Reflections

"You must give everything to make your life as beautiful as the
dreams that dance in your imagination."
—Roman Payne, The Wanderess (2013)

C ONTEMPLATING MY CURRENT STATE, I sift through the various encounters and
obstacles that have led me here. Life, ever the mentor, has presented a wide range
of lessons, enriching my comprehension of existence.

In the beginning, I was a different person.

Swamped in confusion and agony. Challenges seemed insurmountable, each day a clash
with dread and sadness. Yet, in those struggles, I unearthed my fortitude.

*Every hardship, every tear, shaped a sturdier facet of me, bracing me for tough times.*

Baring my soul was daunting yet liberating.

Revealing my deepest fears and old wounds felt like jumping into a bottomless pit. But
in doing so, I discovered a strength in transparency. It was a healing journey that not
just propelled my growth but also cultivated connections with others. It showed that our
vulnerabilities aren't flaws; they're the ties that bind us in our collective experiences.

**"Stories can conquer fear, you know. They can make the heart bigger."**

—Ben Okri

Creating a space for people to share their trials and triumphs taught me we're never truly isolated. This community, founded on empathy and comprehension, has been a solid rock of support and motivation for me. It highlighted the power of collective stories and the comfort in realizing others have tread similar paths.

Self-examination and confronting my inner battles were key in working my way through tough times. By validating and addressing the neglected parts of myself, I began to heal genuinely.

This internal work was challenging; it involved facing harsh realities and enduring difficult moments. Yet, by wrestling with these tough elements, I came to understand myself better.

I've learned that healing isn't a destination but an ongoing journey—a path with ups and downs. It's about welcoming each step, drawing wisdom from challenges, and growing with each experience. *Healing isn't about erasing the past but comprehending it, learning from it, and using that knowledge to shape a brighter future.*

**"The only impossible journey is the one you never begin."**

—Anthony Robbins

This book encapsulates a phase in my life when I grappled with anxiety and imposter syndrome, showcasing my growth and the capacity to effect positive change. I believe it will provide comfort, understanding, and inspiration to others. Going through this process revealed to me that setting out on this path doesn't require an abundance of solutions. The essential thing is to trust in oneself and make that pivotal first step.

_ele_

## More Than a Memoir

**"Writing is a struggle against silence."**
—Carlos Fuentes, The Death of Artemio Cruz (1962)

I pour my soul into these pages, divulging wisdom and encounters that have molded me. Each chapter mirrors the hurdles I've leaped—the victories that have buoyed my spirit and the obstacles that have fortified my determination. Yet, deep down, I sense this isn't the magnum opus of my aspirations. It's a noteworthy landmark, undoubtedly, an integral part of my odyssey and a significant aid to others in their healing. But it's not the ultimate goal. This book holds value, offering solace and direction to others on their personal healing journeys, yet if I am being perfectly honest, it's kind of a veil. It reveals segments of my life while concealing the raw, unfiltered saga of my existence.

**"To write is to plant a flag, to say, 'I am here; this is what I believe.'**
**It is an act of courage, an act of faith, a throwing of the self into**
**the whirlwind of life."**
—Isabel Allende, The Sum of Our Days: A Memoir (2008)

Sitting here, reflecting on all of this, I've hit a realization. Writing a book has always been my ultimate dream. And This book achieves just that, however, the book I envision is more than a brief collection of insights. It's a vessel for my entire life story, laid bare. It's crafted from my intense battles, the wisdom from each fall and triumph, and the spiritual revelations that have steered me.

## The Dream of a Magnum Opus

The book I've always wanted to write is still out there, a comprehensive work that fully captures my life—the honest, the genuine, and the yet-to-be-discovered depths of my soul. It's a book that will demand I uncover every aspect of myself, face every hidden part, and share every high and low with complete honesty.

**"The true alchemists do not change lead into gold; they change the world into words."**

—William H. Gass, A Temple of Texts (2006)

This book, while not the endgame, is a key step towards it. It's a compilation offering glimpses of my path, interwoven with the daily messages that have resonated with many. It illustrates that having it *"all figured out"* isn't a prerequisite for making a difference. It serves as a reminder to me and others that initiating, taking that first leap, is often the crux of any voyage. This book is more than a showcase of endorsement or a collection of insights. It's a tangible testament to my belief in the power of starting, of taking that jump even when the future is shrouded in uncertainty. It reflects my commitment to growth, both personally and collectively. Most importantly, it's a vital leap towards fulfilling my ultimate aspiration—a book that genuinely encapsulates the essence of my life's narrative, shared with the intention of guiding others on their own paths.

_ele_

## A World Transformed by Light

**"Compassion is the radicalism of our time."**

—Dalai Lama

Imagine a future where healing shines bright, transforming the shadows of our struggles into the light of resilience. Envision a world where challenges remain, but our responses are altered. The scars of battles no longer signify pain; they become symbols of strength and wisdom.

Picture waking up each morning with a sense of purpose and tranquility. The pain that once tied us to our history now imparts courage and awareness. Our past burdens—traumas and sorrows—serve as the groundwork for liberation, enabling us to embrace life.

Consider societies that openly have discussions on well-being. Compassion permeates these dialogues, empowering individuals to share their stories without fear, reassured by the knowledge that they're not alone in their journey.

"The only way to make sense out of change is to plunge into it, move with it, and join the dance."

—Alan Watts

Visualize a community dedicated to progress where our paths intertwine with support and encouragement. Here, healing is a shared voyage, with each person's experiences guiding others along the way.

In this envisioned future, personal development is viewed as an evolving journey. Challenges are seen as opportunities for introspection and growth, emphasizing that individual growth is an evolution. Each step taken, whether forward or backward, enriches the narrative of our lives.

"Healing may not be so much about getting better, as about letting go of everything that isn't you – all of the expectations, all of the beliefs – and becoming who you are."

—Rachel Naomi Remen

Our hidden scars now serve as testaments to our strength and adaptability—serving as guiding lights of optimism and guidance for ithose beginning on their path to recovery.

This is the vision we strive to realize—a society rooted in compassion, restoration, and progress.

It's not just a dream.

*It's a reachable goal through effort, kindness, and a commitment to spreading healing thoughts!*

"I alone cannot change the world, but I can cast a stone across the waters to create many ripples."

—Mother Teresa

# THIS IS THE END

## But it is Also, the Beginning of a Much Larger Journey

THIS ISN'T A FINALE—IT'S the threshold of a fresh chapter. The tail end of this story isn't a conclusion. It's the onset of something much grander.

This book is a collection of cherished sayings from our daily texts, sorted by theme, each paired with deep reflections and motivational lectures.

As you work your way through this book, see yourself not just as a reader but as an adventurer on a quest of self-discovery.

You might decide to read it from start to end, letting each theme enrich your insights. Or you could zero in on specific sections that catch your interest.

Or—maybe you'll decide to take a chance and open a random page, trusting it has just what you need in that moment.

Whatever your approach, this book is crafted to be your sanctuary, a gateway to deeper reflection.

## Engaging with Emotions and Insights

Read through these pages. Letting the words and the emotions that follow cascade over you. Notice how they stir the depths within.

*What memories flash back? What long buried emotion comes up to the surface for you?*

This book is yours for the soul-searching.

There is no right way to use this book. Think of it like a tool, and you're the artist. Use it in the way that helps you the most. Scribble in the margins, the headers and footers, claim this space. Each time you open it, you're taking a step toward understanding yourself better and embracing who you are.

## Turning the Page with Anticipation

As I reach the end of this chapter and close this story, I want to reach out to you. This isn't just about sharing my own experiences; it's an invitation for you to explore your own path of healing and self-discovery. Let's journey together, not just as author and reader, but as companions.

Together, we'll navigate through our life stories, unravel the complex aspects of ourselves and cultivate growth and knowledge. Your narrative intertwined with mine adds to something greater—a collective exploration towards a deeper understanding of ourselves and the world.

## Join Our Community

Step onto this journey with us, where every step brings new understanding and every challenge is a chance to grow deeply. Come be a part of our *Healing Thoughts Community*, a place full of empathy, support, and shared wisdom.

Whether it's through our newsletter, our daily texts, or our lively TikTok interactions, joining us is like becoming part of a family. A family dedicated to healing, understanding, and growing personally.

In our community, we listen to you, value your experiences, and share in your adventure.

**Begin today—visit: HealingThoughts.com**

Together, we tackle life's ups and downs, strengthened by our united spirit. We're a mix of different stories, all coming together as we aim for healing, growth, and discovering ourselves.

## Your Voice Matters

Your experiences, thoughts, and views are treasures in our group. Every story, hurdle, and win you bring to the table adds layers to our collective expedition. Sharing your battles does more than help you heal; it lights the way for others, offering hope and encouragement. Your personal stories add depth and insight, enriching our group's understanding of life. I urge you to share your experiences—they're crucial for our joint exploration and insight. Your voice is important; it significantly shapes our communal path to healing.

**This adventure is a group project, not a solo mission.**

Joining our community boosts you and fortifies us collectively. We back each other up, whether we're navigating storms or reveling in victories. Your journey is a vital chapter in our collective saga, deepening our collective wisdom and making our group's bond stronger.

## A Call to Action

Come join us on this exploration with open arms and an open heart.

**Begin today—visit: HealingThoughts.com**

There, you can sign up for the *Healing Thoughts Newsletter*, become part of our daily text community, follow me on TikTok and other social media platforms or simply reach out. Whichever way you decide to join, it's a step towards healing, understanding and positive change. Together, we can build a world filled with empathy and kindness, where we all have the courage to confront our obstacles, celebrate our accomplishments and welcome our whole selves with confidence and elegance.

Let's begin on this beautiful journey together, brimming with hope and bravery; knowing that our shared struggles are actually our greatest strengths.

**Begin today—visit: HealingThoughts.com**

## The Beginning of Your Next Chapter

This isn't the end; it's just the start.

It signals the beginning of a new chapter, not only in this book but also in the grander narrative of your life. These messages have helped many people through tough times. I hope you find clarity in their simplicity and inspiration in the thoughts they express.

**"The purpose of human life is to serve, and to show compassion and the will to help others."**

—Albert Schweitzer

So let's get off our high horses and start lifting each other up, one act of kindness at a time!

—*ell*

# Me, Myself, and I

**Navigating the Inner Self**

**"The only journey is the journey within."**

– Rainer Maria Rilke.

S ELF-DISCOVERY AND PERSONAL GROWTH: Discover motivation in these quotations and musings. They're designed to spark your self-awareness adventure.

Each one is a guidepost toward understanding your true self.

Allow them to nudge and energize you.

Dive into the reflections. Let them carve out a path to a richer life.

*Question your viewpoints.*

Welcome this expedition of introspection. Let each message ignite a fire within you.

**As you walk this path, remember:** *your growth is infinite, your potential boundless.*

I've walked in shoes that never fit,
along paths that never called my name,
feet blistered and sore,
the crunch of gravel underfoot a constant reminder,
I am but a ghost, adrift in my own story,
seeking the place where my soul might dwell,
where the air smells of home and the light feels like belonging.
I've recited words not mine,
a parrot paralyzed by fear,
hesitant to soar into the uncharted horizons of my thoughts,
my breath catching with every unspoken word.

Awareness seeped, like a slow bleed—
a bittersweet revelation of the chains I bore,
not cast by others,
but crafted by my hands,
in a desperate bid to belong,
the metallic taste of conformity on my tongue.
But fitting in was a puzzle with missing pieces,
a picture never quite complete.
Through fragmented friendships I found
my true voice suffocated
smothered by a society too loud to hear my silent cries.

Thinking for oneself is rebellion,
a breaking free from the orbit of external influence,
to chart a course into unexplored territories
of the mind
and heart,
each beat like a drum guiding my way.
This path is unmarked,
soft underfoot, like moss beneath the trees,
etched by my soul's unique vibration.
In this quest for self,
I've recognized the power of my voice.
*The real triumph isn't finding where I fit,*
but in shattering the mold to sculpt my destiny,
crafting a masterpiece that needs no validation
to be whole, to be radiant, to be authentically, irrevocably me.

**"To find yourself, you need to start by actually thinking for yourself."**

— June 12, 2022

Figuring out your own complexities isn't effortless. It's about exploring deeply and questioning what lies beyond the apparent.

Revealing your true self begins with independent thinking. This isn't just breaking from the herd; it's an invitation to explore your inner depths. We're constantly slammed with other people's opinions, the latest trends, and societal must-dos. Falling in line is too darn easy.

*Many grab beliefs off the rack without a second thought, leading to a life of resentment.*

Dare to be different.

Dare to question.

Dare to scrutinize your beliefs, values, and motives. See if they genuinely mirror your authentic self.

This exploration isn't just about finding the answer or understanding yourself completely; *it's about the adventure.*

Roll with the changes.

Grow. Evolve.

Trust your gut, even when it takes you into unexpected turns.

In a room draped in stillness,
I found myself ensnared by time's ticking,
its relentless rhythm sharing secrets through the silence,
each tick a stark reminder of my past self.
A lost soul, lingering on the lonely edges of my existence,
haunting the hollow spaces I've outgrown.
I've clung to old photographs,
fingers tracing the lines of laughter
that feels like it belonged to someone else.
Nostalgia, a bitter pill to swallow,
hoping to reclaim a self,
as comfortable as an old, worn sweater,
yet confining like a butterfly caught in a jar.

The journey from then to now
has been a series of departures,
each step forward a farewell
to versions of me that no longer fit.
Through the raw discomfort of change,
I've come to realize there's no turning back,
no former self waiting to be revived.
*Life propels us onward,*
*demanding growth,*
*the rise of new identities*
*from the flames of fresh trials and triumphs.*
*Embracing this endless metamorphosis,*
*I find peace not in the shadows of what was,*
*but in the luminous vision of who I am becoming.*

**"There is no past version of yourself that you need to get back to. Life is all about moving forward and growing from the new lessons learned."**

— December 18, 2021

You might think you need to get back to an old version of yourself.

But that's *bullshit.*

Life's not about rewinding. It's about progressing, evolving, transforming.

Your experiences and lessons aren't just memories—they're the fuel propelling you forward. *Understand this.* It's how you adapt, improve, and welcome the new.

Each chapter in your life paves the way for the next.

*Adopting this mindset changes everything. You always grow forward. You're not meant to backtrack; you're changing for the better.*

With each moment, you're not losing your old self. You're creating a deeper, more intriguing you.

This isn't about throwing away your past. It's about mixing your experiences into the person you're becoming.

*Every day is an opportunity to add to the incredible person you are.*

I've stood at the threshold of tomorrow,
clutching the fragmented shards of yesterday,
a guardian of ancient ruins,
haunted by the yawning emptiness they leave behind,
a void too vast and dark to fill.
The pain of letting go,
a silent scream through the hollows of my soul,
resounding against walls built from memories
and postponed dreams.

In this desolate landscape of loss,
I've glimpsed the faint outline of possibility,
a nebulous shape forming in the swirling mists of the unknown.
With each goodbye, I find a fragile relief,
a weight lifting,
as if shedding old, weathered layers
makes room for new breath, new life,
for the birth of something fresh.

Every ending is simply the dawn of a new beginning,
each loss, an opportunity for discovery,
every discarded fragment of me,
a step toward the blossoming of who I am becoming.
*This perpetual cycle of death and rebirth,*
*a dance to the relentless rhythm of time,*
*demands not my resistance,*
*but my surrender,*
*to the inevitable rise and fall*
*of the selves I embody,*
*each new chapter an invitation*
*to rise from the smoldering ashes of the old,*
*to embrace the becoming,*
*and to welcome the dawn of a new self,*
*forged in the searing fires of transformation.*

**"Each new chapter of our lives requests an old part of us to fall and a new part of us to rise up."**
— October 17, 2023

Life is a constant shuffle.

We shift, ditching the dead weight, and snagging bits that push us forward.

Each new scene in our saga calls for a fresh us, throwing curveballs and new chances our way. It's a balance between letting go and grabbing hold, needing guts and having a keen sense of self.

Yet, these words might as well be air when it's time to cutting ties.

Maybe it's a piece of who you are, a thought you've clung to, a habit, or a buddy you've been tight with for ages. Right then, it hits you—what felt like your ally might've actually been your anchor, dragging you down.

You're on a mission to unlearn, peeling off layers until your raw, authentic self stands out.

As we drop our old self, we make room for new facets.

It's like cracking open a fresh chapter, nudging us towards a version of ourselves that fits right with where we're at and where we're headed.

This shift is proof of our grit and our knack for rolling with life's punches.

Stepping from one chapter into the next is no small chore, especially when you are also brimming with what-ifs and jitters.

It's about leaping into the unknown, stepping out of the cozy corners. This stretch zone is where we find our muscle and the room to grow.

It's where we learn to bet on ourselves and the ride, even when the road's a blur.

Each chapter is a chance to meet ourselves again, to chisel our mission, and to sync up with our truths.

It's a shot at crafting a life that's deeply ours, vibing with the core of our being.

I've bent and folded,
a human origami,
shaping myself to please all but my own heart.
Each fold marked a chapter I didn't author,
a tale of diminishing myself,
a story of self-abandonment.
I passed through the days, an apparition,
dwelling in the remains of my true self,
grieving the bright colors I'd washed out
to match the world's subdued shades.
In the mirror, a stranger's eyes bore into mine,
questioning, accusing,
a silent cry for recognition.

The truth struck like a sudden frost—
cold, sharp, unmistakable.
I had been watering dead plants,
pouring pieces of myself into the void
of others' comfort,
starving the roots of my being
for the fear of outgrowing the pots I was planted in.

But no more.
I declare a renaissance of the self,
a bold reclaiming of space,
an expansion beyond the confines
of who I was told to be.
I will not shrink,
will not dilute my essence
to make room for others' ease.
This is my rebellion,
a manifesto of growth,
an oath to never again confine my spirit
for the sake of another's comfort.
*I rise, unapologetically whole,*
*a testament to the wild, untamed beauty*
*of being fiercely, unreservedly me.*

**"Don't water or shrink yourself down just to keep a version of yourself that you have already outgrown alive, in some desperate attempt to make others feel comfortable."**

— August 29, 2023

Life is a continuous stream of choices and directions.

Yesterday's *you* might not quite match up with today's edition. That's just how things roll—a sign of getting better and leveling up.

As we transform, there's this pull to dilute ourselves. To backpedal.

*Why?*

Comfort. Familiarity.

*Playing it small so others can keep up is selling yourself short.*

We tell ourselves, *"Better they're comfy than I rise."* It's like wearing an old sweater that's two sizes too small. Snug, but completely absurd.

Look, here's the thing—growth is awkward.

For everyone.

As you stretch and broaden your horizon, so does everything around you.

And sure, it freaks out the old gang. But that's the deal with evolving. When you dial down your shine, you're not just stunting your growth but cheating the world out of the full you. Each time you dim that light, you're hiding a masterpiece.

You're not meant to be watered down.

You're here to be all-out, celebrated, *unapologetically.*

In the stillness of a room too familiar,
I lingered over the pages of a chapter
read and reread,
the learned lines lingering in my thoughts,
a script too familiar to surprise,
yet held onto like a lifebuoy in vast seas.
I've traced the contours of routine,
a path well-trodden, safe, yet suffocating,
where the comfort of known miseries
outweighs the fear of unseen joys.
In this cycle of sameness,
my reflection faded,
a shadow among the living
longing for a spark
to ignite the gray.

The realization, subtle—
life should not be a single story,
but a collection of tales,
each chapter an entry to the next,
a gateway to the unforeseen.
I stood on the brink of change,
reluctant, with the weight of past pages anchoring my feet,
yet the hint of unwritten lines
spurred a curiosity greater than fear.
*To stay is to vanish,*
*but to move forward is to blaze*
*into a story yet untold.*

**"You will never know how amazing your story can be if you keep living the same chapter. It's time to turn the page."**
— March 4, 2022

**Life's a novel:** *and each day, is a fresh page.*

Your saga will be a mix of triumphs and goof-ups, unfiltered and real, seasoned with laughs and hardships.

Sure, comfort zones are snug, but replaying the same old scenes wears thin quickly. The thrill is in the leap, venturing into the unknown. The future is the exciting bit.

Envision endless blank pages waiting for your touch. Adventures, friendships, challenges, and golden life adventures await. Changing things up doesn't have to upend your life. Try a new hobby, wander through undiscovered paths, meet someone new, or switch your morning brew.

*Small changes, big impacts.*

These moments propel you into new chapters, sparking growth and insights.

**Remember:** *You're the boss.*

Starting anew—*that's on you.* The real magic lies in recognizing that you're the one holding the pen. You dictate the narrative, full of twists and turns. Life's journey is replete with new beginnings, adventures, and growth.

*An entire universe of experiences awaits its role in your story.*

Flip the page with confidence, eager for what's ahead. After all, the stories worth telling are brimming with unexpected turns and endless what-ifs.

I've witnessed beauty in fleeting moments:
sunsets suffusing the sky with hope's tender hues,
joy sparkling in a child's eyes,
divine glimpses
in life's mundane grace.
Each wonder observed
left me more hollow,
a bystander on the brink of amazement,
longing for a magic I couldn't grasp,
a miracle I could not claim.
The inward journey began
not with a step, but a tumble,
a fall into the depths of my own despair,
where in the darkness,
I finally glimpsed a faint light—
not from the surroundings,
but shining quietly from within.

The realization came slowly,
a truth long buried under layers of self-doubt:
the miracle lies not in sky, sea, or flower,
but in the breath that carries me through grief,
in resilience rising like a phoenix
from the ashes of defeat.
To understand oneself as a miracle
is to awaken to a new existence,
where every heartbeat is a masterpiece,
every breath is proof of the extraordinary beauty
of simply being.
This understanding, once accepted,
turns every moment into a miracle,
not because of what I observe,
but because of what I am—
a marvel, not for the rarity of my existence,
but for the sheer, improbable reality of it.

**"Seeing a miracle may inspire you, but finally understanding that you are a miracle, that will change your life."**

— September 6, 2021

We're all amazed by life's high points.

Those epic sunrises, serendipitous encounters, and jaw-dropping feats. These moments ignite our hearts, making us yearn to be part of the magic. They're glimpses of the extraordinary, a break from our daily snooze fest.

But the real magic show isn't just around us—*it is us.*

This realization isn't just a fleeting thought. It's a soul-shaking revelation that upends our self-perception.

*Being alive is a cosmic jackpot.*

From the atoms partying in your body to the mind-blowing sync between your brain and soul, you're a walking miracle.

This new perspective is a call to live differently.

Knowing you're the star of the show, you treat yourself like royalty. You become your biggest fan, accepting your flaws and quirks as part of your unique story. You start pursuing your passions and trusting your gut.

Every moment, every encounter is a chance to learn, adapt, and expand your horizons.

Welcome the magic that is you.

You're not just along for the ride—*you're the star attraction.*

**"He who knows others is wise; he who knows himself is enlightened."**

– Lao Tzu.

Going after self-knowledge is like signing up for a class called *'Who the Heck Am I 101'*—noble, sure, but mostly it's about finally understanding why you're weirdly good at remembering song lyrics from 10 years ago when you don't even know why you walked into the kitchen moments ago.

# SCARS TO STARS

## The Journey of Healing

> "Although the world is full of suffering, it is also full of the overcoming of it."
>
> – Helen Keller.

**H**EALING AND RECOVERY: STEP into a world of healing. Here, you'll encounter quotes and musings on dealing with trauma and moving towards the emotional wellness that awaits you.

This collection gets it—*healing's a wild ride.*

It's here to back you up and cheer you on through this tough but hopeful adventure.

*Welcome the path of recovery.*

Let each nugget of wisdom light your way. Recognize that healing is not a straight line.

It's a journey marked by unexpected twists.

**As you read these thoughts, remember:** every step brings you closer to peace.

In the depths of my own striving,
where each hard-won achievement scales a ladder into the void,
I recognize the drive isn't born from a desire to tower over others,
nor from the vanity of accolades.
This relentless push, nearing burnout,
stems from a mix of fear and hope—
a frantic bet that climbing high enough,
doing enough,
being enough,
might secure a place of belonging,
a haven of acceptance,
a sense of safety in a world that once showed its cruelty.

It's not ego that fuels these midnight oil burnings,
these far-reaching aims towards the stars.
It's the haunting memory of traumas past,
the chilling repercussions for simply being,
and the faint, flickering hope that maybe,
just maybe,
if I can dazzle the world enough,
I can outrun the shadows,
earn my place,
carve out a corner where love,
in its most unconditional form,
finds me,
accepts me,
tells me, *"Here, you are safe."*

*In this relentless pursuit,*
*I often forget*
*that maybe,*
*just maybe,*
*I am already enough.*

"**Trauma survivors who push themselves to the brink of burnout in pursuit of overachievement aren't motivated by ego. Instead, they are often propelled by a mix of fear of repercussions and a hope that, by being sufficiently impressive, they might finally attain love, acceptance, or safety.**"

— January 30, 2023

Healing and self-discovery walk a rocky road.

Trauma-touched souls, driven by fear and hope, aren't seeking glory. Their hustle isn't about loud proclamations but rather, it's about confronting pain's shadows.

Fear of failure looms for those marked by trauma, weary of past wounds.

*It's not just avoiding another stumble; it's silencing the voices of old scars.*

Striving for excellence becomes a shield, a fortress of achievements guarding against past hurts. Yet, beneath this armor lies a tender quest for love, acceptance, and refuge.

They often equate worth with actions, believing love and safety are trophies earned, not given. This stems from a past where affection and protection were conditional. So, they aim high, chasing the dream of unconditional support and security.

Their pursuit of excellence reveals bravery, but it also comes at a steep cost. Racing towards exhaustion for approval or love which leads to burnout.

The healing journey is uniquely intricate for trauma survivors.

It involves dissecting why they relentlessly pursue success. It's understanding that their value isn't tied to a list of wins. And learning gentler ways to seek love, acceptance, and safety.

Most importantly, it's realizing they're worthy of these gifts.

Not because of their accolades—*but by being simply human.*

The day the ground beneath my feet quaked,
I plummeted into a subterranean river of my own making.
within the shadowy depths and hidden currents,
I learned to breathe among the ruins of shattered dreams and silent fears,
each breath, sharp, like the jagged rocks along the riverbed,
redefined my being.

In solitude, I battled the waters,
fought the relentless currents of anxiety, their force my own,
their secrets sharing lies through the dripping caverns.
The demanding drift through darkness
weighed my bones with more than pain—
it sculpted an identity I reluctantly wore.
*"Broken,"* the currents labeled me, *"Lost,"* the waters declared,
and I responded.

*"I am not my scars or the agony endured."*
Healing isn't returning to a past untouched by trauma,
but navigating the discomfort of unbecoming.
It demands courage to let go of known sorrows,
to shed an identity molded by misery,
standing bare in self-reflection's dim light.

I am the observer, steadfast beneath emotional disorder,
a lone mariner in these hidden currents.
In this awareness, I find freedom—
not by erasing pain,
but by recognizing I am much more
than the sum of my traumas.
Witnessing, not claiming,
I move through life, healing, ever whole,
a subterranean river flowing towards the surface,
where light meets the water, and I rise.

> "Healing can be uncomfortable because we have become accustomed to the despair and assumed the identity of our trauma and pain. But you are not your trauma, your anxiety, or any of your emotions or thoughts. You are the presence, the observer behind these things. Don't claim them, witness them."
>
> — April 3, 2023

Healing is about diving into the deep end of the pool. Not just floating around in the shallow waters.

We're talking about swimming into those hidden, dark corners where discomfort and vulnerability hang out. This deep dive prods at our core, especially when knotted up in pain and loss.

*You're more than your scars or worries. You're the observer, the person sitting back, watching life's storms roll by.*

Healing dares us to loosen our grip and see beyond the hurt. It's like stepping back, witnessing your emotional drama without getting swept away. It's about shedding the old sob stories and stepping into uncharted, scar-free zones.

Observing your emotions from the sidelines is a new level of awareness. It's being a mindful spectator of your inner chaos, free from judgment or entanglement.

In this space, healing thrives, and peace quietly enters.

As you walk this healing path, view discomfort as a sign of growth.

You're not your pain or emotions. You're the witness, observing with compassion and insight.

*Don't flaunt your pain like some medal.*

*Witness it, soak in the lessons, and let it guide you to a richer understanding of yourself.*

After unforeseen storms,
I sit amid my life's remains.
Bare, a raw chaos exposed,
every exhale echoes endless—silent skirmishes.
No tales of heroism, just days passing,
each nodding to uncelebrated resilience.
Laughter lingers like a relic of forgotten joy,
sarcasm, once a shield, now too heavy to wield.
They say healing is a journey,
but don't tell of the rough paths,
strewn with remnants of what was.
No markers, no signs of progress,
just endless attempts, setbacks, perseverance.

Alone, I've learned:
healing wears no hero's cape,
bears no cinematic gloss.
It's sitting with discomfort, recognizing pain,
not as a guest, but as a part of me needing to be heard.
It's a silent, simple affair, magic-free,
an effort that continues unnoticed, without praise.
Exhausting, draining, sometimes feeling futile,
yet there's a raw beauty, a hidden strength in this truth.
Letting go isn't graceful, but hesitant, shaky,
a brave act against the unknown,
choosing to face the storm with openness, not defiance.
To heal is to exist within chaos and confusion.
So, I affirm to my reflection,
this path is yours alone, no need for pretense.

*True healing is quietly recognizing your vulnerability,*
*finding strength in facing yourself, judgment-free, fully there.*

"It doesn't have to look magical or pretty. Real healing is hard, exhausting, and draining. Let yourself go through it. Don't try to paint it as anything other than what it is. Be there for yourself with no judgment."

— July 23, 2022

Healing is no easy task.

Picture a battlefield littered with hurdles, setbacks, and a good ol' dose of self-doubt. Yet, it's also your golden ticket to growth and self-discovery. We all have a thing for painting our healing in rosy hues. We aim to make it look peachy, to flaunt a seamless recovery.

**But let's face it:** *healing can be quite rough around the edges.*

It's about tackling those deep-seated scars and darkest fears head-on. It's about feeling every emotion, raw and unfiltered. Bad days will come with the territory—feeling lost or overwhelmed is part of the deal. *And that's okay.*

Shower yourself with kindness and support.

Healing is not a sprint.

Healing is not a one-size-fits-all solution.

It's a custom, tailor-made suit that you rock on your own terms. This journey is about you, your growth, and your self-discovery.

Forget keeping up appearances.

Lean into your genuine, unpolished self.

*Believe in the magic of growth and change, even when it's messy.*

You're leveling up, getting stronger and wiser by the day.

True healing isn't about spinning a perfect story for the audience. It's about honoring your path and healing on your own terms.

Within the silent stage of my decisions,
I've faced crossroads where each path
carries the weight of potential heartache,
decisions demanding pieces of my heart
as the toll for passage.
With each step taken,
I dance delicately with destiny,
feeling the deep cut,
my heart's tender parts
wounded by choices
meant to steer me toward growth.

In this space of pain,
opened wide by the scalpel of decision,
I've found space to breathe,
to allow healing to unravel gently,
a paradox where loss cultivates new strength.
These bittersweet moments,
teach a tough lesson:
*the path to soulful healing*
*often passes through heartache's valleys.*
Here, in the shadows of pain,
lie profound opportunities for transformation—
where light seeps into broken places,
guiding the soul
toward deeper, truer wholeness.

**"There are moments when you are called to make choices that may wound your heart, yet in the process, they create space necessary for the healing of your soul."**

— May 27, 2023

We often have to face tough choices that can fray the edges of our hearts, leaving them tender and bare. However, it's right there, in the thick of it, that the seeds of our soul's mending are sown.

Choosing the path sprinkled with thorns isn't a masochistic ritual; it's an open invitation to growth, to carve out a nook within us ripe for healing.

This trip isn't for the faint-hearted.

It demands the courage to lock eyes with our fears, to wade into the murky waters of the unknown. It's about wrapping our arms around the discomfort, accepting it as a transient pain with the promise of a lasting serenity on the horizon.

These choices aren't about self-destruction.

They're a quest for authenticity, a realization that sometimes, our hearts need to traverse the shadows to truly appreciate the light. They need to be acquainted with the sting of loss to fully relish the warmth of love; they must endure the ache of goodbye to comprehend the beauty of connection.

**At life's pivotal moments, remember:** *the choice that grazes your heart might be the salve for your soul.*

It's a paradox. An enigma.

A truth that opens its petals only to those brave enough to walk the path less taken.

*Welcome this journey.*

Let it steer you, and have faith that, in the end, it will guide you to a place where your heart and soul resonate in perfect synergy.

RYAN PUUSAARI

Crushed under expectations,
I mastered the art of wearing masks,
each a nebula concealing my inner light.
The turning point,
realizing the heaviest chains
are the gravitational forces we choose.
Healing began with a daring question,
*"Who am I beneath these cosmic clouds?"*
A question so powerful it triggered
a supernova of self-awareness.

Layer by layer, I shed expectations,
a gas and dust collapsing inward,
lightening the load on a core ready to ignite.
Old doctrines, now foreign,
belonged to someone else—
not the protostar forming within.
With each layer removed,
a radiant truth surfaced:
*the authenticity of my stellar core.*

Healing wasn't fixing broken pieces
to fit an old constellation,
but discovering the constellation was never mine.
In unmasked solitude,
my voice radiated with the power
of its own nuclear fusion,
expressing through actions, choices,
each a burst of helium light,
reclaiming a narrative long hijacked.
*Healing is an act of cosmic defiance,*
*a commitment to be brilliantly, beautifully real.*

"Healing is not simply a matter of attaining emotional well-being,
but rather it's a process of shedding that which is not truly a part
of one's self - the societal expectations, the ingrained ideologies -
and embracing one's whole authentic being."

— November 9, 2022

Healing is about stripping away the societal stickers and norms that make us feel like strangers in our own skin.

Picture yourself as a statue, originally crafted with unique features. Over time, society, family, and culture plastered on layers of stickers and paint. Sure, these might have felt like armor or a tribe emblem at first, but they slowly buried the masterpiece underneath.

Healing is about gently scraping off those extra layers to unviel the real you beneath.

*If you're looking for an easy ride, you better sit this one out.*

It takes courageous introspection—facing the parts we've hidden away.

It's about evaluating inherited beliefs and seeing if they resonate with our core.

It's ditching the old and welcoming the new.

Shedding those societal layers might leave us feeling bare, like we're streaking in public. But that's when our truth and raw power shine. That's when we discover our actual values and passions, free from the crowd's judgment. Embracing our whole, unadulterated selves isn't about hitting perfection or living on cloud nine every day. It's about accepting all our sides—the bright and the dark, the strengths and the flaws. It's about being in tune with our authentic rhythm, making choices that resonate deeply, and expressing ourselves in ways that are purely us.

In this process of unraveling and self-renewal, don't be surprised if your social circle, career path, or hobbies start to shift. You might gravitate towards new scenes and people who reflect your genuine vibe.

That's the beauty of dropping the act.

It frees us to live more authentically, more in sync with our essence.

In the serene stillness of post-recovery,
my interests, like seasons, have irrevocably shifted.
It's not a sad goodbye,
nor a fiery rejection of past ties.
Rather, it's a gentle unclasping of hands,
releasing connections that no longer suit
the evolving self, like a phoenix rising from ashes.
This newfound clarity, a dawn breaking,
illuminates faces and phases
once deemed essential to my essence.
Now, I see them as they are—
no longer pedestals of longing and belonging,
but simple truths in the story of my soul.

It's not a loss, this shift in interest,
but a liberation.
A shedding of illusions that once clouded my vision,
a breaking free from the gravitational pull
of influences that dimmed my essence rather than amplifying it.
Healing has taught me
to hold my connections up to the light,
to discern the genuine from the fleeting,
to see where my energy is nourished
and where it is depleted.
*In this new clarity,*
*I find not void, but space—*
*space to expand, to breathe,*
*to welcome what aligns*
*with the deepest truths of my being.*

"**Healing makes you lose interest in many things you once connect-
ed with. Not even out of sadness, but out of finally seeing people
and things for who and what they really are.**"
— May 21, 2022

Healing remixes the track.

Suddenly, old jams just don't groove the same. This isn't about the blues. It's like we're
rocking fresh lenses. As we piece ourselves back together, priorities shift. Fake glitz loses
its shine, and we crave real talk and genuine vibes.

At first, it feels like we're a snake shedding skin in the hot dry sun. But we're actually
digging deeper into our own essence, understanding the big picture with eagle like eyes.

This clarity is liberating.

It causes us to stop wasting time on what doesn't spark joy.

We get picky in the best way.

*Choosing depth over a crowded room doesn't make us snobs. It means we're aiming for
connections that truly feed our souls.*

Healing equals power.

Ditching the façade, we find our true might and grit. It's not about bossing others around.
It's about steering our own ship, following a compass that points to our true north. On
this road to healing, let's not be too hard on ourselves. Severing bonds can sting. A tad
of sorrow is normal—it's all part of the glow-up. As we heal and grow, doors open. New
adventures await.

*Healing is really about returning to home base.*

Acknowledging our worth and hugging our true selves tight. And as we do, we naturally
drift towards folks and experiences that mirror our inner truth.

**Past attachments we once clung to might fade, but the treasure we find is pure:** *a
life authentically ours, rich in connections that genuinely resonate.*

**"What happens when people open their hearts? They get better."**
  – Haruki Murakami.

Be open to the process of healing, even when it feels like you're trying to solve a Rubik's Cube in the dark.

# Now and Zen

## Mastering the Art of Presence

**"Mindfulness isn't difficult, we just need to remember to do it."**
– Sharon Salzberg.

**M**INDFULNESS AND AWARENESS: THE quotes and musings in this collection emphasize the significance of being present and aware of our environment.

They prompt us to slow down, breathe deeply, and truly appreciate the splendor of the moment and the world around us.

*Welcome the power of now.*

Let these messages guide you to a state of mindfulness.

**As you reflect on these words, remember:** *the beauty of life is in the here and now. Savor each moment, and let it fill your soul with wonder and gratitude.*

I've been drifting through life,
an archivist lost in dusty tomes, trailing the same old paths
etched deep by the quills of routine.
Each day a repetition, each choice
a mimicry of the one before, guided not by the curiosity of my soul,
but the inertia of a wounded self.
*"How long have I wandered these corridors of memory,*
*my decisions reflections of an unexamined heart?"*
Each step, each turn, blindly taken,
leading further from my truth, further from the light I once knew
in the clarity of youth's unburdened dawn.

In the silence of forgotten chambers,
it dawns on me, amidst the dust of archives, the power of a pause,
the strength found in a single breath.
*"Does this move me forward,*
*closer to the manuscripts I hold dear,*
*or is it another step in the dance of distraction?"*
To ask is to awaken,
to choose with eyes wide to the ancient scripts' unveiling.
A simple question, a moment's halt,
yet in it lies the path back to myself,
to the halls filled with intention, leading not to the remnants of past wounds,
but forward, towards the light of conscious choice.

The library of my life, once a maze of repetitive aisles,
now reveals hidden compartments,
filled with forgotten manuscripts and untold stories.
And so, I begin again, with every dawn,
an archivist more aware,
walking the journey of my days
not as a ghost cataloging the past,
but as a soul awakened,
discovering hidden manuscripts
that guide my course by the stars of my own values.
I dust off the cobwebs of old habits,
and find within the pages of my own being,
the ink of new intentions, the parchment of possibility,
steering my course by the stars of my own values.

"If you continue to go through your life unconsciously on autopilot, you'll keep making choices based off the wounded perception of who you are. Start making choices consciously. Bring awareness into your day, stop and ask yourself, "does this choice move me forward toward my core values or away from them?" Then act accordingly."

— August 7, 2022

Life's a wild ride, and let's face it: *it's not always luxury seating.*

Sometimes, it feels like we're just coasting, not really in the driver's seat. *Have you ever caught yourself just going through the motions?* That's autopilot for you. It's comfy, sure, but it can also lead you off track.

It's time to seize back the controls. Hold up. Reflect.

When faced with a choice, hit the brakes and ask yourself, *"Is this propelling me towards what I really care about, or is it a detour?"*

Your big things—honesty, kindness, courage—are your north star. Align with them, and you're cruising in the right direction. Every decision is your chance to steer your existence towards what you truly want. It's tough—absolutely—but oh, so rewarding. Staying true to yourself, to your core values, means you're not just existing.

*You're leveling up.*

Slipping into this groove of deliberate living doesn't just click overnight.

It's more of a grind-it-out daily kind of thing. Start simple.

Pick a better snack, say no when you need to, and take a minute to just breathe. Small tweaks can lead to big shifts over time. And sure, tripping up is part of the script. The trick is to learn and press on.

Stick to what's right for you and make choices that mirror that, and you're not just growing; you're thriving.

Finding joy and contentment on this path—*that's the jackpot.*

In moments dark,
entangled in the web of decisions left unmade,
I felt like a kite without a string.

Silence, my new companion,
taught me the weight of words unspoken,
dreams unchased, loves unclaimed.
It was in this void, I learned the heaviest truth—
the shackles binding me were forged
from my own fears, doubts, my own iron will to sink.

Within the silence, a truth—
*"I am..."* holds power,
a key to break free from chains unseen.

With each "I am," a step towards light,
choosing, shaping,
the architect of my existence.
The night, a patient sculptor,
molded my resolve with every heartbeat.

Empowered, I learned to say,
*"I am..."* and in doing so,
crafted a path of my own.

"**The more you realize you get to choose, the more empowered you become. You get to choose how you respond. You get to choose the meaning you assign to what happens to you. You get to create who you are every time you speak: 'I am....'**"

— July 15, 2023

Our choices shape our life.

Every moment, reaction, and decision is in our hands. This knowledge is empowering. Suddenly, we're not just onlookers; we're in charge of our story.

When faced with surprises, remember that we pick our responses. It's not about stifling emotions but thoughtfully choosing our way forward.

The lessons we draw from what happens are where our true might lies. The same event has different takes. It's our perspective that colors our world.

The words *"I am" are* like casting spells. With each *"I am,"* we define and redefine ourselves. *"I am strong," "I am worthy,"* these are choices that lift us.

Choosing consciously takes mindfulness.

It's easy to slip into autopilot, so pause.

Reflect.

*Is this reaction, this story, this identity truly what I want?*

As we harness this power of choice, its potential becomes apparent. We're not drifting on fate's tides. We're sculpting our life, one decision at a time. We can't control everything, but how we respond—*that's our territory.*

The power is in your hands. Your reactions, the meanings you attach, the person you become—these choices shape your existence.

*Lean into this power, and feel your strength grow.*

I've long lived in the shadow of my emotions,
fearing the storm they promised with every darkening cloud.
I built walls to shelter from the rain,
doors to close against the howling wind of grief,
windows to shield against the lightning flash of anger.
Here, in this fortress against feeling,
I discovered deeper solitude,
a silence not of peace but of avoidance,
a stillness not of calm but of escape.

In surrender, in opening the door,
I learned the truth of transformation—
emotions, once adversaries, became guides,
lighting the path to self-awareness
with their intense glow.
*Acceptance was the key,*
*turning fear into understanding,*
*anger into energy,*
*sorrow into depth of compassion for myself.*

No longer do I fight the tidal wave,
but dive into its heart,
finding in its center not the chaos I feared,
but the peace of deep waters,
where every emotion is but a wave
on the surface of a sea that is me—
deep, vast, and ultimately calm.
*In this acceptance, I am free,*
*no longer a prisoner*
*but a traveler,*
*guided by my emotions*
*on a journey to the center of my being,*
*where lies the stillness of inner peace.*

**"By accepting your emotions, rather than avoiding them, you strip them of their power to control you, transforming these once-feared forces into allies on your journey toward self-awareness and inner peace."**

— June 29, 2023

Accepting your feelings can be a powerful shift. When you fully experience your emotions, you realize they're not foes to be feared but signals offering valuable insights. Instead of running or shoving them under the rug, you give them a nod.

For instance, when you feel angry, you might acknowledge it by saying, *'I'm feeling angry right now, and that's okay.'* This validation and acceptance is critical to gaining control.

Think of your emotions as ocean waves. Some are calm and chill, while others are wild and throwing a temper tantrum. Fighting the waves or ignoring them leaves you drained and eventually drowning. But if you learn to ride the waves and go with their flow, you'll hit a sweet spot of zen and poise.

*Facing up to your feelings is enlightening.* You begin to crack the code of your emotional patterns, paving the way to some serious soul-searching. This insight is dynamite. It lets you zero in on why you feel what you do and tackle any sneaky issues under the surface.

Turning your emotions from frenemies to allies takes a lot of work.

It's like building a fortress of chill inside you, a mental space where you can remain calm and composed even in the face of strong emotions. Being at peace with your feelings means life's curveballs are less likely to knock you off your feet. You morph into this nimble ninja, prepped for whatever life throws.

*To ignite this change, mindfulness is where the magic begins.*

Watch your feelings like you're binge-watching a drama series—*interested but not absorbed.* Sure, it's a challenge, but stick with it, and it'll start to feel more like a routine.

Your emotions are part of the package deal that is you, but they don't slap a label on you. By welcoming them, you're not handing over the keys; you're actually steering the ship. You transform potential roadblocks into launchpads for self-discovery and inner zen.

We believed in our strength,
but time unveiled harsh truths,
like storm clouds cloaking a clear sky.
Our paths diverged, leaving silent voids of regret,
empty halls in a forgotten mansion,
I move through memories of a bond now broken.
In this emptiness, the truth of change is clear,
sorrow has shaped me,
molding my soul, a blacksmith's forge,
grief, a relentless fire, altering my very being.

This journey of solitude guides me within,
through shadowed forests of introspection,
learning to let go, a river releasing to the sea,
choosing transformation over clinging to the past.
Life calls us onward, not to cling to the past,
but to bravely move forward, allowing thoughts to roam free,
like wild horses on an open plain.
In this release, I find my road to healing,
a path illuminated by the gentle glow of newfound freedom.

**"Instead of trying to control, reason with, or react to thoughts, let them enter and leave your mind freely, without engaging them or getting attached to them."**

— September 12, 2021

Life is complex, and often, our thoughts love to steal the show, twirling around like they own the place. We try to boss them around, convinced we're in charge. But imagine if we just let our thoughts cruise by, with no interference from us.

Envision your mind as a vast sky. Thoughts are just clouds floating by—some fluffy and light, others stormy and brooding. We often want to run after these clouds, analyze them, and predict their next move.

But that just kicks up a storm.

*What if we just watched them, acknowledged their presence, and didn't cling?*

This isn't about zoning out of our own stories.

It's learning to keep a chill distance, grasping that thoughts are just that—thoughts.

Not gospel, not eternal.

Letting them drift through our minds, we open up room for clarity and peace. We start to tell apart uplifting thoughts from the downers, deciding consciously where our vibes go. This path asks for patience and gentle persistence.

It's like learning to float—relax into it, and trust you won't drown. At first, it's weird, maybe even tough, to let go of our control itch. Yet, with time, we hit upon a sweet freedom in our psyche. We grasp that we're not our thoughts; our core stays untouched by the mental buzz.

The next time you're swept up in your thoughts, remember you can just step aside and let them flow.

Breathe in awareness, breathe out attachment.

Within this release, tranquility has been chilling, just waiting for you to notice.

I've raced with the wind,
breathless,
always chasing the next moment, never in the now,
a heart beating in tune with the city's relentless pulse.
The world, a blur, slipped by unnoticed,
its colors dim, its voices lost
by the uproar of my inner chaos.
Joy seemed an alien concept,
as distant as the horizon on a foggy morning.
Caught in the storm I created,
I forgot the warmth of sunlight on my skin,
the soft song of the earth beneath my feet.

Then, during a rare pause
in the relentless march of time,
I found a breath, a heartbeat,
a fleeting glimpse of the world beyond my storm.
In the simple beauty of a dew-kissed leaf,
the tranquil drift of clouds across a blue sky,
I rediscovered wonder, amazement.
I learned to stand still,
to let the beauty of the world wash over me,
to allow myself to be moved by its quiet majesty.

In watching, in truly seeing,
I found a peace I thought was lost,
a reconnection to a world alive, vivid, and vast.
This hard-earned insight revealed a truth long overlooked—
in the middle of chaos, there is beauty to be found,
if only we slow down enough to see it.
*To allow awe, to let presence fill the spaces between our thoughts,*
*is to open the door to a world where every moment holds a miracle.*

**"In all the chaos and hurry, do not forget to notice the beauty and miracle of this world. Slow down. Notice. Observe. Be aware. Allow presence and awe to come back into your life."**

— December 30, 2021

In our everyday hustle and bustle, we often miss the marvels around us. Life teems with beauty, yet we're too caught up to notice.

Slow down.

Notice.

Observe.

Be aware.

The beauty of the world awaits on the doorstep of your soul.

Knocking softly.

Patiently.

Until you open the door.

Watch the dawn break, painting the heavens. Notice a butterfly flaunting its colors, nature's artistry at work. Listen to kids laughing, their joy ringing through the air. Feel the sun's warmth, a simple nod from the universe. Slowing down lets us see what's always been there. It's more than just looking—it's truly seeing and being in the moment. This brings wonder, a sense that we're part of something bigger.

Welcome this awe into your life.

Despite the chaos, beauty abounds. In pockets of stillness and wonder, we uncover a richer love for our world.

So, pause, inhale, and be astonished by the everyday miracles.

In the dimming light, I pause,
reflecting on the day's missed cues,
the weight of unmet goals, anchors dragging in the night,
the pain of unseized moments,
the sting of unsaid words,
actions halted by fear's tight grasp.
It's often easier to tally lacks and losses,
to focus on what's missing,
rather than seeking the light
among the clouds of might-have-beens.

But then, as night takes hold, I shift—
from dwelling on darkness to gazing at glittering stars,
from voids to the sparks of good
that broke through today's gloom.
A shared laugh, a burden lifted,
a balloon released to the sky,
unexpected beauty in the mundane,
a reminder of life's hidden pearls.
This shift, a quiet defiance against despair,
guides me from the allure of the abyss.
'Hunting the good stuff,' they call it—
a search for the specks of gold
in the silt of daily existence.

It's a journey back to myself,
to the belief that even in the darkest of days,
there are victories to be claimed,
joys to be savored, lessons to be cherished.
In this act of searching, I find not just the good,
but a path through the night,
a way to balance the scales
between what is lost and what remains.

**"At the end of each day, reflect on what went well. This practice, known as 'hunting the good stuff,' can help shift your focus from what's wrong to what's right."**

— July 19, 2022

Stuck in the daily hustle, it's easy to fixate on the flubs. We often stew in the slip-ups, the bumps, and the *"what-ifs."*

But here's a savvy switch: *spotlighting the wins.*

Each evening, throw it in park and sift through the day's highs. This isn't about glossing over the rough patches or playing pretend. It's about acknowledging that, within the turbulence, there were sparks of brilliance.

The charm of this tactic is its utter simplicity.

There is no need for fancy ceremonies or hour-long meditations. Just a moment or two to replay your day, seeking out those bits that brought a smile, a sense of achievement, pride, or even just a breather from the chaos. These highlights could range from a heartfelt conversation to a delicious bite or maybe even just the way the sunset paints the sky.

Actively hunting the positives tunes our brains to spotlight for life's sunny sides. With time, this mindset makeover can shift how we view our day-to-day. Rather than being bogged down by gloom, we begin to notice life's abundant positives. It's not about wearing rose-tinted glasses or sidestepping growth.

It's steering through life with a more hopeful, balanced lens.

Plus, this habit is resilience gold. Making a habit of spotlighting the bright bits builds up a stash of good vibes, a buffer for when the going gets rough. It reminds us that, even in the gloom, rays of light are piercing through.

So, as each day winds down, make a point to celebrate the wins.

Jot down those triumphs, relish the replays, and let a wave of thankfulness wash over you.

*This no-fuss routine could seriously revolutionize your vibe and outlook on life.*

**"Awareness is like the sun. When it shines on things, they are transformed."**

– Thich Nhat Hanh.

Realize your awareness is like a magic wand for your life. Wave it around, and poof! That Monday morning feeling turns into, *'Actually, I got this.'*

# Bouncing Back

## Chronicles of Grit and Grace

**"It's not that I'm so smart, it's just that I stay with problems longer."**

– Albert Einstein.

**R**esilience and Perseverance: Quotes and profound insights to help us navigate hurdles, setbacks, and letdowns. These messages act as rays of hope, brightening our path when we feel engulfed in darkness.

They inspire us to stand tall after every tumble and see each obstacle as an opportunity for growth, molding us into sturdier individuals.

*Welcome resilience.*

Let these words lift you from the shadows.

**As you reflect on these words, remember:** *every challenge you face is a stepping stone, molding you into a stronger version of yourself.*

Rise, grow, and transform into the powerhouse you're destined to be.

I've danced with despair,
its icy fingers familiar on my waist,
leading me through a waltz of shadows.
The music, a haunting melody of secrets and sighs,
not quite sadness, nor despair,
but something in between.
Laughter, once a constant companion,
now feels like a distant visitor,
its bright quips lost in a self-made haze.
However, in this chaos,
a spark stubbornly flickers—a reluctant defiance.
It speaks of dreams not extinguished,
but dormant,
of love not lost, but lingering,
buried under layers of fear and doubt.

Through tears and trials, I've realized
healing isn't a place to reach,
but a path—endless, twisting.
And so, I stand,
a little broken, a bit jaded,
but fiercely clinging to the belief
that I am not defined by my fractures.
*For even fragmented,*
*I can love, dream,*
*strive for that elusive next level.*
I don't need wholeness
to engage the world, to find acceptance.
*Healing, I've found, is not a prerequisite for living,*
*but a companion on the journey,*
*teaching me that even in my imperfection,*
*I am enough.*

**"You don't have to be *'fully healed'* to give or receive love, to go after that dream, to get to that next level. Healing is a constant state."**

— February 14, 2022

Healing is not a roadblock.

It doesn't shut down the way to affection, goals, or personal growth.

There's this tall tale floating around that says, *"You need to be all fixed up, perfect, before you can grab your dreams or find love."*

*Healing's part of the adventure, not a pit stop.*

It's all about evolving, bit-by-bit.

This mindset is liberating.

There's no need to hold off on joy until you're *"all better."*

Being a masterpiece and a work in progress at the same time is totally cool.

Your path is not about hitting some mythical healing finish line. It's about the trek, with healing as your sidekick, not your end goal.

Adopting this perspective lets you soak up the now. It nudges you to chase those dreams and love life, scars and all. Start gunning for your goals today. Begin opening your heart, even if it's still on the mend. Believe in your right to happiness and success, regardless of your healing stage. Happiness and progress are up for grabs every step of the way.

You're solid, just as you are.

Each tick of the clock is a chance to expand, cherish, and live to the fullest.

Seize this kick-ass truth.

Your value is not tied to being all pieced together or hitting perfection.

You are worthy of your desires and love right now, not off in some polished, healed-up tomorrow.

In the quiet hours,
I've doubted the strength within,
fighting silent battles against shadows,
where my own voice turned against me.
Days stretched into nights,
in an endless cycle of self-questioning,
each *"what if"* a dagger, cutting through the calm,
each *"if only,"* a chain, binding me tight.
Belief, so delicate,
swayed, a candle in a breeze,
flickering, threatened by the storms
of my own making, hurricanes of doubt.

Through this struggle,
a truth quietly surfaced,
taught by scars, by tears,
by the very doubts that aimed to crush me.
Belief in oneself is not a fortress,
impenetrable and fixed,
but a garden, fragile and constantly growing,
the rich black-earth soils fertilized with hope,
but often watered with moments of fear,
each flower a bold badge of endurance,
each weed a reminder of battles fought.

On days when the light dims,
when the garden withers,
it's not a defeat, but a part of the cycle,
the ebb and flow of a practice
as essential as breathing.
*Thus, I learn,*
*to nurture this belief,*
*to accept the imperfections,*
*the days filled with doubt,*
*as necessary steps*
*on the journey to who I am becoming.*

**"Believing in yourself is a practice. Some days it feels impossible, and that's okay."**

— September 23, 2021

Believing in yourself is not something that happens overnight.

It's a continuous effort.

Some days, it might seem like an insurmountable challenge and that's completely normal.

Self-confidence isn't always about being sure of yourself. It's about adapting to setbacks. It involves acknowledging that doubts will arise. You'll question your abilities, choices, and path—it's all part of the process.

The key is not to let those tough days define you.

Don't allow moments of uncertainty to overshadow moments of strength. Recognize that self-belief is a journey with its ups and downs, twists and turns. During times when belief feels out of reach, remember it's okay to feel that way.

Doubts are natural.

The important thing is to keep moving forward—keep pushing yourself and maintaining faith in your abilities. Because believing in yourself doesn't mean never facing challenges; it means getting back up after every fall. It involves learning from doubts, growing through obstacles and coming out stronger on the other side.

So, on those challenging days when self-belief seems hard to grasp, take a moment to breathe. Recall your past triumphs and reflect on the hurdles you've overcome.

Remember, it's perfectly fine to experience those days. They are simply a natural part of life's ups and downs. It's the challenges we face along the way that shape who we are and build our character.

Self-belief is all about staying true to yourself consistently. It means choosing to focus on your strengths, especially during tough times when it seems daunting.

Those moments are when self-belief truly matters the most.

In the theater of my failures,
I've played the lead—a marionette,
dancing to the discordant tune of setbacks,
each fall a curtain call in a play I never auditioned for.
The ground and I became reluctant companions,
intimate in the way of warriors and their wounds,
each scar a story, each bruise a lesson
in the art of falling, and the science of rising again.

They say true strength is not in the never falling,
but in the always rising—
each time a little higher,
a phoenix reborn not from absence of ash
but because of it.
I've learned to accept the fall,
to view each tumble not as a loss,
but as the setup for a greater leap,
a prelude to the act of soaring.

With eyes set on the boundless blue,
where twilight's hues kiss the horizon,
I understand now—
the sky is not the limit, but the invitation,
each setback a gust under my wings,
lifting me higher,
towards the endless expanse of possibility.
Here, in the aftermath of falls,
*I find my strength,*
*not in remaining unmarked,*
*but in the resilience of rising—*
*ever upward, ever hopeful,*
*a sign of the unyielding spirit*
*that resides within.*
*I keep soaring,*
*for every fall is but a step*
*on the staircase to the stars.*

**"True strength is in picking ourselves up after we fall. And every time we rise, we soar higher. Remember, every setback is a setup for a comeback. Keep soaring, the sky's the limit."**

— July 10, 2022

Life is a series of ups and downs.

Every time we rise, we go higher than before.

Setbacks may seem scary, but they're not the end.

They're hidden chances.

Chances to grow, to strengthen, to stand tall, and to stage an epic comeback.

It's in these challenging times that we really become strong.

Like a phoenix rising from the ashes, we come back smarter and tougher.

This process is anything but a straight line. It's full of twists and turns, and these twists shape us into who we are.

They school us in the art of bouncing back.

So, welcome the setbacks. They're just steps to your comeback.

Keep flying high.

The sky's just the start.

Every fall and rise teaches us more about ourselves, our strengths, and what we can do.

True strength is about accepting the falls, mining the lessons, and standing taller.

It's about reaching new heights, undeterred by the stumbles that once seemed insurmountable.

In the shadow of setbacks, I linger,
cloaked in the crimson dusk of shattered ambitions,
each misstep a reminder of dreams deferred,
paths blocked by the rubble of faltered attempts.
In the aftermath of disappointment,
solitude stood as both captor and companion,
a place where hope felt as distant
as stars to a grounded soul.

In the stillness, a shift—
the realization that each pause,
each detour carved from trial and error,
was not a barrier but a guide,
pointing toward unseen roads.
This pause, once burdened with the weight of defeat,
transformed into a space for introspection,
a moment not of conclusion but of inception,
where obstacles turned into stepping-stones,
each a call to rise, to reflect, to refine.

Viewed through this lens, setbacks transformed—
not as road ends,
but as bends in my path,
each presenting a view of new possibilities,
a landscape rich with the promise of progress,
turning once-dreaded blockades
into gateways of opportunity.
Each step forward a testament
to resilience, to the enduring spark within,
that strives not just to survive but to thrive.

**"A setback can be a stepping-stone in disguise, a pause in your journey that invites reflection and recalibration, turning what are first seen as obstacles into opportunities for growth."**
— October 30, 2022

Setbacks are not roadblocks; they're launchpads.

Think of them as the universe's way of saying, *"Time out!"*

It is a golden opportunity to take a breather and map out a new course.

This isn't just about tackling obstacles; it's about rolling out the red carpet for them as harbingers of growth.

When life decides to throw a wrench in your plans, it's easy to think about throwing in the towel.

**But wait a second**—*every trip and fall is just setting the stage for your epic rebound.*

It's an invitation to pause, ponder, and pivot. This timeout is your chance to reassess with a fresh set of eyes.

Here's where the magic happens.

In those quiet moments of introspection, you discover your grit. You recognize your arsenal to brave the storms. You learn that each bump in the road is not just a chance to beef up your character and hone your skills but also a stepping-stone toward personal growth and self-improvement.

So, next time you hit a snag, give it a big ol' bear hug.

See it as a stepping-stone, a necessary pit stop on your adventure.

Spin it into a moment for reflection, fine-tuning, and growth.

Keep in mind that nestled within each obstacle is your ticket to the big leagues.

It's up you to grab it and make it your springboard to greatness.

In the shadow of towering puppeteers,
I've felt small, a mere ant in a cavernous hall,
overwhelmed by challenges vast and insidious,
each a giant mocking my strings,
their jeering laughter a thunder in my ears.
With every setback, a string pulled,
my spirit, a marionette
being guided to a show of doubt and fear,
each step faltering under the weight of unseen hands.

But, in this performance of trials,
a shift occurred, a spotlight beyond center stage,
a realization that I am no puppet,
bound by strings to an unseen master's whim.
By breaking mountains into stones,
each obstacle a puzzle to be solved,
I learned to move, not with fear, but with purpose,
each step a question, each answer a step forward,
the path beneath my feet
solid and reassuring.

With conviction guiding me,
I made my way off the stage,
the scent of fresh earth and possibility filling my lungs,
replacing fear with curiosity—
each obstacle now a gateway
to growth, learning, and victory,
illuminated by the soft glow of determination.
I pressed forward,
no longer a puppet,
but a trailblazer,
uncovering the vast potential within,
each heartbeat a drum, steady and relentless.

"Tackle your challenges with conviction; don't let them puppeteer your emotions. Deconstruct their complexity into manageable pieces, and with each step, approach the journey with an inquisitive spirit, replacing trepidation with the thrill of discovery."

— January 5, 2022

Life is full of challenges. Big, scary ones.

They love to toy with our feelings, making us their marionettes.

- *But what if we took control?*

- *What if we faced these giants head-on, with grit?*

Imagine every challenge as a towering puppeteer, trying to pull our strings. Instead of succumbing to its manipulations, we can become the puppet masters of our own lives.

Start by dismantling those behemoths. Break them down into manageable chunks. It's like tackling a puzzle: start with the edges and work your way in, piece by piece.

Jump in with a curious heart.

Swap out fear for the thrill of the hunt.

Embrace the unknown. Savor the journey of learning and growing.

Every obstacle is an invitation to push our boundaries and level up. Think of each challenge as a scene in a grand play, and you're not just an actor but the director.

So, let's not let these giants push us around.

Let's take them on with grit, break them down, and tackle the journey with curiosity and zest. With every step, we reclaim our strings, turning what once felt overwhelming into a series of small, conquerable tasks.

Remember, adventure is just around the corner. The stage is set, the spotlight is on, and it's time to shine in the face of those towering puppeteers.

In quiet moments, I tread the event horizon of self-discovery,
solitary, shadowed by memories of those who once stood beside me.
Their absence—a void not of distance,
but of diverging trajectories.
I am drawn into the black hole's darkness,
where pictures of the past speak softly,
ghostly remnants fading into the cosmic hum of transformation.

Personal growth feels like nearing
the event horizon of a black hole,
a point of no return,
crossing the threshold into unknown realms.
The gravitational pull of my past—once a tether—slips,
its grip weakening, like stars being stretched
and consumed by the singularity's embrace.
I ventured into my depths, seeking solace, seeking growth.

With each step forward,
the gravitational boundary expanded
between myself and those I cherished,
their voices drowned by the singularity's resonant call.
My healing,
a journey they could not accompany,
my growth,
a reflection of paths they never took.
Not all hands that let go do so out of malice;
some simply cannot grasp the gravitational pull that propels us forward.

**"Always keep in mind that not everyone will applaud or accept your journey of healing and growth. At times, your progress may act as a mirror, reflecting their own stagnation or challenges they haven't yet faced."**

— May 18, 2022

Your mission to grow, heal, and shine isn't about amassing likes or nods of approval.

It's your epic tale of leveling up, patching up your spirit, and stepping into your prime.

If your growth casts a giant shadow over someone else's inertia, that's their puzzle to solve, not yours. Swallowing this bitter truth is brutal but crucial. Don't you dare dim your light or hit the brakes for the sake of keeping everyone on an even keel.

*This journey has your name on it.*

It's about owning your strides, soaking in the lessons, and striding ahead full tilt.

Keep your eyes on your lane, particularly when you hit a wall of indifference or pushback. This isn't a competition; it's your solo mission of self-polish.

Lean into the grind, high-five your wins, and never stop moving.

Your path is yours alone, and it's golden.

Stick to it, stay tough, and above all, keep it real.

Your climb is a shout-out to your grit and commitment, and believe me, it's all worth it—every single step, every hurdle, every win.

*So, keep striding on.*

*Keep lighting up the room.*

*And let your journey flaunt your relentless drive.*

**"Out of suffering have emerged the strongest souls; the most massive characters are seared with scars."**

– Khalil Gibran.

Those struggles aren't just for dramatic effect. They're your personal boot camp, sculpting a tougher you. So, next time life throws a curveball, remember you're in training to throw it right back!

# CROWN THYSELF

## The Coronation of Excellence

"You have power over your mind — not outside events. Realize this, and you will find strength."

– Marcus Aurelius.

**E**MPOWERMENT AND SELF-WORTH: THIS set of quotes and messages highlights the need to recognize your value. They help build a positive self-view and strong personal toughness.

Think of them as high-fives to your soul, nudging you to keep tabs on your own awesomeness and the cool skills you bring to the world.

*Celebrate your uniqueness.*

Let these words reinforce your inner value.

**As you reflect on these words, remember:** *to stand proud in your uniqueness and let your spirit shine—you're a key piece in life's big jigsaw, with unique abilities and strengths that matter.*

In the dim light of sacrifice's shadow,
a river flowed, its waters clear and deep,
its currents, winding through a forest dense,
reflecting dreams of others, not my own.
I thought that shrinking, folding inwardly,
and fading into the currents of their lives,
would weave me into hearts, indispensable,
more cherished.

Each time I did give in, a stone was cast,
and ripples spread unseen,
my needs a bygone breeze—
a language lost, a dialect of absence, silent plea.
This neglect—a quiet, steady erosion,
like banks worn smooth by ceaseless, silent flow,
did not bridge gaps but widened, deepened rifts,
between the love I gave and love I sought.

*"Why must I always bend?"*
I asked myself, as shadows grew and screamed through the night.

Through anguish, then reflection, at the river's edge,
I saw, at last, the truth,
that love, like water, should not be confined.
True love, pure,
demands no shrinking souls,
but a celebration of our fullest selves.

Through anguish, then reflection, at the river's edge,
I saw, at last, my worth,
a flame unquenched by others' fleeting needs.
The river flowed within me,
strong and free,
no longer bound by shores of sacrifice.

My heart, a vessel, held its waters clear,
reflecting now my dreams,
my voice,
my life.

**"Neglecting your own needs does not make you easier to love."**
— February 28, 2023

Neglecting your needs won't make you more lovable.

It's a common trap: *thinking that sidelining our wants makes us more attractive.*

We often believe that by prioritizing others over ourselves, we'll be seen as desirable. It is standard to believe that being undemanding and self-sacrificing will make it easier for us to stay in someone's life. However, this belief is flawed.

Skipping over what you need doesn't make you more liked; *it makes you less seen.* You shrink back, silencing your voice and erasing your boundaries. In doing so, you turn into a mere outline of your true self, robbing others of the chance to love you for who you really are.

Love isn't about finding someone who requires nothing from you; it's about discovering a partner whose needs complement yours—a person you can support while receiving support in return. It involves creating a reciprocity-based partnership, a give-and-take deal, building a bond where both feel seen, heard, and valued.

Neglecting your needs harms yourself and damages your relationships. It paves the way for resentment, miscommunication, and imbalance in the dynamics between people.

You are showing others that it's acceptable to disregard you, diminishing the foundation of your relationships over time.

*So, what steps can you take?*

Start by recognizing your worth. Understand that your needs matter. Give yourself the green light to voice what you need, to reach out for it. Communication is key. Engaging in heart-to-hearts with those around you about boundaries, expectations and how you feel supported is crucial. Get clear on what fills your love tank and tune into what others need. Remember, neglecting your needs doesn't make you more lovable; it just makes you less understood.

Let's champion self-love, honor our needs, and let our true selves shine.

Taking this step opens the door to deeper, more genuine connections.

In the vast expanse of the solar system,
I've often feared the silent void,
mistaking its stillness for emptiness,
a barren Martian world with whirling alien winds.
I've bartered with the emptiness,
traded fragments of my identity for the illusion of companionship,
fearing that without another's gaze upon me,
I might dissolve into the crimson dust.

However—to stand alone,
to embrace the silence of my solitude,
is not a fall into desolation,
but an opportunity to cultivate
a thriving colony of self-worth.
With each solitary step, I uncover
that the Martian habitat of my soul
is rich with laughter, tears, and insight,
a biosphere where no compromise is tolerated,
where every shadow is dispelled
by the brilliance of self-acceptance.

In this thin atmosphere of introspection,
I build protective habitats,
shielding my essence from the radiation
of external judgment.
I generate warmth from within,
like terraforming my heart
to create a livable climate,
where self-love can thrive even in the harshest conditions.
I extract the waters of wisdom
from the icy reservoirs of past experiences,
nurturing the growth of self-awareness
in controlled environments of contemplation.
I stand now,
an unwavering pioneer, with the rover of reflection,
learning to cherish the autonomous life of my own being,
discovering in the stillness, not fear,
but a celebration of the self, whole and radiant in its solitude.

**"Don't allow the fear of being alone dim your worth. It is better to bask in the company of your own self-respect than to dwell in the shadows of compromise and dissatisfaction."**

— August 25, 2022

Society nudges us towards the crowd, suggesting we're incomplete on our own. But at the end of the day, loving yourself beats getting lost in a sea of faces.

Fear of solitude is tricky. It's too easy to let it take the wheel, which is a trap.

*Getting cozy with solitude can switch things up big time.*

Silence is where you meet your true self, unearth desires, and recognize your power. It means acknowledging your value on your own, establishing your standards, and refusing to compromise.

You are better off alone than in poor company.

Compromise is okay, but not at the expense of your peace.

**Feeling unsatisfied is a clear signal shouting:** *"Stay true to you!"*

Your worth isn't tied to how many people you surround yourself with. It's about how you value and treat yourself and how you expect others to do the same. This path is rugged, sprinkled with doubt and loneliness, yet it's incredibly fulfilling. Beyond the fear is self-affection and genuine happiness.

Alone time is an opportunity for growth, a learning path, and a season of flourishing.

Building a solid bond with yourself is priceless. Don't let the fear of solitude eclipse your shine.

With self-respect as your guide, you're never truly solo.

On the day I wrapped myself in self-respect,
the world didn't pause, there was no applause—
it was a vibration, a tender yet seismic shift
within the caverns of my too-long neglected soul.
For years, I danced with self-doubt,
a shadow waltz of questioning worth,
each step lighter, less certain,
more of a drift than a stride.
Then came the moment,
soft as dusk yet clear as dawn,
when I chose to view myself through a kinder lens,
to adorn my spirit with the dignity it deserved.

Reflections in the mirror subtly shifted,
eyes once critical now showed quiet understanding,
and words, those double-edged swords,
began to build rather than berate.
I felt the warmth of self-acceptance,
like the gentle embrace of morning sunlight
filtering through lace curtains,
casting delicate patterns on the floor.

With each new day, I saw—the world,
tinged by the hue of my newfound respect,
each interaction a reflection of my inner change.
The air seemed crisper, the colors more vivid,
as if nature itself acknowledged my transformation.

This path, defined by the quiet, powerful choice
to honor my essence,
brought a poignant awareness of time lost
in the shadows of self-neglect.
With each day's passing,
in this slightly longer walk through life's complexities,
I found not just sadness in the time it took to arrive here,
but a quiet joy in the journey forward,
each step a declaration:
I am, at last, my own ally,
in a world that waits to reflect what I choose to shine.

**"The moment you decide to start respecting yourself you'll notice a major shift in your everyday life."**

— May 3, 2022

Take your life up a notch with some serious self-appreciation.

This isn't just about treating yourself to spa days or setting boundaries. I am talking about a radical, soul-deep transformation here.

Realizing your value is huge.

You are inherently deserving of love, kindness, and respect—*both from yourself and those around you.*

Digest this truth and witness your world shift magnificently.

In matters of the heart, self-esteem is your all access pass.

Say *"so long"* to the negatives. You're on the hunt for positives now.

In your career, self-esteem is your trump card. Stand firm, express your needs, and snatch those golden chances. Next thing you know, you will be cueing that career upgrade.

When it comes to mental and emotional well-being, self-esteem involves making self-care a priority and knowing when to draw the line.

Less stress, more bliss—*that sounds sweet, doesn't it?*

Starting on this path of self-esteem requires courage and a lot of introspection. But the payoff is a is absolutely priceless.

You're sculpting a life filled with joy and fulfillment.

*Now, isn't that the goal?*

In the silent struggle with self,
a sudden burst of birdsong at dawn,
taught me
love ignites with a gentle sizzle,
a deep exploration into the soul's
hidden wonders—
that to love others,
I must first accept my own self,
laying a foundation for bonds to build upon.

Self-love, the root from which affection grows,
as sweet as the scent of blooming jasmine at dusk,
turns out to be the strongest bond,
a gentle hum of morning birds
greeting the new dawn,
a refreshing breeze caressing tender leaves,
fingers tracing the outline of a cherished memory,
welcomes me warmly.

As I bask in this self-affection,
the rustling leaves, the patter of rain,
resonate within, reflecting the realness of being.
Love, I discovered, blooms like the wildflowers,
each petal unfolding, reaching towards the sun,
revealing a mosaic of colors, a spectrum of emotions.
Thus, with each beat of my heart,
a thump-thump of acceptance rings true,
binding me to the universe,
as the gentle buzz of bees on a summer day
blends seamlessly into the symphony of nature,
synergizing love and life.

**"To love oneself is to truly understand the depth of your own soul. It's the foundation upon which all other love is built."**
— June 20, 2023

Self-love isn't just fashionable—*it's fundamental.*

It's about genuine respect and appreciation for yourself, stepping way beyond simple vanity into genuine self-regard.

Consider self-awareness your north star, guiding you towards purposeful living and clarifying your aspirations and fears, thus influencing your choices and interactions.

Self-love dictates how you expect to be treated, establishing boundaries, and demanding respect. This vibe of self-respect broadcasts to others how they should interact with you, leading to healthier bonds.

When you're filled with self-love, you're no longer on a hunt for external validation and you don't waste any time trying to patch up inner voids; instead, you simply radiate love, enriching your relationships.

*The irony is that loving yourself increases your capacity to love others.*

The journey to self-love is a marathon filled with self-discovery and facing truths head-on, where obstacles become stepping-stones for growth.

It's about owning and polishing your imperfections and knowing your worth.

Self-love is merely the launch pad for the epic journey of life, an endless cycle of self-discovery, acceptance, and care, paving the way for all love.

Dedicating time to self-care is critical; it's what sculpts your most crucial relationship and shifts how you interact with the world around you.

Self-love isn't just a passing trend—*it's the bedrock of a life well-lived.*

In a world eager to shape me,
to mold me into a version more palatable,
I've carved out an act of rebellion—
*the radical choice to love myself.*
This defiance isn't loud,
nor does it carry the hallmarks of revolution,
but it's present—in every step I take
without apology, in every choice
that declares *"I am worthy."*

It's a silent skirmish,
fought in the shadowy alleys of creeping doubt,
where the air hangs heavy with the scent of rain,
in the fraught gaps between self-acceptance and the world's oppressive hand,
a line etched in the shifting sands of my soul,
gritty and resolute.
To love myself in a world
that equates worth with conformity
is my resistance, my heartfelt declaration
that I will not be diminished.

In this act of defiance,
I find not just strength but a profound liberty—
the courage to exist on my own terms,
feeling the warmth of sunlight breaking through the stormy clouds,
affirming the unyielding belief in my inherent value.

**"Loving yourself is an act of rebellion in a world that often demands conformity. It's the affirmation that you are worthy of love, respect, and kindness. In this act of 'defiance', you find the strength to live life on your own terms."**

— February 2, 2023

Be bold.

In a world of copy-paste, self-love is your battle cry.

It screams, *"I'm worth it!"* With every act of self-appreciation, you carve your own trail.

Society loves its molds.

It's all about the *"shoulds"* and *"musts,"* boxing us into corners of doubt.

Smash through with self-love. It's your declaration of independence, claiming your space and rocking your true colors.

Self-love is deeper than a pat on the back. It's honoring your needs, drawing lines in the sand. It's the kindness you'd show a friend, now turned inward.

*Welcoming this self-love, you unlock the cage, letting your authentic self soar.*

This rebellion reshapes your world.

It's your green light to chase what lights you up, never mind the peanut gallery. Self-love lays the groundwork for a life that's rich, painted in shades of genuine joy.

Yet, it's a climb.

This path demands you to face the mirror, swapping out criticism for cheers. It's about self-care as a non-negotiable, crafting boundaries like an art. On this trek, you blossom, growing into your full splendor.

*Choosing self-love in a world hung up on sameness is revolutionary.*

It's declaring loud and clear that you're worthy of the finest. And in this stance, you find the grit to live by your own script.

I've built a gallery of could-have-beens,
a painting of accomplishments deemed too small, too insignificant to count.
I've wandered these halls like Alice,
a critic harsher than any voice from the outside,
dismissing each achievement, overlooking the milestones.
Down the rabbit hole of self-doubt I tumble,
dark, twisting tunnels spiraling into the depths of uncertainty,
where every twist and turn reveals more layers of my Wonderland.

The Mad Hatter's tea party of thoughts,
teacups and saucers spinning wildly, clinking in sync with my doubts,
tries to convince me I am mad, yet in madness, there is clarity.
The Cheshire Cat's grin, a symbol of my potential, appears and vanishes,
a wide smile fading in and out of the mist, eyes gleaming with cryptic wisdom,
reminding me that my path, though curious, is my own.
Beneath layers of self-doubt lies a treasure,
not of silver and gold, but of skill, determination, and spirit
far more precious than any external praise I've denied myself.
The Queen of Hearts screams, *"Off with your head!"*
each time I falter, her voice trembling with imperious commands,
yet I am not her subject.
I wield the vorpal sword of self-belief,
a gleaming blade, sharp and precise, cutting through the playing cards of fear,
slaying the Bandersnatch of self-doubt,
a monstrous figure with gnashing teeth and fiery eyes,
revealing the caterpillar of creativity and the dormouse of determination,
hidden in the tulgey woods of my mind,
dense foliage and twisted paths where light and shadow prance in a confusing maze.

The truth, a revelation bright and bold,
shines through the cracks of my self-imposed limitations:
I am capable,
endowed with a wealth of potential
that waits not for recognition from the world,
but acknowledgment from within.
With each step forward, I vow to honor this wealth,
to give credit where it's due—to myself,
for the journey isn't just about reaching peaks,
but valuing the climb, every grueling, beautiful step of the way.

"We tend to undervalue our own accomplishments and overlook our potential, leading us to believe that we are not capable of achieving great things. But the truth is that you possess a wealth of talent, skill, and resilience that far surpasses the recognition you give yourself."

— October 2, 2021

We tend to downplay our successes, crediting luck or timing.

But the truth is—*you're a genius in disguise.*

Caught in the hustle, it's hard to see our wins, especially against the flashy success stories online. But your path is yours alone, peppered with victories that matter. Reflect on your wins, write them down, and focus on what you've achieved, not what's pending.

Every success, no matter how small it seems, deserves to be celebrated. Each step forward, each goal met, is a testament to your hard work and determination.

*Trust in your magic. You've nailed more than you admit.*

Own your talents and tenacity. Your potential is on the brink of bursting forth.

It's time to root for yourself—*you're on track for greatness.*

Your story is unique, and your accomplishments are significant. Don't let the noise of comparison drown out your own triumphs. Keep pushing forward, acknowledging your progress, and believing in your capabilities.

The world is waiting for you to shine.

Your path to success is paved with your own efforts and determination.

Stand tall.

Recognize your worth.

And continue to strive for the greatness that lies within you.

You've got this—*every step you take is a step toward a brighter, more fulfilling future.*

**"The most common way people give up their power is by thinking they don't have any."**

– Alice Walker.

Realize you're the superhero of your own story, with the power of choice in your utility belt. Use it wisely, or you might end up accidentally super-gluing your life to a path you didn't mean to take!

*—ele—*

# SERENITY SPECTRUM

## Shades of Inner Peace

> "Peace is not the absence of conflict, but the ability to cope with it."
>
> – Mahatma Gandhi.

**I**NNER PEACE AND CALM: Explore these quotes and insights. They're your spark for finding peace inside. Each one acts as a guide, leading you to a haven of calm.

Begin this journey of tranquility.

Light up your inner fire with each word.

*Change your perspectives.*

Discover the hidden jewels of serenity in your soul.

**As you journey, remember:** *your ability for peace knows no bounds, your potential for calm is endless.*

There I stood, within the ruins of my own creation,
a fortress built from sleepless nights and relentless thoughts.
In chasing dreams, I lost more than I gained—
time, peace, fragments of myself left on the battlefield of ambition.
I wore exhaustion like a medal,
a misguided mark of honor in a world that praises the relentless,
those who persist without pause.

In rare moments when the world fell silent,
I heard the voice of my own frailty,
a reminder that even the strongest storm
eventually yields to tranquility.
I laughed in the face of my limitations,
a hollow sound in the empty room of my resolve.
*"Surrender,"* I mocked,
but each day, that notion seemed less like a defeat
and more like a relief.

In the mirror, I saw not a conqueror,
but a soul pleading for respite,
for a pause in the relentless progression of days.
It was a bittersweet revelation—
in my rush towards tomorrow,
I had left myself behind.
Now, I chose to stop,
to breathe, to rest, to heal.
Not a defeat, but a declaration—
that I am worth more than the sum of my achievements,
that my value is not tethered to tireless toil.
It's okay to take a break, to retreat into the haven of self-care,
to mend the wear and tear of a spirit stretched too thin.
*Burnout is no badge of honor,*
*but a sign to seek the quiet,*
*the peace,*
*the space to simply be.*
*For in this pause, I found not weakness,*
*but strength,*
*not defeat,*
*but wisdom.*

**"It's okay to take a break. If you feel like you need time to focus on you, then you probably do. Don't wear burnout like a badge of honor."**

— January 15, 2023

Pause the chaos!

We live in a non-stop hustle culture, fooled into thinking that endless grinding is the secret sauce to success.

Spoiler alert—*that's bogus.*

If you're itching to chill and focus on you, listen up. Brushing off that feeling is a one-way ticket to Burnout City, and trust me, it's not a place you want to visit.

Burnout is often worn like a medal, a sign you're working your tail off.

*But what's the price?*

Your sanity and health, that's what. When burnout hits, your get-up-and-go gets up and leaves, your imagination dries up, and life just isn't as peachy. It's a lose-lose deal.

Taking a breather is self-love. It's hitting pause to juice up and get your head straight. It's not a sign of weakness; it's wisdom. It's knowing you have to be in tip-top shape to be on top of your game.

If you're feeling the pull to hit pause, do it. Step off the never-ending merry-go-round.

Now's the time to do you.

Dive into things that make you happy, chill, and feel complete. Whether it's getting lost in a book, wandering in the woods, or just vegging out, it's your moment to refresh.

Remember, taking a break isn't waving the white flag; it's refueling your tank. It's key to keeping you on your A-game and chasing your dreams with all you've got.

So, don't brag about being burnt out.

Instead, rock your self-care moves like a boss, knowing they're what really keep you balanced and kicking butt in life.

In the rush of days,
I've lost myself,
a boat without a rudder in a storm,
where motion blurred into insignificance,
and stillness felt like a forgotten language.
Each day bled into the next, indistinguishably,
a relentless sequence of actions without intent,
where the voice of my own thoughts
was lost in the pace of constant activity.

But within this unending flow,
a realization, quiet, life-altering—
the courage it takes to stop,
to stand firm in the storm and find peace in the eye.
In that pause,
a world opened up,
rich with the colorful hues of moments unnoticed,
where breath became a bridge
between my soul and the infinity of life.

This stillness, a defiance
against the praise of perpetual motion,
a reminder that in the spaces between,
we find the depth of our own existence.
Daring to pause,
I unearthed the richness that emerges
not from doing,
but from being,
from the silent observation
of the world in motion,
the rustle of leaves in the wind,
the scent of rain on dry earth,
the warmth of sunlight on my skin,
the taste of morning dew on my lips,
the soft caress of a gentle breeze,
the distant chirping of morning birds,
and the realization
that I am part of it all,
whole and present.

**"In a world that glorifies busyness, dare to pause. The richest moments often come when we are still enough to notice them."**
— July 28, 2022

Hold up, wait a minute.

Sometimes, the best play is no play at all.

Sitting still in this nonstop world, screaming for our eyeballs and energy, can feel pretty weird. But hear me out—*it's in the zen of zero action where we find our mojo and muscle to move forward.*

When trouble or choices stare us down, our knee-jerk reaction is to jump in, fix things, and be the hero. We're wired to think our values are all about what we do.

But what if the power move was to just pause and absorb the scene?

Throwing it in park lets us sync up with our core. It's like going on a deep dive inside, tuning into our own channel, raw and real. Here, we square off with our demons, our dreams, and our wants. It's giving ourselves the green light to be 100% us, quirks and all.

This isn't about dodging duties or taking the easy route. It's about giving ourselves a hot second to figure out what really needs doing. Often, the answers we're hustling so hard to find are right there, chilling in our own backyard, just waiting for us to stop and notice.

Plus, hitting the pause button is radical self-care.

In a world that is all *"go, go, go,"* standing still is like saying, *"I matter. I'm more than my to-do list."* It's a shout-out to our own worth beyond the hustle.

Next time you're drowning in the what-ifs or the what-nows, remember it's totally cool to just hit pause.

Chill.

And take a breath.

In that silence, in that space, you might just stumble upon the clarity and calm you've been chasing all along.

In the haste of days, I tread a high wire,
feet kissing cold steel, teetering in the wind.
Each breath short,
a wavering step;
each release hurried,
a faltering shift.
My body trembled,
a tightrope walker in chaos,
telling tales of turmoil without rest.

In the haste, I overlooked—the power of a slow breath,
the steady pole that counters the wind's roar.
I learned to listen,
to recognize the gentle sway,
to slow my steps,
to find my pace.
With each purposeful breath, I steadied the line,
a dialogue of calm with gravity's pull.

This new mastery,
a tightrope across opposing buildings,
taught me to embrace the unruly winds,
a steady hand to guide the balance in the night.
In the language of breath, I found my equilibrium,
a quiet space to exist,
to be,
to heal.

And so, I breathe—deeply, fully,
a conversation with my nervous system,
learning to regulate,
to balance,
to be.

**"Breath is the language of the nervous system. Learn to slow it down to help regulate."**

— November 27, 2023

Breathing serves a purpose beyond keeping us alive. It acts as a form of communication with our nervous system.

When you slow down your breathing, you signal to your body that everything is okay, promoting a sense of calmness. This simple practice can help regulate emotions and alleviate stress.

Think about it.

When we feel anxious or scared, our breathing quickens as our body reacts to perceived threats. However, modern stressors like work deadlines or difficult conversations are not life-threatening situations.

That email isn't a saber-toothed tiger.

By starting to slow down your breathing, you can immediately feel a sense of control and relief, even in the middle of these stressors. Slowing down those breaths is you taking charge, telling your body the coast is clear and it's time to kick back. Slowing your breath involves taking steady breaths, which is not just doable but highly accessible anywhere, anytime, making it the ultimate chill pill on the go. Whether you're prepping for a talk or drifting into dreamland, focusing on your breath can do wonders.

Incorporating breathing into your routine can affect your mental and physical well-being. It sharpens focus, slices through anxiety, and can even dial down your blood pressure. Stick with it, and this tactic only gets easier, becoming second nature.

So, the next time you're feeling stressed out, remember that breathing is the language spoken by the nervous system.

Get the hang of deep breathing.

It's like tuning into your body's calm center, easing the edginess, and sprinkling some peace into your day-to-day hustle.

In the chaos of days blurred into nights,
like a time traveler lost in temporal flux,
where peace seemed a concept,
as elusive as 88 miles per hour on a deserted road,
I found myself adrift,
caught in the storm of relentless thought,
the DeLorean's tires igniting the asphalt in a blazing trail of fire.

Lost, until a revelation pierced the noise,
*"Great Scott!"*—
*the creation of calm lies within my own hands,*
*each action a step back in time, restoring balance.*

I built a time machine in the everyday,
finding ritual in the simple act of water meeting skin,
hands covered in grease, creating a miracle,
the fading ink of a photograph clipped to a guitar string, restored,
details sharpening with each moment of clarity,
in stretching towards the warmth of the flux capacitor—
each spark a reminder of Hill Valley, my home,
the glowing time circuits on the dash guiding my return.

Through this practice, I uncovered a revelation—
peace is not a far-off land to seek,
but a space within,
like the hidden components of the time circuits,
accessible with each intentional act,
a haven built from the ritual of returning,
to the present,
my personal 1985.

"**Create a 'peace ritual' for yourself. This might involve a warm bath, reading inspiring literature, journaling, or a gentle yoga sequence. Use this ritual to return to a state of calm whenever you feel unsettled.**"

— October 23, 2023

In the tornado of the everyday, snagging a bit of peace is essential.

Caught in the endless spin of to-dos, it's easy to skip over chill time.

Enter the *'peace ritual,'* your VIP pass to Tranquility Town—a sacred place and time to kick back, ponder, and hit the reset button.

Your *'peace ritual'* is not bound by any rules. It's all about you and what brings you tranquility.

Perhaps it's a luxurious soak in a hot bath, with the gentle sounds of the water urging you to relax. Enhance the ambiance with your favorite tunes or the soft glow of candlelight. This is your escape from the hustle and bustle, a time dedicated solely to you. Crack open a book that feeds your soul. Poetry, essays, whatever floats your boat. Let the words wash over you, sparking joy and wonder. Journaling could be your friend here, too. Pour out your heart on paper—fears, dreams, the whole shebang. No holds barred. This is your no-judgment zone to sort through the mental clutter. Maybe even something like yoga can join the party as well. It's not just about pretzel shapes; it's fluid peace. A stretch here, a bend there, dissolves tension, aligning you with your center.

**Bottom line:** *Your peace ritual is whatever flips your calm switch. Bath, books, pen in hand, yoga—whatever makes you happy.*

The main thing is to make it a habit.

When life's all go, go, go, gift yourself a slice of slow.

That's where you'll catch glimpses of real, unshakeable peace.

# RYAN PUUSAARI

In the balance lost,
I wandered, a castle under siege,
between the body's trembling walls and the soul's desperate cries,
each neglected, a step closer to invasion,
a shadowy battlefield where memories haunt, ghosts of past battles.

The catapults of doubt crashed against my mind,
stone upon stone, crashing through the night,
as the soul's archers fired arrows of hope,
slicing through the air,
seeking targets in the shadows of despair.

The battering ram of anxiety pounded relentlessly,
each strike a thunderous boom,
reverberating through my being,
cracks forming in the walls of my resolve.

Yet within the chaos, I glimpsed
a banner of peace fluttering in the breeze,
the scent of wildflowers, the sound of distant waves,
a gentle reminder of the union I yearned for.

I sought harmony, a truce
over chasms wide of neglect,
found truth in simplicity,
an essential treaty between the physical and spiritual,
the key to unlocking mental peace,
a quiet integration like sunlight filtering through crumbling battlements,
warming the cold, trampled ground beneath.

Strength was reborn in this union,
a path to wholeness,
where health is not just of body or spirit,
but the seamless blending of both,
a fortress rebuilt from the ruins,
standing resilient, serene, and whole.

**"Balance between your physical health and your spiritual health is critical to your mental health."**

— November 14, 2022

Balance isn't an afterthought; it's the main event.

It's the art of aligning your mind and soul with your body.

While the gym and a healthy diet are beneficial for your physical well-being, it's equally crucial to address your spiritual needs.

Physical fitness can be clear and measurable. But spiritual wellness dives deeper, asking *"Who am I?"* and syncing with life's rhythm.

*Your body and spirit are a dynamic duo. Neglecting one is like missing a beat.*

Focusing solely on physical fitness without nurturing your soul is like a hit song without heart. Your goal should be a harmony between physical health and spiritual vibe, custom-mixed for you.

Keep up with the basics for your body, but also nourish your soul with what gives it wings—*be it quiet moments, wild escapes, or belly laughs.*

Balance is a dynamic mix, ever adjusting.

It's not just about clocking years; it's about adding depth and color to life. Take care of your body, sure, but don't skimp on nurturing your spirit.

*Find your balance, and with it, you've got your life's hit track.*

I've made a home in mayhem,
familiar walls constructed from turmoil,
where peace feels like a foreign concept,
a language I've never learned to speak.
Wrapped in the false comfort of constant chaos,
I've danced with disruption,
a flirtation with the known,
fearing the quiet, the calm,
like a stranger at my door.

This comfort in chaos is a self-made cage,
bars forged from fear of the unknown,
of the peace that beckons just beyond the strife.
I stand at a crossroads,
a future of tranquility within reach,
yet I pause,
caught in the gravitational pull of familiar disorder.

With a self-mocking laugh,
I acknowledge my own self-sabotage,
the future peace I've held at arm's length
for fear of losing the devil I know.
No longer.
*With a step forward, I choose the unknown,*
*the path of peace over perpetual pandemonium,*
*a leap of faith into a future*
*where calm is not the enemy,*
*but the most intimate friend I've yet to meet.*

**"Don't sabotage your future peace because familiar chaos is comfortable."**

— April 21, 2023

Comfort loves to play dress-up as chaos.

A sneaky little imposter, making us cling to messes like they're life rafts in the ocean of the unknown. But clutching onto chaos is like feeding the monster that's eating your peace for breakfast.

Picture your life as a garden.

Chaos—that's the weed. It sneaks in, choking out the good stuff, hogging all the sunlight.

You might think, *"Eh, pulling weeds is a hassle."*

But guess what?

Ignore them, and your garden's going to look like a before picture in a home makeover show. Your peace is like a seed with potential written all over it. But here's the catch, seeds can't grow in the shade of chaos. Pick chaos, and you're basically slamming the door on any chance of your peace seed sprouting. You're stuck in a loop, thinking it's your cozy blanket when it's actually a straitjacket.

Busting out of this chaos cycle is not a walk in the park. It's more like hiking up a mountain in the rain without a map. It's about figuring out that you're worth more than endless reruns of *"Days of Our Chaos."*

**And it all kicks off with a decision:** *putting your future peace in the driver's seat.*

Get cozy with change; it's the only ground where peace can take root. Ditch the chaos, and your life garden's going to bloom like it's on a time-lapse.

Future you will be throwing you a parade, grateful for the quiet you've sown, for the chaos you kissed goodbye.

Peace isn't just some pie-in-the-sky dream.

It's right there, arms open, waiting for you to take the leap.

**"Peace comes from within. Do not seek it without."**

– Buddha.

Life's ups and downs, much like a yo-yo in the hands of a hyperactive toddler, are utterly random. The only peace you'll find is in how you decide to roll with it. So, strap in, and maybe learn to meditate or something.

# Hearts Aflame

## Kindling Compassion and Love

**"Love and compassion are necessities, not luxuries. Without them, humanity cannot survive."**

– Dalai Lama.

**L**ove and Compassion: These deep insights on love, kindness, and empathy spotlight how deeply connected we are and the strength of empathy to heal and unite.

They nudge us to extend a hand in friendship and care, to see beyond our differences, and to acknowledge the shared humanity that connects us.

Begin this path of compassion. Let each message inspire you to adopt love and kindness.

*Understand that our bonds run deep.*

Empathy is the bridge that links hearts and minds.

**As you ponder these words, keep in mind:** *that your ability to love and understand is limitless, and it's the key to a more unified and peaceful world.*

In my endless giving, I dwindled,
a candle burnt at both ends, sputtering out,
leaving mere glimmers of warmth
in the chill of depletion's shroud.

Gradually, a realization took hold—
caring for oneself isn't selfish; it's salvation,
a revival of the inner flame
that had dimmed within my soul's frame.

This act of self-preservation,
my emancipation's gentle bloom,
a homecoming to my inner nation,
cultivating the garden of my spirit's room.

From this self-care, a phoenix arose,
bestowing the world not with scraps,
but the fullness of a soul
replenished, glowing, and whole.

In tending to my essence,
I found the purest form of benevolence—
not from a barren well,
but from a cascade of abundance,
overflowing with the best of me.

**"Self-care allows you to give the world the best of yourself, instead of what's left of yourself."**

— April 17, 2022

Self-care is no fancy extra; it's a core kit for a smashing life. It's about offering the world your A-game, not just the dregs.

In our pedal-to-the-metal reality, the self often hits the back burner. We hustle, aiming to ace tasks, charm the crowd, and one-up the game. In the rush, we sideline numero uno: *us*.

Enter self-care.

It's not just a spa day; it's our recharge zone, ensuring we don't just run on fumes but sparkle. Self-care is the ultimate self-rescue. It's clocking what you need and making it happen, setting boundaries, saying *"no thanks"* when necessary, and keeping burnout at bay. It's your strategy to not just get by but flourish.

Neglect self-care and it's not just you who suffers; your circle feels it, too.

When you are running on empty you're not up to playing your roles—be it ace friend, top-tier family member, or stellar workmate. You can't dish out your best.

But make self-care your jam, and watch how you light up the room. You're all in–present, perky, and on-point; gifting everyone the cream of you, not just the crumbs.

What does self-care look like? It's personal. It could be sinking into bubbles after a long day, a quiet walk, stretching it out, or scratching something off the list. Hunt down what clicks for you and lock it in your daily beat.

Self-care isn't an ego trip.

It's standard procedure, your pass to a rich, even-keeled life. So, treat yourself. Both you and the world deserve nothing less than to peak you.

The need to express, to be acknowledged,
beats within me like a drum, a longing deep in the heart,
resonating with our universal desire for validation,
for the honor of being seen
in the light of our own truths.

We stand alone, each against the sweep of history,
holding tightly to our stories,
our character built on moments of joy and pain,
painted with the colors of our laughter like a sunrise,
and our tears like a soft evening rain.

This deep longing to be recognized, to be heard,
is as inherent as the air we breathe,
the scent of fresh earth after a storm,
a necessity, not a luxury.

For within the act of sharing, of listening,
we find connection,
the acknowledgment of our shared humanity,
the affirmation that, in this infinite, indifferent universe,
we matter.

Today, I release my stories into the void,
a firm assertion of my being,
staking claim to the space I fill,
the breath I take, the taste of morning dew on my lips,
the life I lead—all deserving to be told,
all deserving to be heard.

**"We are all worthy of telling our stories and having them heard. We all need to be seen and honored in the same way that we all need to breathe."**

— October 6, 2021

Stories.

We've all got them. Hidden away, itching for the spotlight.

They're not just past events; they're the heartbeat of who we are.

Every single soul, with its unique path, has the right—no, the need—to spill their tales.

It's as vital as the air we breathe.

These narratives are snapshots of our souls. They spill the beans on our highs, lows, and victories. Telling our story, we offer a piece of our soul, hoping to be truly seen. When we share, it's like saying, *"Hey, you're not alone."*

Our struggles, aspirations, and fears resonate, binding us.

Sharing is our secret sauce for healing, allowing us to piece together our history and truly own our path.

So, let it out.

Never doubt the might of your voice.

By sharing, we liberate ourselves and light the path for others.

Let's salute our stories and, by doing so, salute our shared humanity—our collective spirit.

I've carried the weight of words,
the sting of actions, a cloak heavy with the burden
of another's hidden wounds.
Each look, each phrase, a reflection
not of who I am, but of their inner conflicts,
fields I roamed, mistaking their battles for my own.
How heavy the heart grows,
how bent the back,
believing their struggle
was etched into my being.

But in a moment of clarity,
the ground shifted beneath me—
a liberation from the tangled web
of misplaced blame and misinterpreted motives.
I then saw not only my own pain
but also the shadows of theirs,
casting patterns on the barriers around our hearts.
With this realization, the air lightened,
and the words, the looks, the hurts,
became less like chains and more like water—
flowing past me, around me,
but no longer piercing through me.

I stand now, not as a target for their pain,
but as an observer of our shared journey towards healing,
learning to recognize not just the projection,
but the projector—
each of us a mirror
to the other's unspoken battles.
*And in this light, empathy finds its foothold,*
*a gentle understanding*
*that none of it was ever truly personal.*

**"Once you realize that almost everyone is projecting their own pain, trauma and limitations onto you, it becomes much easier to stop taking things so personally."**

— October 8, 2022

People have a knack for hurling their personal chaos your way.

It's an involuntary reflex that has the ability to make you feel like you are gazing into one of those wacky, distorted carnival mirrors.

Then comes your lightbulb moment when you realize their drama is just that—their drama, not a verdict on your worth. People rarely realize they're dumping their emotional baggage on your doorstep. Grasping this little nugget lets you keep your cool, responding with a grin rather than a scowl. You're basically decrypting their code, understanding the frets and fears underneath.

This doesn't mean you roll out the red carpet for their gloom and doom. Stand your ground, but try to also see things from their perspective.

This balancing act is pure gold. It nurtures self-love and helps you empathize without losing yourself in their drama.

When you feel like you're under fire, hit the pause button.

Remind yourself, *"That's their circus, not mine."*

Be your own cheerleader.

Take a step back.

Breathe in. Breathe out.

This little breather is your shield.

It's not about being immune to every snide remark or side-eye. It's about fortifying your sense of self so well that those jabs just bounce off.

We parade our victories,
yet within us, battles rage—silent, unseen,
*each of us bearing the weight of our own worlds,*
*a universe of pain and sorrow, hidden in plain sight.*
From this realization, compassion emerges—not forced,
but as a natural response, seeing my own struggles
reflected in the eyes of another.

Beneath every layer of resilience,
there lies a fragility, a human vulnerability,
binding us together in a quiet pact of shared existence.
*No one walks this earth untouched by the thorns of adversity,*
*we are all made of both steel and sorrow,*
*and in this shared heritage,*
*I find not just empathy, but a fierce kind of love,*
*a compassion driven by the deep understanding*
*that we are all, fundamentally, beautifully,*
*tragically,*
*human.*

**"Compassion is fueled by understanding and accepting that we're all made of strength and struggle - no one is immune to pain or suffering."**

— December 5, 2021

Compassion is what stitches society together. It recognizes our blend of strengths and stumbles—no one's immune to life's downpours.

Compassion starts with you. It's about owning your flaws and scars.

Acknowledging our own rough patches helps us grasp others' battles. It's a whole *"I get you"* vibe because, let's face it, we've all been in the trenches. Genuine compassion isn't about pity. It's about connection. It says, *"I see your struggle because I've been there too."* It's reaching out, no judgment, just pure, shared human experience.

Acknowledging our struggles feels like a faux pas in a world of invincibility.

Yet, true grit is found in vulnerability. It's this unguarded truth where connections deepen.

Compassion is action, not just sentiment. It's kindness in motion, lending a hand, and showing up when it counts. It's choosing empathy, even when turning away seems easier.

But hey, compassion isn't just about giving. It's also about opening up, welcoming help with open arms.

That's real courage.

The magic of compassion is a domino effect. A little kindness goes a long way, reminding us we're not alone in this battle.

It's what makes us human, bridging divides, uniting us in mutual care and understanding.

Through compassion, we find hope and healing.

It's what makes us, well, us.

In a world quick to offer solutions,
where advice flows freely, unsolicited,
I've felt the weight of words meant to solve, not soothe,
a barrage of fixes for a soul not broken but aching to be understood.
I've stood within the noise—buzzing, booming, banging—
longing not for the sharpness of answers, but the softness of empathy,
a space to be seen, heard, like a shelter in the storm,
not as a puzzle to be completed, but a story unraveling at its own pace.
The art of listening, once a gentle river, now a lost treasure,
becomes a precious rarity,
a quiet validation of worth beyond mere words,
an understanding that sometimes, the heart speaks in silences
that no solution can fill.

The heart, a fragile flower in a thunderstorm, speaks in silences,
its voice like a gentle breeze, swaying the branches,
its petals stretching towards the sun of understanding,
not solutions, but pure, radiant empathy.
In the act of genuine listening, I find not just my own voice,
but the depth of connection,
a bond formed not from advice, but from shared humanity,
a reminder that on this large, spinning globe,
being seen and heard is all any of us truly desires.

The leaves rustle, sharing secrets with the wind,
each rustle a story, a sigh, a silent cry for connection.
The art of listening, lost in the rush to respond,
becomes a rare jewel, shimmering in the depths of human interaction,
a quiet validation of worth beyond mere words,
an understanding that sometimes, the heart speaks in silences
that no solution can fill.

In the act of genuine listening, I find not just my own voice,
but the depth of connection,
a bond formed not from advice, but from shared humanity,
a reminder that on this large, spinning globe,
being seen and heard is all any of us truly desires.

**"People want to be seen and heard, not solved. They long for understanding and empathy, rather than quick fixes and unsolicited advice. Learn to listen."**

— August 13, 2021

In a world bombarded by endless chatter and unsolicited advice, it's important to remember, what people truly desire is not a solution, but to simply feel seen and heard. Within the rush to offer answers, we sometimes overlook that genuine connection is built on understanding and empathy.

When someone opens up about their struggles, they're not just fishing for repairs. They're often searching for a space where their feelings get a nod and a place on the shelf. It's a decisive difference, being seen as a person deserving of empathy rather than just a problem to solve.

Authentic listening means hitting mute on our internal monologues and biases.

It's about being there, really there, with the person sharing their world. This brand of listening isn't about zoning out; it's active. It's about shelving agendas and immersing ourselves in someone else's view without getting our feet wet.

This active participation with listening paves the way for empathy—a knack for feeling someone's experience, grasping their feelings without slapping on our own verdicts or fix-it badges.

Empathy transcends agreement or disagreement; it centers on comprehension. It serves as the link that binds our encounters.

It's the glue that bonds us.

Listening and showing empathy may appear like a luxury in a society that prioritizes solutions and productivity. But actually, they're the bricks and mortar of all that's real between us. They enable us to transcend surface-level exchanges and to partake in truly authentic connections.

So, next time someone shares their tale, tune in, solution-free.

In day-to-day moments,
I've voiced the phrase,
*"I'm okay,"*
a mantra more for others than for myself,
a veil thinly draped over the turmoil within.
Behind this façade, a storm rages,
a tempest of doubts and fears,
silent screams swallowed by the night.
The taste of salt from unshed tears,
bitter and stinging on the tip of my tongue.

I've played this charade of pretense,
smiling through the ache,
laughing off the pain,
while longing for someone to see
the truth that lies beneath the surface—
the not-okayness that clings like a shadow,
cold and clammy against my skin.

Sometimes, I yearn for just a glance,
one that sees through the mask I wear,
a look that says without words,
*"I see you—beyond the façade, beyond the forced smiles."*
I crave a hug that speaks volumes,
arms that wrap around me, offering refuge
from the battles I fight alone.
The comfort of warm fabric,
fresh from the dryer, feeling like home.

To hear,
*"I know you're not okay,*
*and that's okay,"*
would be a balm to the wounds
hidden from view,
an acknowledgment of the struggle
that goes unseen,
a recognition that it's okay
to not be okay.

**"Sometimes when I say I'm okay, I just want someone to look me in the eyes, hug me tight, and say, '*I know you're not and it's okay.*'"**
— March 10, 2023

Sometimes, my *"I'm okay"* doesn't mean I am smooth sailing, it's really a secret SOS, hoping someone will come along and decode my emotional distress.

Imagine me flashing a rehearsed grin, tossing *"I'm okay"* around like confetti at a bash I never wanted.

What I'm really fishing for? Not just a head nod and move on.

I'm on the lookout for that emotional Sherlock Holmes. Someone to peer a bit deeper, glimpse behind the curtain, and maybe, just maybe, offer a hug that says, *"Life's a show, but you don't always need to be on stage."*

I fantasize about the moment someone hits pause, locks eyes with me and says, *"Hey, I hear 'I'm fine,' but it's screaming 'help' to me."*

And then comes the hug.

Not just any hug, but the kind that feels like it's pulling every bit of gloom out of me—a hug that says, *"The lone wolf days are done."*

I'm craving that rare, straightforward connection.

It is a time when words take the backseat to a silent *"I get you"*—validating it's cool to be a beautiful mess. In our fast-forward world, where *"I'm okay"* slips out robotically, I long for that standstill, that touch that says, *"I see the real you, and hey, it's perfectly fine to unravel."*

So, if one day you catch my *"I'm okay"* thrown out with mechanical ease, stick around a bit longer. Dig a bit deeper, squeeze a bit tighter, and let's share a moment of silent understanding.

Because often, *"I'm okay"* is really just my way of wishing someone would spot the *"not really"* hidden inside.

**"I have found that among its other benefits, giving liberates the soul of the giver."**

– Maya Angelou.

Doling out love and compassion like Halloween candy might just be the best life hack. Not only do you make the world a tad less grumpy, but you also feel like a super-hero—cape and tights optional.

# Lens Shift

## The Power of Perspective

**"If you change the way you look at things, the things you look at change."**

—Wayne Dyer, You'll See It When You Believe It (1989)

**P**ERSPECTIVE AND ATTITUDE: QUOTES about how adjusting your viewpoint and mindset can transform life experiences, highlighting the impact of changing our perspective.

They encourage us to view obstacles as opportunities and failures as lessons, enabling us to navigate life's complexities with greater ease and positivity.

*Welcome the power of perspective.*

Let these quotes inspire you to shift your mindset.

Understand that challenges are stepping stones and setbacks are valuable insights.

**As you reflect on these words, remember:** *your outlook shapes your journey, and a positive perspective is the key to a more fulfilling and optimistic life.*

I walked as an outsider,
hovering on the fringes of circles I couldn't join,
a shadow in a world filled with laughter and light.
My anguish, like Iceberg Alley,
where colossal chunks of glaciers drift from distant Greenland,
looming, immense and grand,
forged a divide between my heart and the world.
This pain, like the submerged mass of an iceberg,
rendered me invisible,
turning bright emotions into the pale, frosty silence of winter,
transforming joyous music into the eerie, distant creaks of cracking ice.
I moved through the cold, dark waters of my mind,
where the frigid ocean mirrored the vast emptiness within me,
each wave a reminder of the barriers between me and the warmth of others.
Beneath the silent, static expanse of ice, the waters held life,
each hidden current hinting at the connections I longed to feel.

I navigated each day as a glacier,
isolated by an ocean of unshared sorrows,
believing my grief was an icebound fortress,
an unbreachable barrier to belonging.
But, over time, tides shifted, a subtle transformation began.
As the tides of time warmed my frozen heart,
the icy fortress began to melt,
revealing the currents of life beneath the once impenetrable surface.
I realized my unique yet universal story
was not a barrier but a bridge,
not a sign of isolation but a signal for connection.
The very pain that carved deep crevasses in my soul,
like the unseen base of an iceberg,
wove me into the broader human experience.
In sharing my scars, wounds, and healing,
I found not only comfort but community—
a foundation built on the profound, on the bedrock of shared experience.
Through these narratives of pain and recovery,
we discover the ties that bind us, the empathy that unites us,
turning pain from a source of alienation
into a catalyst for connection and understanding.

**"The pain that made you feel like an outsider is the very narrative that ties you to a world of healing and empathy. It's through these shared stories of struggle that we find common ground, fostering connections deeper than surface similarities."**

— January 7, 2023

The hurt that once set you apart isn't just a solo burden.

It's a bridge to a realm of healing and understanding. Through these common tales of hardship, we discover a deeper bond, more meaningful than just surface-level likenesses.

In our darkest moments, we often stumble upon our most significant connections.

It's not just the suffering itself but the resilience, evolution, and compassion that bloom from these trials.

Envision a place where our scars are emblems of valor, where openness signals fortitude. Your story turns into a bat signal for others, a message that solitude isn't their only companion.

Welcoming your tale changes suffering from a lone journey to a shared expedition.

Each story told is a lifeline, a glimmer of hope in the gloom.

Your pain isn't just a shadow; it's the north star, shining bright in the night sky.

When shared, it guides others out of their own darkness. Showing that we're all part of a greater human experience.

In this shared space, we find comfort and strength, turning individual scars into collective courage.

I am more than the battles I've braved,
my essence not confined by scars;
a blend of light and dark, joy and sorrow,
Crafted into a soul far richer than struggles suggest.
challenges form part of my journey, not its entirety,
forged by varied experiences, with tears and laughter too.
Like a phoenix rising from ashes grey,
my spirit, a radiant gold, soars beyond the confines of pain.
Today, I step beyond the shadows,
refusing struggle's narrow definition.
I welcome the emerald of my growth,
the crimson of my passion, and the azure of my tranquility,
rewriting my story with a broader palette—
each shade painting the horizon of tomorrow.

**"Don't let your struggle become your identity."**

— June 28, 2023

Hurdles, life's scrapes and bumps, mold us.

They're like the shadows adding depth to a painting, enhancing the contrast and making the light bits pop.

*But you can't let those shadows hog the whole scene.*

You're not just a sum of tough times; you're a work of art in the making.

Picture trekking through a forest. It's thick, dim, and the trail is all uneven. That's your ordeal. But the forest isn't the entire world. There's sky above, clearings in the distance, and so much more out there. Don't miss all that by just eyeing the dirt path.

Sure, challenges come and go, but they leave marks on us, schooling us in resilience, empathy, and fortitude. But they shouldn't morph into the bedrock of our persona. Your scars, hurdles, or history do not define you.

You're a being in bloom, poised for a dazzling metamorphosis.

Letting our struggles become our label boxes us in, shutting the door to fresh experiences and chances. We end up circling the same old sorrows, missing out on the beauty and wonder that life flings our way. It's crucial to acknowledge our battles, learn from them, and then push ahead.

Marching on doesn't mean erasing our struggles.

It means incorporating them into our tale without giving them all the limelight. It means acknowledging that we're more than our challenges, that we've got the chops to sculpt our lives in spite of them.

See your challenges as just one part of your journey but not as your whole story.

You're not your battles.

You're a unique, evolving soul packed with potential brimming with promise, poised for greatness.

In the shelter of survival,
I crafted habits like armor,
each a shield against the harshness
of an unpredictable, overwhelming world.
They were my safe haven,
where I hid from fierce storms
and the life outside walls too dense
to let in any light.

But as the battles quieted
and I faced my fears,
I saw these walls not as safeguards,
but as barriers—
a cage of my own making,
crafted from fear and avoidance.
As the dust settled,
and new horizons beckoned,
I stood at the fork between survival and truly living,
realizing my shields now held me back.

Letting go—
scary yet freeing—
meant dismantling the fortress,
brick by brick,
habit by habit,
to step into the light, defenseless,
open to the possibility of thriving.

For survival tools,
essential in the dark,
become shackles at dawn,
binding us when it's time to soar.
Thus, I chose to unlearn,
to build anew—
not fortresses, but bridges
leading to a life of fullness.

**"The habits you created to survive may no longer serve you when it's time to thrive."**

— March 26, 2022

Surviving is all about building fortresses, being on guard, and pinching pennies like there's no tomorrow. We become pros at side-stepping life's curveballs, our senses on high alert.

But when the sun's out, and fortune's smiling, those same fortresses might block out the warmth, and penny-pinching can choke off our growth.

Switching gears is like grooving to a new beat. The moves that kept you steady in the storm might trip you up in the calm. It's not about ditching the survival dance; it's about mixing in some new steps. Thriving is about letting go, trusting, and daring to invest in your dreams.

Remember, habits are the silent puppeteers of our days, steering our actions and shaping our tomorrows. Their real mojo is not just in setting them up but in our power to tweak them.

Asking, *"Is this feeding my growth?"* —is the bridge from just getting by to living large.

Thriving is also about connections. In survival mode, flying solo can feel like the safest bet. But in growth mode, that same solitude can turn into a cage. Sharing the ride, absorbing the lessons others offer, and exchanging support turns success from a lonely quest into a collective celebration.

Also, thriving made-to-order for each of us. What elevates one soul might not lift another. Owning your personal journey and tempo is crucial. It's not a sprint; it's a marathon. The real shift is from a mindset of scarcity to one of abundance—in thoughts, deeds, and vibes.

The habits we pick up in the trenches are medals of our grit. But as we step into the spotlight of thriving, it's crucial to reassess, to let go of the old, and to welcome new habits that match who we're evolving into. It's about rewriting our story from just scraping by to shining bright. Remember, growth is not just about where you're standing but how you spread your wings.

In the maze of avoidance,
I wandered, seeking paths around pain,
thinking each detour might spare me
the heartache of direct confrontation,
each turn from trouble a defense against despair.
But the paths of evasion,
winding and endless,
led not to safety, but deeper into a wilderness
of lingering memories and unaddressed shadows.

*Here, in the silence of fleeing what troubled me,*
*I found no peace,*
*only the growing realization*
*that avoidance is a loan taken against the future,*
*its interest compounded in solitude and silence.*
The brief relief yielded
to a landscape more formidable,
where issues left untended
grew wild and untamable,
a thicket of thorns from seeds of neglect.

In the courage to face what I feared,
a lesson learned—
the cost of avoiding's temporary relief
is a debt paid through lasting challenges,
and in turning towards, not away from, problems
lies the path to true peace,
a route that, though demanding, leads to healing,
to growth, and to the subtle strength
found in meeting the storm head-on,
not in the shelter of avoidance,
but in the commitment to persist and prevail.

**"Avoidance trades short term relief for long term suffering."**
— July 4, 2022

Dodging the tough stuff has its allure. A swift sidestep can be a fast track out of the ick.

But, oh boy, does that short-lived chill come with a hefty tab. Before you know it, you've traded a molehill for a mountain of worry.

Avoiding a tough convo feels like a win, but that nagging issue is still there, festering, cranking up the tension. Or, shelving a daunting task, feels like a breather, until you remember the deadline's still ticking, and now the pressure's dialed up.

Avoidance is like slapping a band-aid on a gash, screaming for stitches.

Sure, it hides the mess, but healing, it's not happening. In fact, it's likely to get gnarlier. The more we dodge, the beefier our fears grow, turning avoidable issues into behemoths.

Notice when you're in evasion mode and flip the script. It's about squaring up to those bogeymen, even when your knees are knocking.

This isn't about being fearless.

It's about grabbing the reins, facing the music, and coming out tougher on the other side.

Next time you're itching to bail, hit pause and ask yourself:

*"Am I just brewing a storm in a teacup?"*

If the answer's a big fat yes, then maybe it's time to bite the bullet.

It's a rocky road, but the jackpot at the end is worth every bump.

I've lived within the confines of expectations,
a world defined by lines drawn not by me,
but for me—each a barrier to boundless possibility,
a cage of shoulds and musts, a prison of propriety,
limiting the sky to a sliver of dreams,
a narrow beam of light breaking through the clouds.
In this self-made prison, days blurred together,
each one a photocopy of the last,
where dreams shrink to fit
the small realities prescribed by others,
a bird with clipped wings in a cage.

Then, in a moment of rebellion,
a spark of curiosity flickered to life,
challenging the walls I've built from expectations,
questioning the why,
the because,
the should.
With open curiosity as my guide,
I stepped beyond the familiar,
into a realm rich with the unknown,
where possibilities expand endlessly,
a horizon unbound by the constraints of expectation.

Here, in this expanse of potential,
I find not only the freedom to explore
but the thrill of discovery,
free from the chains of predetermined paths,
the cold, hard bars of expectation melted into the soft,
open air of possibility,
in a reality crafted not from what is expected,
but from what could be—
infinite and limitless.

**"Expectations create limitations. Open curiosity creates infinite possibilities."**

— September 27, 2021

Expectations are ninja-like. They creep up on you, disguised as goals, dreams, or societal standards. We chase them with gusto, but in the frenzy, we might miss the cool stuff just off the path. It's as if we've got blinders on, focused on the prize, oblivious to the show around us.

Enter curiosity.

It's your ticket to ditching those blinders.

It invites questions, fuels wonder, encourages detours.

It's not about abandoning your goals; it's about being open to the journey, to the detours that might lead to something unexpected. With curiosity as your guide, you're not confined to that narrow path. You're in the wild, open, where every step could reveal a new path, a fresh opportunity, a different perspective.

Imagine diving into a new project. You could go in rigid, with a fixed plan. Sure, you might hit your target, and that's great. But what if you let curiosity lead? You're not just checking boxes; you're in uncharted territory, creating something uniquely yours. It's the difference between coloring inside the lines and painting your own mural. One's following the script; the other's writing your own story.

*So, how do you ignite this curiosity flame?*

It's all about turning the tables. Instead of asking, *"Will this meet my goals?"* try asking, *"What's out there to explore?"*

It's about enjoying the journey as much as the destination. It's being at peace with the mysteries ahead. This mindset shift takes time, but stick with it, and it'll start to influence how you approach not just projects, but life as a whole.

It's not about giving up on your goals or lowering your standards. It's about redefining success. It's about understanding that the best moments often come from the unexpected, from those times when you ditch the script and let curiosity lead.

In rooms too small for my spirit,
I've folded into corners,
believing less space meant less pain,
a heart shrunk to avoid the touch of sorrow.
Each day, a call,
to shrink, to fade,
a voice convincing in its insistence
that to be unnoticed was to be safe.

But life, in its relentless march,
taught harshly,
that time is a river swiftly flowing,
and to hold oneself back
is to watch the world pass by in a blur of might-have-beens.
In the pain of what I lost by diminishing,
a realization, stark and bright—
life is too vast,
too rich to be lived from the sidelines.

To live fully is to expand,
to take up space,
to welcome the breadth of possibility,
to grow beyond the confines of fear,
and in doing so,
to step into the brilliance of becoming,
unfolding into the immensity of life,
a flower stretching towards the sun,
too short for anything less
than the fullness of being.

**"Life is *too short* to keep yourself *small.*"**

— January 1, 2023

Life's zooming by like a final clearance event, and well, the truth is, staying in your little box, playing it small, is like clutching a winning lotto ticket but never making the dash to cash it in.

You weren't crafted to fade into the scenery.

You're here to throw splashes of color across life's canvas, make it pop, make it scream *"you."*

Understand, you're the lead in your own epic saga, not just some easily skipped-over side character.

*Why settle for a minor role when you could be the one directing the show?*

Playing it safe might feel cozy, like curling up in a quiet corner of a vast library. But, remember, you're not meant to be a mere footnote or a stand-in—you're the main attraction, the unexpected twist, the climax that leaves everyone breathless.

It's time to raise those sails, catch the wind of ambition, and sail across the sea of possibilities. Display your full spectrum, your panoramic brilliance to the world. Life moves too fast for you to dim your light.

*Why whisper when you're built to resonate across generations?*

Stand tall, claim the spotlight, and remember this: in life, you're destined to shine, not just fade into the background.

On this brief tour we call life, minimizing yourself is like sidelining the epic saga you're supposed to narrate. So crank that volume, claim center stage, and etch your mark so deep that the universe won't soon forget.

Because truth be told, life's too precious to play yourself down, it's time to scale up, or else it's like you have already taken the final bow.

**"If you change the way you look at things, the things you look at change."**

– Wayne Dyer.

Your perception's basically your reality's fairy godmother. A little bibbidi-bobbidi-boo, and bam—your pumpkin of a day just turned into a carriage. Glass slippers not included.

_ele_

# Joy's Recipe

## Ingredients for a Happy Life

"Happiness is not a station you arrive at, but a manner of traveling."

– Margaret Lee Runbeck.

**H**APPINESS AND CONTENTMENT: THESE quotes have the power to infuse your life with joy, teach you to value that you possess, and guide you in discovering happiness in fleeting moments.

They encourage you to slow down, savor the present, and appreciate the beauty in simple things like a smile, a kind gesture, the sun's warmth, or a familiar tune.

*Welcome the joy of the moment.*

Let these quotes remind you to cherish the small pleasures in life.

Understand that happiness often lies in the simplest of things.

**As you reflect on these words, remember:** *the key to a joyful life is finding delight in the ordinary and toasting to the everyday miracles we often breeze past.*

In the pursuit of joy,
I discovered a rhythm,
a flow,
a cascade of golden light born from a single choice,
radiating warmth like the morning sun
that begins within and spreads outward,
rippling—laughter across a silent pond.
Feeling good became not just a state,
but an action,
a force,
propelling me beyond myself,
into spaces where my joy could reach others.

It's remarkable how a heart
inclined towards joy can start
a chain reaction, spreading brightness
in a world often dim.
In this act of doing good,
I've seen the reflection, joy mirrored in the eyes of another,
a sparkle in a dew-kissed meadow,
the scent of fresh rain
on dry earth,
underscoring
its contagious
nature,
its ability to transform not just one life,
but many.

**"When you choose joy, you feel good and when you feel good, you do good and when you do good, it reminds others of what joy feels like and it just might inspire them to do the same."**

— January 9, 2023

Picking joy is a bold move in a world that often feels like a ton of bricks. It's not just about chasing the grand slam of happiness but also savoring the little, everyday wins. When we swing for joy, we light a spark within.

This spark is contagious, a bona fide bliss bug, scattering cheer far and wide.

Feeling upbeat isn't just a passing mood; it's a vibe that shapes how we act and connect.

When we're riding the joy wave, we're more likely to spread kindness, lend a hand, and leave a positive mark.

It's a cycle of goodness ignited by the simple act of choosing joy.

But how do we latch onto joy when life is like a never-ending rollercoaster of ups and downs?

It starts with being all in the moment and spotting the magic in the little things. It's about counting our blessings and focusing on our bounty instead of the voids. And it's about bouncing back with a hopeful vibe after a tumble.

Spreading the good isn't just a personal boost; it also sets the stage for others.

It's the gentle push, reminding us joy's in the mix, even when the grind gets real. And when others catch a glimpse of that glow within us, they're inspired to ignite their own. It's a chain reaction of joy, rippling from one heart to another, brightening the globe.

So, let's go for joy.

Let's feel good, spread good, and fire up others to do the same.

It's a choice that can flip not just our own script but also the stories of those around us.

I've walked, unconsciously through my days,
a feather adrift on a gentle breeze, swaying softly through sunlit meadows,
my steps silent on ancient paths, worn by time and countless lost souls,
"run, Forrest, run!"—through the woods trails,
chased only by memories of the past.
Laughter rang hollow through empty valleys,
smiles fading like a box of half eaten chocolates,
in a world drained of its colorful hues,
sepia tones shadowing the long, solitary wait on the bench.

In this desolate landscape of loss, where hope flickered like a mirage,
comfort blossomed in the smallest gestures—
a hand extended, a lifeline for Bubba in the jungle's chaos,
or a gentle offering, a chocolate sweet and unexpected,
showcasing life's simple,
significant gifts.
Within the rubble of my grief,
I discovered the power of a single act,
unassuming, yet profound,
a carrying of Jenny's burdens without question.

It was then I understood,
as Forrest, with his silent, steadfast grace,
taught us: in giving, we receive;
in comforting, we are comforted,
just as Jenny found solace in his unwavering love,
her chaos quieted by his enduring embrace.
Today, I chose to be that first drop,
as deliberate as lacing up shoes before a cross-country run.
In kindness, I forged a legacy,
not of what was lost,
but of what could be offered—
a ripple effect,
reaching far beyond grief,
a shrimp boat, casting nets that gathered more than just shrimp,
healing broken lives and broken dreams.

And in that moment, I knew: *love endures, and so do we.*

**"Kindness is like a ripple effect—it starts with one act and can spread to touch many lives. Be the first drop in the water."**
— March 9, 2022

Kindness rocks.

It's more than a nice gesture; it's the whole vibe.

Think of it as that one pebble causing a splash, sending out ripples—sparking a kindness revolution.

Think of our planet. We're all droplets in this massive pond. Choosing kindness is like tossing pebbles in, making ripples that reach far and wide. These ripples have the power to flip scripts, brighten dark corners, and encourage more folks to join the party.

There is no need for fireworks.

Kindness lives in the low-key moments—the smiles, the casual *"hey, how's your day,"* the lending of an ear—tiny seeds of goodness that can blossom big time. You toss these seeds out; you never know where they'll sprout or who'll get a piece of that warmth.

Kindness is infectious.

Witness one act, and you're likely to pass it on.

Boom, a chain reaction of good vibes, lighting up a whole crew, neighborhood, even towns.

Being that pebble is about stepping up and sprinkling kindness even when it feels like a stretch. It's about giving a darn, even when the worlds in a funk. It's about being the glow in the gloom. In a world sometimes dimmed by downers, we're the crew to flip the script.

Kicking off a kindness wave, we have what it takes to send out ripples that can rock the globe, one kind deed at a time.

So, let's be the pebble, start the splash, and watch as kindness ripples outward.

In the solitude of my four walls,
with no eyes to judge,
I become a version of myself unfiltered,
a spirit unleashed,
dancing with the abandon of youth untouched by skepticism,
a soul momentarily free from the chains of indoctrination.

It's here, in the chaotic whirl of limbs,
where the scent of sweat mingles with
the cool,
stale air,
the breathless laughter following a song,
a melody echoing off the barren walls,
that I find a piece of what was thought lost—
a joy unfiltered,
a reminder that sometimes,
the simplest acts
carry the greatest power to heal.

In this dance, this return to simplicity,
I'm reminded of the purity of happiness,
one that requires no explanation,
no restraint—
just the freedom to be,
to feel the soft carpet between my toes,
the soft swoosh of my clothes as I sway,
fully alive
in the purest sense.

**"Never underestimate the healing power of listening to your favorite music on full blast while dancing around the house like a five-year-old on a sugar fix."**

— November 19, 2022

Music is not just beats and melodies. It's a portal to pure joy, a bridge to our playful side, and a serious mood-lifter.

**Picture this:** you're solo at home, the day's been a drag, and you're feeling blue. *What's your next move?* You could mope around, or you could blast your go-to jams and bust out some living room dance magic.

Music has this uncanny knack for pulling us out of the funk. It's like a time warp, zapping us back to those carefree, golden days. I remember a time when I was feeling down, and I put on my favorite song. Suddenly, I was transported back to a summer day from my childhood, running around the backyard without a care in the world.

That's the vibe you're chasing.

When you're dancing in your space to that killer track, you're not just moving your body; you're shaking off the heavy stuff, the worries, the gloom.

It's not about nailing those dance moves or keeping the beat. It's about letting loose, getting goofy, and soaking up some joy. In those moments, your mind's not bogged down by your to-do list or life's hiccups. You're right there, at the moment, totally alive. And that's where the magic of healing kicks in.

This whole dance-like-nobody's-watching thing?

It's a big ol' middle finger to the stress and anxiety life chucks at us. It's our way of saying, *"Hey, life, you've got your games, but here's my secret stash of cheer and peace."* In these moments, we're reminded that life, for all its twists and turns, is also brimming with simple joys that can lift our spirits and mend our hearts.

So, next time you're in a slump, turn that music up to eleven and dance like a five-year-old post-candy jackpot.

It just might be the pick-me-up you never knew you needed.

In nature's cradle,
where the hum of gadgets subsides,
I found a refuge to breathe,
to listen to the earth's orchestra—
its rustles, murmurs, and sighs.
Amidst the green, under the endless sky,
I discovered an ancient language,
a dialogue in the rustling leaves,
the babbling streams, the gentle hum of the wind.

The world, often hidden behind screens,
unveiled its beauty layer by layer,
unseen, unheard, unfelt,
revealing life's simple truths
carried by the breeze,
painted in the sky, stomped in the soil beneath my feet.
The scent of pine and damp earth filled the air,
cool grass tickled my skin,
sunlight filtered through the canopy,
casting dancing shadows on the forest floor.
Birdsong filled the space, a melodic chorus,
while the brook's soft murmur
added a soothing bassline, each note a reminder of ancient rhythms.

This break from the electronic tether,
a reconnection to the world's pulse,
rooted me in the present,
in the real,
in the tangible essence of life.
In this quiet simplicity,
I realized all that's missed
in the clamor of living,
and felt a sweet sorrow for the time lost
to the artificial,
when the world, in its purest form,
offers a profound connection,
rooting me in the present,
in the heart of what it means to truly live.

**"Spend time in a natural setting without electronics. Pay attention to the sounds, sights, and smells. This practice can help ground you in the present and reconnect you to the simplicity of living."**
— May 6, 2022

Think back.

When did you last stand in a forest, surrounded by towering trees, their leaves rustling in the wind? Or sat by a creek, watching water frolic in the sun's glow?

These moments, pure and simple, form the essence of life, yet we often overlook them in our day-to-day rush.

Powering down our gadgets isn't just a break for our eyes; it's a sanctuary for our souls. In nature's hush, we find space to breathe, think, and feel. Here, we touch base with life's basics, with the joy often buried by the constant barrage of notifications and screens.

As you nestle in nature's arms, let its subtleties wash over you.

Observe the countless shades of green, the elaborate dance of leaf patterns, and the delicate charm of wild blooms. Allow the orchestra of nature—the chorus of birds, the sighing of leaves, the gentle babble of water. Inhale deep, let the fresh, earthy scents ground you in the present.

This ritual is more than just a sweet time-out. It opens the door to being fully present, forging a deeper connection with both the external environment and our inner selves. In nature's simplicity, we find clarity. We're reminded that life isn't just a series of tasks but a collection of tranquil, captivating moments.

So, take a step away from the fast pace of modern existence.

Wander into the wild, even if it's just a city park.

Ditch your phone and be all in, right in the moment.

You might find that in the gentle rustle of leaves, you'll catch the voice of your own soul.

In my relentless rush,
I overlooked the lesson
in every sunset, every moonrise,
in the slow bloom of flowers
and the steady change of seasons—
that life moves not at the speed of schedules
but at the pace of the turning earth.

I found peace in the quiet observation
of nature's unhurried grace,
the way light shifts across the sky,
trees cycling through seasons,
how rivers carve canyons
not in haste, but with persistent flow.

*In Earth's cycles,*
*I saw my own phases,*
*a gentle reminder that growth*
*takes time,*
*that healing and becoming*
*are as natural*
*as the moon's wax and wane.*

**"Observe the natural world's cycles and rhythms. Just as seasons change and plants grow at their own pace, understand that your life also has its own natural rhythm."**

— June 8, 2023

Life hums, mirroring the rhythm of the cosmos.

As seasons change and plants flourish on their own schedule, our lives dance to a beat of their own. Caught up in the daily grind, we often forget that we're stitched into nature's vast scene, not standing outside it.

Look around.

Notice how each tree grows at its leisure and how every flower blooms in its own season. The oak isn't in a rush to lose its leaves, and the rose doesn't scramble to show off its petals. They sway to Earth's tempo, aligned with life's cycle.

*So why do we push ourselves into endless activity, into a relentless pursuit of more?*

We're schooled to compete, to excel, to keep winning. Yet, in this sprint, we lose touch with our own rhythm. We overlook that, similar to the changing seasons, our lives ebb and flow.

Welcome your life's seasons.

There will be high points where everything just works, and you're buzzing with drive. And there will be lulls, seemingly still, yet underneath, strong foundations are being laid.

In the rush for achievements, don't forget to actually live. Allow your life to unfold at its natural pace, confident that each phase arrives at the ideal time. Just like a caterpillar becomes a butterfly when it's ready, your life's episodes will naturally progress.

Nature doesn't rush, yet all is accomplished.

Let this be our take-home message. Every element has its place; every pulse holds significance.

March to your own beat, and have faith in the timing of your life.

In life, joy and pain intertwine,
polarities of light and shadow on the canvas of being,
crafted by the meticulous hand of an unseen Architect.
I have learned not under the bright rays of sun,
but in the grip of shadows, where pain etches deeper meaning into my soul.
Each ache, each tear, is a line of code—
a promise encrypted in suffering,
a potential for growth, for profound insight,
like the glitches in the first Matrix, imperfections revealing hidden truths.
The Architect, in his quest for perfection,
designed a utopia devoid of suffering, serene and pure,
yet humanity rejected it, craving the depth of feeling.
*"We tried to create a paradise, but it was a disaster,"* he confessed,
for we need pain to define our joy, to appreciate the vibrancy of our existence.

These glitches, these sorrows, are vital anomalies,
lines of code embedded within our psyche, invisible to eyes clouded by grief,
yet tangible, a silent pledge that from this pain,
something meaningful will emerge,
just as Neo discovered his purpose through adversity.
Life reveals its truths not at the zenith of joy,
but in the quiet aftermath of sorrow, where the heart, once fractured,
becomes fertile soil for lessons only struggle can impart.
We are like the rebels of Zion, finding strength in the stark reality of our battles,
each scar a testament to our resilience.

Thus, I cherish not only moments of clear joy
but also the trials, for in the narrative of my life,
each tale of pain contributes to the intricate beauty
of a life richly lived,
a code written in both binary and the blood of experience.
The Matrix could not exist without its anomalies,
and our lives would be hollow without shadows.
In the depths of suffering, we find our truest selves,
emerging from the darkness,
reborn, enlightened, ready to confront the Architect
and grasp that true power lies in the equilibrium of light and dark,
joy and pain,
illusion and reality.

**"Life's beauty is not just in joy, but in the lessons learned from pain. For in every moment of pain, lies a promise."**

— May 10, 2022

Life is a mixtape of highs and lows. We've got the laughter tracks and then those tearjerkers.

The real beauty is not just in the fist bumps and victory dances but in the face plants that have us tasting dirt.

*The jackpot—growth, insight, a whole new vibe—is buried beneath our hardest face-offs.*

Pain often crashes the party like an uninvited guest, making us wish we could show it the door, pronto. But flip the script for a sec. *What if pain is that sage, that old wise mentor?* It's packed with lessons, sharing secrets of a more prosperous life, if only we're game to tune in.

Now, don't get it twisted. I'm not saying we should chase pain like it's going out of style. It's more about recognizing that pain has a role. It nudges us to peek inside, face the music, and come out the other side not just intact but stronger, inner iron.

Consider heartbreak, it feels like a sucker punch to the gut, right? Everything's grayscale. But give it time, and eventually, you realize heartbreak was schooling you in love's hard knocks—what you want, what you stand for, what kind of heart you want to sync up with.

Then there's failure, that reality check that burns. But it's also prime time for a playbook overhaul, a chance to redraw the map with a sharper pencil and a clearer head.

Each sting comes with a promise—a heads-up that learning's on the horizon, that growth's brewing, and that even in the dark, there's a glimmer waiting to be seen. It's the universe's way of saying the toughest lessons come dressed in shadows.

Next time pain drops by, try looking beyond the discomfort. Hunt for the lesson lounging in the shadows. Claim it as your ticket to level up, to enrich your soul's understanding of this wild ride we're all on.

'Cause truth is, it's in the tumbles and falls that we dust off our true grit and shine.

**"The more you praise and celebrate your life, the more there is in life to celebrate."**

– Oprah Winfrey.

Party for the little things, because every day deserves its own confetti moment. It's like saying 'thank you' to life, but with more sparkle and possibly cake.

# Valor Vignettes

## Tales of the Fearless

"Courage doesn't always roar. Sometimes courage is the quiet voice
at the end of the day saying, 'I will try again tomorrow.'"
— Mary Anne Radmacher.

**C**OURAGE AND **B**RAVERY: THESE quotes on overcoming fears, embracing risks,
and staying true to oneself are incredibly powerful in igniting growth and authenticity.

They underscore that courage isn't about being fearless but about conquering fear, inspiring us to step out of our comfort zones and embrace our vulnerabilities.

*Welcome your bravery.*

Let these quotes motivate you to face your fears and take risks.

Understand that true courage lies in acknowledging your fears and pushing forward.

**As you reflect on these words, remember:** *the journey to self-discovery and authenticity is paved with challenges, but it's through overcoming these obstacles that we find our true strength and purpose.*

In comfort's familiar hold,
I lingered too long,
like Newton beneath the apple tree,
bound by the gravity of the known,
a bird in a cage with the door wide open,
too hesitant to explore the skies beyond.
The vast, uncharted world outside
beckoned with the promise of unknown heights,
its crisp air carrying the scent of potential,
yet fear rooted me in place,
an apple clinging to the branch,
unwilling to release and fall to the earth.

Discomfort, ever hovering at my edge,
loomed large,
like the apple's inevitable descent,
the step into the void, a leap too daunting
for a heart schooled in the safety of sameness.
But the voice of potential,
soft yet insistent,
urged me to confront the confines of my making,
to challenge the boundaries I had drawn
around the contours of my life,
like Newton's curiosity defying the limits of gravity.

In the discomfort of stepping beyond,
I found not the fall I feared,
but wings I never knew I had,
lifted by the forces of enlightenment,
strength forged in the act of leaving behind
the worn paths of the familiar.
Growth, I learned, does not flourish in the shade
of familiar trails but in the bright, open spaces just beyond,
where triumph lies not in avoiding discomfort,
but in its willing acceptance—
a validation to the bravery
found in venturing from the known to the beyond,
like Newton's apple revealing the laws of the universe,
transforming fear into the flight of discovery.

**"Welcome the discomfort of stepping out of your comfort zone. Growth and success lie beyond the familiar boundaries we set for ourselves."**

— October 14, 2021

Step into the unknown. That's where the magic of expansion and the jackpot of victories hang out, way past the cozy corners of routine.

We're creatures tuned to the rhythm of the known, lovers of comfort, champions of the *"been there, done that."* The big-time transformation, the kind that skyrockets you, is sneaking around just beyond the boundaries you've boxed yourself into.

Stepping out of your bubble isn't just about making the jump; it's about befriending the butterflies that come with it. It's about seeing that flutter of nerves as the welcome mat to your new level, punching through the glass ceilings you once saw as the firmament.

Comfort is the snooze button on life's alarm clock. It doesn't prod you to change lanes, rethink your route, or approach the puzzle from a new angle. But, step off the beaten path, and bam! You're in the land of what-ifs. This is where the prize lies, in those nerve-wracking steps forward, with trepidation as your backdrop but not your script. When your knees are knocking, you march on. When you're out in the deep end, crafting your own float.

*So, how do you cozy up with discomfort?*

Switch things up. Instead of dodging unease, welcome it as your plus-one to the growth gala.

Pursue the enigmas, not the exits.

Unclench your grip on the tried-and-true; dive headfirst into the new wave.

Sure, it's a tall order. It's about mustering up the guts, building resilience, and staring down the scare-fest. But oh, the spoils! Beyond the bounds of snug lies a realm ripe with expansion, victories, and an unmet you just itching to say *"Hey."*

So, make the move. Cozy up to the discomfort. And witness your world stretch in vistas unimagined.

In the domain of comfort, I once built a home,
like Da Vinci's sketches, the blueprints of my known.
Walls lined with the familiar, a haven from the unknown's roar,
yet within these walls, restlessness brewed,
a soul longing for the light beyond the safety of its self-made prison.
Small acts became my rebellion, each day a step into the uncharted,
a word spoken in fear, a path walked alone,
tiny triumphs in the expanse of existence,
as if each brushstroke revealed a new invention,
each discovery pushing boundaries once set in stone,
mirroring Da Vinci's relentless pursuit of knowledge,
his notebooks filled with the mechanics of the human heart,
the flight of birds, the mysteries of motion.

With each challenge, a layer shed,
revealing strength hidden beneath complacency,
muscles of bravery flexing, previously dormant, untested,
like Da Vinci's contraptions, emerging from the mind's depths,
his designs for flying machines daring to touch the heavens,
each mechanism a testament to brilliance concealed
in the consciousness of imagination, each sketch defying gravity.
This daily embrace of discomfort, a gradual crafting of spirit,
expanded my vistas, pushed the walls of my haven
until they vanished into the horizon,
much like Da Vinci's vision transcending the canvas,
his Mona Lisa smiling enigmatically,
his Last Supper capturing the divine and human,
each piece breaking free, touching the sky.

Over time, the once daunting became the norm,
a testament to the growth found
in the accumulation of moments,
each small act of courage a brick in the fortress of my becoming,
each innovation a leap towards a future unbound,
where dreams and reality intertwine, in the intricate dance of creation,
as Da Vinci's Vitruvian Man stands,
arms outstretched, a symbol of perfect proportion,
harmony found in the union of art and science,
a blueprint for the limitless potential within us all.

**"Build courage through small acts. Challenge yourself daily with tasks that push you slightly out of your comfort zone. Over time, your threshold for bigger challenges will grow."**

— September 3, 2021

Tiny steps lead the courage charge.

It's not about grand gestures but the day-to-day nudges that push us a smidge past our comfort cocoons. These little challenges, stacked over time, beef up our bravery for the big jumps.

To whip up courage, sling together daily mini-missions that push your limits, even by a whisker.

Start small.

Voice an opinion, try something new, or simply say 'no' when 'yes' is your go-to.

These might seem minor, but they're mighty in molding your courage muscle.

Stick to this path, and you'll watch previously towering tasks shrink down to size. Your knack for wrangling uncertainties and diving into risks grows. You become a resilient being, more sure-footed in weathering life's rollercoasters.

The trick is to never stop pressing forward and to keep stretching your comfort zone. It's not about banishing fear but learning to stride ahead despite it. It's picking growth, choosing to act when you'd rather not.

So, lean into those tiny acts of bravery.

They're your stepping-stones to the mammoth dares.

Remember, each step outside your cozy circle carves out a fiercer, bolder you.

I try to take the leap,
but fear tells tales of caution,
a chorus of what-ifs and buts,
holding me at the edge of change.
Inside me though, a voice dares to defy,
with a soft insistence that stirs my spirit:
*"It's daunting, yet the path—oh, the path
will forge you anew, into something greater."*

Accepting this challenge,
this invitation to step beyond what's known,
I find courage in the acknowledgment
that failure, should it come, is not defeat,
but a gateway to greater resilience, wisdom, and strength.

This leap into the unknown
is driven not by the assurance of success,
but by the hunger for growth,
for life beyond the confines of fear.
With a deep breath,
I step forward,
into the breadth of possibility,
eager to meet the version of myself
that waits on the other side,
sculpted by trials,
radiant with the sheen of courage
earned on the pilgrimage through fear.

"I know it's scary, but it will be worth it. Because even if you fail, you'll be better, stronger, and more capable for it. You need this change, this challenge, this growth. Go find out what life is like on the other side of your fear."

— March 12, 2023

Facing the unknown is a beast, isn't it? All those *"what-ifs"* circling like vultures, casting shadows of doubt and fear.

**But get this:** *it's supposed to rattle you.* Because that's where the magic happens; beyond those shivers and shakes lies evolution, change, and a you that's itching to break free. You might trip, and you might even eat dirt. But when you haul yourself up, you're doing more than just standing; you're climbing a notch higher, tougher, ready for the next round.

Diving into the unknown isn't about keeping score. It's the journey, the change that blossoms within when you step out from the cozy, known confines. You crave this. The challenge, the shift, the chance to stretch your wings and really see what you're capable of.

So, suck in that breath, round up every ounce of courage you've got, and take the plunge. Welcome the fog of not knowing, the excitement of possibility, the raw thrill of the expedition.

**And here's the thing:** *no matter how it pans out, you win.*

*Why?*

Because you had the audacity to stare down those fears, chase your dreams, and live full throttle. That's the meat of it:

- Finding out what lies beyond fear.

- Tapping into your true grit.

- Transforming into the mightiest version of yourself.

So, take that leap. It might be terrifying, but oh, the ride is going to be epic.

In the war with my shadows,
where fears speak with voices I know well,
I've mastered not the art of evasion
but of standing, eyes locked, fists ready,
matching the thunderous clap of courage.
Confronting these apparitions,
each a mirror to my deepest unrest,
I've found not the comfort of safety,
but the exhilarating discomfort of growth.

Courage, a torch flickering in a storm's fury,
does not dispel fear but confronts it,
face to face,
a silent acknowledgment of its presence
and a refusal to be defined by it.
*With each fear faced,*
*I transform,*
*each challenge refining my spirit,*
*reflecting a strength born of adversity.*

> "Facing our fears helps us find our power. For courage isn't the absence of fear but facing it head-on. And with each challenge faced, a new strength is born. Fear is the shadow; courage is the light."
> — July 17, 2022

Bravery isn't about dodging fear; it's about choosing to lock eyes with it.

With each face-off, we shed a layer, revealing our inner might.

Fear shadows us, while bravery shines the path forward, transforming us into unbreakable badasses.

Our story is filled with scenes where fear looms large, urging a step back. But it's exactly these scenes that call for a dose of daring.

Accepting our fears isn't a sign of surrender—it's the first step toward flourishing.

When we dare to meet our fears eye to eye, we unlock doors to new beginnings and a fiercer version of ourselves, filled with potential and self-discovery. Fear is the dark earth cradling the courage seed. Without it, our valor finds no foothold, no ember to ignite its flame.

Every brush with fear is a chance to nurture our courage, to let it bloom, spotlighting strengths we never knew we had.

So, let's not shy away from our fears.

Face them, learn from them, and turn them into the foundations of our grit.

It's not about erasing fear from our lives.

It's about acknowledging our fears, challenging them, and discovering the relentless light of courage that lies within.

They said healing was a journey,
yet no one mentioned the darkness
that devours the path,
or the silence that magnifies doubts.
Each hesitant step,
weighted with a heart
trying to heal,
stitch by invisible stitch,
through the worn fabric of a soul.
Ahead lay a vast expanse of maybes and what-ifs,
a blend of fear and hope.

In this walk,
with each cautious step,
I discovered strength not in the ground covered,
but in the act of moving,
the bravery to face what's next
the next breath
the next break in the trees
where just enough light slips through
to reveal the next step.
I realized,
healing isn't arriving,
but the ongoing stride,
choosing to move
when stillness feels safer.
A tribute to the resilience
of a spirit chasing wholeness.

**"Walking the healing path is about consistently taking small steps into the unknown."**

— August 2, 2022

Treading the path of healing is all about baby steps into uncharted territory. There is no need for dramatic leaps or overnight makeovers. It's the subtle, everyday choices that nudge us forward.

Healing is a marathon, not a sprint, pieced together by moments that gently steer us toward feeling whole. It kicks off with that single, brave decision to shake things up. That choice is a vow to keep pushing, even when the roads are foggy. Each move we make is a win, showcasing our grit and bounce-back game. We're stepping into the unknown, banking on the hope that each step is a move closer to where we want to be.

Healing's path is far from straight. It's a trail with bumps and detours, packed with moments of second-guessing and huffing in frustration. Yet, it's these hurdles that give us a peek into who we are, our limits, and what we're capable of. They teach us that healing is more about the trek and the discoveries made, not just the finish line.

*This road is paved with mini acts of courage.*

It's about staring down our ghosts, facing our hurts head-on, and being open to new paths. It's letting go of dead weight and welcoming growth. Each step is a leap of faith, a trust-fall into our own ability to heal and transform.

Navigating this path means getting cozy with ourselves. It's about understanding what works for us, tending to our needs, and constructing a more robust self, one step at a time.

Healing's trek is deeply personal, tailor-made for each soul wandering it.

There's no one-size-fits-all suit here.

What matters is the motion, those tiny yet bold steps.

With each one, we edge closer to healing, to a fuller, more tranquil state of being.

In the hush of twilight, I sit,
surrounded by the remnants of what could have been.
Each shard glints in the fading light,
a reminder of paths not taken,
of words swallowed by fear,
and dreams deferred in the face of doubt.
I've felt the oppressive weight of expectations,
a burden that bends but never breaks.
My journey, a series of starts and stops,
a map inked more by detours
than by the straight lines of success.

But within the chaos of missteps and might-have-beens,
a realization dawns, quiet and enlightening:
the beauty of my path lies not in its perfection,
not in its flaws,
but in the raw, unedited truth of my story.
The scars I bear,
the salty tears I've shed—
not failures, but evidence of a life fiercely lived.
They are the ink in the pen of my life,
writing a story rich with perseverance.

*Now, I choose to see each twist and turn*
*as chapters of a grander tale.*
*For in the complexity of my journey,*
*there lies an amazing story,*
*one only I am destined to create.*

**"Instead of getting entangled in the complexities of your journey, focus on the amazing story it is destined to create."**
— April 7, 2023

Life's ride is a web of complexities.

We focus in on the bumps, the twists, and the bends, missing out on the epic story unfolding. Instead of getting hung up over the intricacies of our path, we ought to hug the saga that's gradually taking shape.

Each obstacle, each minor setback, isn't a roadblock but a step up, crafting a story that's uniquely ours. It's the rugged, winding paths, not the smooth, straight ones, that create compelling stories, challenging our resilience and character.

These are the tales that resonate, leaving a lasting mark on our being.

See your journey not as a series of random events but as a carefully curated collection of moments, each enriching your saga. The hurdles aren't there to trip us but to mold us, chisel our spirit, priming us for the pages ahead.

*So, why sweat the complexities?*

Let's toast to the masterpiece we're crafting.

Let's revel in the plot twists, draw power from the tests, and glean insight from the lessons on the way. Our path isn't merely a route we tread but a story we author, one bound to be legendary.

Change your focus from the puzzles to the plot, from the barriers to the breakthroughs. Wrap your arms around the narrative of your journey, for it's in this story we find our mission, our growth, and our essence.

*And it's this very tale that will define our legacy.*

**"Courage is like a muscle. We strengthen it by use."**

– Ruth Gordo.

Keep practicing courage, and soon you'll be so buff in bravery, you might just start wearing capes to the grocery store. Just remember, it's a fine line between hero and needing to explain your outfit choices to security.

# TURNING PAGES

## The Art of Moving On

**"Some of us think holding on makes us strong, but sometimes it is letting go."**

– Hermann Hesse.

**A**cceptance and Letting Go: These messages touch on confronting reality, moving beyond the past, and focusing on the future.

They reveal that while we can't change what has already occurred, we have the power to shape what lies ahead by liberating ourselves from the burdens of yesterday.

*Welcome the present.*

Let these messages guide you in releasing the past and stepping into the future.

Understand that your ability to influence what's to come starts with letting go of what's behind.

**As you reflect on these words, remember:** *the key to a brighter future is found in the courage to leave the past behind and embrace the possibilities that await. It's about giving the old heave-ho to yesterday and winking at tomorrow with both eyes wide open.*

I lingered at the edge of the old,
a chapter worn and well-thumbed,
its pages yellowed and curling,
familiar in its contours,
yet hollow in its comfort,
its words fell flat, their magic spent.
My spirit, restless,
spoke of worlds unseen,
of stories untold waiting just beyond
the fear of turning the page.

But, I hesitated,
clinging to the script of yesterdays,
fearing the blankness of the page to come,
the open space of stories yet to be told.
The call to move forward,
insistent and gentle,
spoke of trust, of faith in the unknown,
a reminder that growth resides
not in the safety of the known,
but in the courage to step into unknown light.

Honoring this call,
I turned the page,
embracing the uncertainty,
the vulnerability of beginnings anew,
an author facing the daunting blankness
of the very first sentence.
I found strength in the act of letting go,
in the belief that the next chapter,
though unwritten,
holds the promise of a journey
worthy of the spirit's longing,
a testament to the power of listening
to the quiet voice within,
guiding towards the unfolding
of new dreams, new paths, new life.

**"When your spirit is telling you it's time for a new chapter, honor it."**

— July 6, 2023

There's this voice inside you, right? Persistent but not pushy, it's hinting at a shake-up. This isn't about whims or passing cravings. It's a profound, gut-level nudge that something has got to give.

That nudge is your green light. It's time to stretch, grow, and really own who you are.

Look, ditching the old you doesn't mean trashing your past. Your story's your backbone, packed with lessons and strength. But clinging too tight to yesterday is like hugging the pool edge, never daring to swim. You'll never savor the thrill of the dive or the grace of the strokes until you let go and trust.

*Change, yeah, it's scary.*

You're stepping off the map, ditching the cozy for the unknown. Yet, real growth is out there, beyond the comfort zone.

That inner poke is basically saying, *"You're set."*

Set to grow, stretch, and really step into your essence. Listen to that inner voice. It's like your soul's internal north star, guiding you, understanding you. When it hints it's time for a new chapter, it's spot-on. You're primed to bloom, tackle whatever's next, and show the world your true colors.

Jump into this change with everything you've got. This isn't just a journey; it's your epic quest. Every step is a step closer to who you're meant to be.

It's less about the endpoint and more about the evolution en route.

So, when your soul signals a new season, stand up and cheer. Dive headfirst into this new adventure, this growth, this endless sea of possibilities.

What-ifs.

Trust me, your future self is already cheering you on.

Behind me, the shadows of *"what was"*
stretch long and deep,
a collection of footsteps in the sand,
washed away by time's relentless tide.
It's a letting go, a release—
an auction of emotions, a bidding farewell
to artifacts no longer needed,
a surrender to the inevitability of change,
to the ebb and flow of existence,
letting the gavel fall with a resounding bang,
selling off each piece to the highest bidder.

Ahead, the horizon blurs with *"what's to come,"*
a blank canvas awaiting the first daring stroke,
a painter's hand trembling
with anticipation and fear,
where faith illuminates the path,
a light in the uncertainty of tomorrow,
each moment an opportunity
to craft a masterpiece from the mist of possibility.

This journey—
of curating, auctioning, creating,
of accepting, releasing, believing,
is marked by the strokes of silent struggles,
a testament to the artistry found
in the openness of trust,
in the bravery to move forward,
to paint new chapters of my life,
with hope as my palette,
and faith as my brush.

**"Accept what is, let go of what was, and have faith in what's to come."**

— January 20, 2023

Embracing the now is all about making peace with the present moment—the feels, the scenes, the whole shebang, even if it's miles off our wish list.

This nod lets us chill, clears the fog, and lays down a rock-solid base for sprucing things up. It's about being present, accepting the highs and lows, and finding contentment in the here and now.

Ditching the has-been means cutting loose from yesterday's tales.

It means offering up a bit of grace—to ourselves and others—tucking those lessons under our belts and strutting into tomorrow lighter and brighter. Letting go of the past involves forgiving, learning, and moving forward without the weight of old stories holding us back.

Believing in the yet-to-be is like trusting the ride, even when the maps are blurry.

It's the hunch that ahead lies a bundle of shots and openings despite the route being a squiggle. This forward-looking belief arms us with the guts to leap, welcome new winds, and chase what sets our souls on fire. It's about having faith in the future, knowing that opportunities will come, and being ready to seize them with enthusiasm and courage.

Stitched together, these truths sketch the map for a more awake, resilient life jam-packed with joy. By giving a nod to the now, releasing the has-been, and banking on the yet-to-be, we can ride life's rollercoasters with finesse and boldness. This approach helps us stay grounded, optimistic, and prepared to face whatever comes our way, turning each moment into a chance for growth and joy.

So, let's practice being present.

Let go of what no longer serves us.

And trust in the adventure that lies ahead.

By doing so, we cultivate a life that's not just lived, but fully embraced and enjoyed to the fullest.

Change, relentless, washes over me,
pushing against my resolve, like Icarus soaring on waxen wings,
leaving me suspended in the cycle
of grasping and letting go,
a dance as timeless as existence itself.
This fierce struggle imparts a tough lesson:
release carries a grief like melting wax, yet within that pain
lies a promise—
the chance for peace, for renewal,
in the embers of our fallen feathers.

We fight to hold on,
clinging to the known, to the loved,
even as it shifts and fades,
like the sun's deceptive warmth,
and in the same breath,
we fight to let go,
to unburden, to step forward
into the uncertainty that freedom brings.
This duality,
this war within the heart,
is the human condition—
perpetually torn between
the beauty of a clenched fist,
holding fast to fleeting feathers,
and the grace of an open hand,
surrendering to the winds of fate.

With each ascent,
we feel the heat of ambition,
the intoxicating promise of greatness,
only to be humbled by the inevitable descent,
as our wings dissolve in the harsh light of reality.
We learn that our flight,
though fraught with peril,
is a testament to our enduring spirit,
a symbol of our unyielding quest
to touch the heavens, despite the fall.

**"One of the hardest lessons in life is letting go. Whether it's guilt, anger, love, loss or betrayal. Change is never easy. We fight to hold on and we fight to let go."**

— October 11, 2023

Dropping the baggage is like the ultimate cleanse, a soul detox, if you will.

**Picture this:** You're juggling guilt, anger, lost love, profound loss, and stabs of betrayal like they're going out of style. That's a hot mess. Changing it up is like swapping out your well-loved, comfy tee for something sleek and new—scary but oh-so-necessary.

Nailing down the art of saying *"goodbye"* isn't about pretending the pain didn't hurt or erasing the past. It's about sashaying forward, full of grace, armed with all those tough-gotten nuggets of wisdom, prepped to rock the heck out of life's next scene. It's about strutting into reality, heels high, lessons learned, ready to slay the next chapter. It's realizing that clutching onto yesterday's drama is like jogging on a treadmill—lots of sweat but going nowhere fast.

Being stuck on guilt is like wearing a *"Kick me"* sign. Dumping the guilt means giving yourself a round of applause for being beautifully flawed and rolling out the red carpet for round two, smarter and with more flair. Anger, the lingering aftertaste nobody asked for. It's the spicy sauce that keeps burning long after the meal's done. Kicking it to the curb means acknowledging the burn and then choosing to chill your palate with peace instead. The love conundrum—letting it go is like finally hitting pause on that tearjerker you've been replaying, making you sob into your popcorn. It's reminding yourself that you're the main character who deserves a plot twist filled with happiness. Grappling with loss is tough; there's no glitter there. But it's about knowing our lost stars twinkle brightest when we push forward, their love our unseen accessory. Betrayal, ugh, the ultimate party crasher. Bouncing back means strutting away with your dignity, patching up the trust cracks, and not letting one bad apple sour your view of the orchard of life.

**So, here's the tea:** Letting go is the secret runway to growth. It's about peeling off the old layers with a flourish and stepping into your power. It's about saying *"Thank U, Next"* to the old tunes and cranking up the volume on life's next big hits. As you let go, you're not just making space; you're setting the stage for life's next grand entrance.

Get ready to take a bow, because the spotlight's on you.

In the silence of my own burden, I stood like Atlas,
bearing the weight of worlds upon my shoulders,
each stone, a fragment of the sky,
guilt, worry, and fear
piled high upon a back bent with strain.
Each stone, a story I told myself,
of duties owed, of expectations unmet,
a collection of burdens gathered along the way,
not all mine to bear, yet clung to
as if letting go would unhinge the heavens.

In the quietest hours of the night,
a gentle voice broke through—
not all that weighs upon you is yours to keep,
not every load is meant for your shoulders.
With tentative hands, I began to unpack,
to set down stones not mine to carry,
discovering, beneath layers of assumed obligation,
the lightness of being,
the liberation in understanding
which burdens were truly mine.

This unburdening, a slow unraveling of years,
taught me that strength lies not in the carrying,
but in the courage to release,
to recognize that some paths are meant to be walked
unencumbered,
with a heart free to rise above
the weights we were never meant to bear.

**"Not everything that weighs you down is yours to carry."**
— June 17, 2023

Just because we've got broad shoulders doesn't mean we should be everybody's coat rack.

It's a fact we often overlook.

We're too busy carrying all the weight—the expectations, the stress, and every little worry the world decides to throw our way.

Let's get real.

Being strong isn't about how much weight we can carry without collapsing.

It's about figuring out what deserves a spot in our backpack and what's just taking up space. We need to learn to pick our battles, to distinguish between what lifts us up and what's just dragging us down. We've got to sort what spurs our growth from what's mere dead weight.

Life is not a contest of endurance. It's about walking light, with eyes wide open and hearts full of fire. When we let go of the excess, we're not just moving; we're soaring, aligned with our true direction. It's about realizing our worth isn't hitched to our burdens but to the buoyancy of our spirit.

It's time to make a choice.

To let go of the clutter, the hang-ups, and the doubts that chain us.

It's high time to embrace the sweet relief of walking our journey with only what belongs in our story. Life's way too short and way too sweet to be a storage unit for stuff that was never ours to begin with.

Let's lighten up and live.

Beneath the burden of toxic ties,
I once mistook chains for safety,
believing in the necessity of their hold,
a self-imposed imprisonment
to the familiar ache of unworthy bonds.
The release seemed simple—
detach, depart, deconstruct
the external sources of my pain.
Yet, the heart of the matter lay deeper,
embedded in the core of my own being,
where shadows of myself
gripped tightly to these harmful bonds.

As a tree, I stood rooted in poisoned soil,
branches heavy with the weight of withered leaves,
each limb a tether to the shadows of my past.
To grow, I must shed the bark that binds,
let go of deadwood, expose my inner rings,
and embrace the sunlight
piercing through the canopy.
Growth demanded more
than just the pruning of outward ties;
it required an excavation,
a gentle but firm uprooting
of the parts of me that fed and were fed
by the toxicity I longed to escape.

With each layer shed,
I found not loss, but liberation—
a disentanglement from the past,
a freeing of the self from the trap of old patterns.
This freedom, a passage
through the heart of transformation,
unveiled the true nature of growth:
letting go of my own shadows,
embracing the lightness found
in the act of letting go,
stepping into the expansive, open field
of new possibilities and beginnings.

**"True growth isn't simply about releasing toxic people or things from your life; it's about shedding the parts of your own self that cling to these elements, liberating the grip of past patterns so that you can welcome the transformation that awaits in the freedom of letting go."**

— April 26, 2022

Revamping your life isn't just about kicking those energy vampires to the curb or saying goodbye to habits that keep you in the mud. Nope, it's way deeper. We're diving head-first into the soul pool here, challenging every inch of ourselves to ditch those comfy yet oh-so-rusty chains of negativity. Not exactly a breezy stroll, but hey, it's the secret ingredient for genuine, earth-shaking change.

*Are you bidding adieu to the old baggage? Letting go of the old junk?*

That's where the bravery shines.

It's about turning your back on yesterday and sashaying into tomorrow like you own the place, heart flung wide open. It's about trusting this wave of change, placing your bets on your own badassery to hit the big red *'reset'* button.

*The sweet taste of freedom comes when you unshackle those self-imposed chains.*

This makeover requires you to switch up the lenses through which you're viewing life. It's about spotting the sparkle in the unpredictable and eyeing change as your new bestie. Growth isn't a straight, boring line; it zigzags, twirls, and dances, each move schooling you in its own rhythm. And this isn't a solo act. It's about vibing with a tribe that boosts you up and sprinkles a little extra glitter on your growth path. Surround yourself with the kind of folks who not only brighten your darkest days but also reflect your own brilliance right back at you.

Growth is about seizing your crown back.

It's about standing tall in your worth, strutting your unique flair. It's a love letter to yourself, a head nod of recognition, steering you towards the freedom and fresh starts waiting just beyond the curtain of release.

So, brush off that old dust and welcome the new you with all the fierceness you can muster.

In the silence that followed your leaving,
I saw the closed door
as a denial of worth, of bonds, of shared moments,
the firm shut of a cocoon,
where caterpillars dissolve into nothingness,
a silent judgment casting me into the past's shadow.

In the quiet of absence,
an enigmatic alchemy,
not of abandonment, but of evolution,
the severing of silken threads that bound me
to a state of stasis, now cracking open,
a cutting free from ties that could not hold
the weight of coming days,
dissolving my self-imposed chrysalis,
unveiling not a void, but an expansive horizon—
fertile ground for renewal, for repair, for blossoming.

Freedom became my new pursuit,
a liberation from my own set expectations,
a pilgrimage to my core,
where each step, light as a feather,
declared my value,
my strength,
my capacity to transcend yesterday's confines.

In this liberation,
I found the essence of being set free,
not by the hands of another,
but by my own,
an ascension into the limitless skies
of self-realization,
where the only approval required
was my own.

**"You were not rejected; you were set free. Now it's time to liberate yourself."**

— December 9, 2021

We're wired to brace for the worst, so when the sun shines our way, we're all like:

*"What's the catch?"*

But guess what? You totally deserve all the happiness and wins.

Sailing through calm waters feels odd, doesn't it? Like, *"Am I being punked?"*

This skepticism acts like a bulky life jacket; sure, it might keep us from drowning in disappointment, but it also dampens the joy of basking in the sunshine.

Life's got its ups and downs.

For every face-plant, there's a high-five waiting. For every tear shed, laughter's lurking around the corner.

Trust in this balance. This give-and-take is life's natural flow.

Riding a high wave, don't second-guess it. Just ride it out with a big ol' thank you.

Now, this isn't about tossing caution to the wind or forgetting your blessings. It's about giving yourself a pat on the back for the hurdles you've cleared. It's a nudge to remind you that you've earned every bit of goodness that comes knocking. It's a little voice saying, *"Hey, you worked for this sunshine."*

Next time luck winks at you, don't give it the side-eye.

Remind yourself of your value and the road you've traveled. Hug the good times and let them power your next steps. Because honestly, doubting every win isn't the vibe.

*You're built for amazing things; no disclaimer needed.*

**"Acceptance looks like a passive state, but in reality, it brings something entirely new into this world. That peace, a subtle energy vibration, is consciousness."**

– Eckhart Tolle.

Sure, acceptance might seem like you're just sitting there, zen and all, but secretly, what you're really doing is sneaking peace into the party and spiking the punch with consciousness.

# Inner Pleas

## Trusting Your Gut

"Every pain, addiction, anguish, longing, depression, anger or fear is an orphaned part of us seeking joy, some disowned shadow wanting to return to the light and home of ourselves."

- Jacob Nordby

**I**ntuition and Inner Wisdom: These messages encourage us to listen to our instincts, trust our gut feelings, and have confidence in our inner wisdom.

By honoring this inner guidance, we navigate life's journey with a stronger belief in ourselves and a clearer sense of our direction.

*Welcome your intuition.*

Let these messages inspire you to follow your inner voice.

Understand that your instincts are a compass guiding you through life's complexities.

**As you reflect on these words, remember:** *the key to a fulfilling journey lies in trusting your inner guidance and having faith in your own path.*

Happiness, so often chased,
proves elusive, slipping through fingers
damp with the dew of morning's hope,
yet purpose, when found,
anchors the soul,
a lighthouse guiding through the darkest storms.

It's in this quest, this seeking beyond the veil of sorrow,
I've discovered the weight of my own existence,
not measured in moments of fleeting joy,
but in the substance of living with intention,
a journey marked not by the absence of despair,
but by the presence of meaning.

*Purpose, a light in the darkness,*
*clears the path ahead,*
*a promise that even in the heart of darkness,*
*there lies a reason, a mission,*
*transforming the heavy shroud of depression*
*into a cloak of resolve,*
worn with the dignity of understanding
that in purpose, we find the antidote to aimlessness,
the true opposite to emptiness.

**"The opposite of depression is not happiness, its purpose."**
— June 2, 2022

The real counter to depression isn't bliss, it's purpose-driven living. This shakes up the usual chase for happiness as the end-all, be-all. It's like saying that what really keeps the gloom at bay is having a solid why, a reason that makes everything click.

*So, what's this purpose thing?*

It's the juice that makes life worth the squeeze. It's the fire that gets you jazzed to jump out of bed each day. It's the spark behind your moves, the searchlight for your choices, and your north star directing you to your genuine flow.

Purpose isn't a cookie-cutter deal. It's as unique as your fingerprint. For some, it's all about making waves in their work or lending a hand to others. For others, it's diving into hobbies, passions, or the people they hold dear. It's about what sets your soul on fire, what gets you stoked, and what makes you feel all lit up inside.

But finding your purpose is no stroll in the park. It's a plunge into the depths of *"you."* Tackling the big questions:

- *What matters to me?*

- *What gets me pumped?*

- *What am I ace at?*

- *How can I leave my mark in a meaningful way?*

Once you've got your purpose in your crosshairs, it's go time. It means aligning your do's with your beliefs, making moves that resonate with your mission, and leveraging your gifts to spread the good. It's about being intentional with your time, energy, and toolkit, ensuring your daily hustle sings in tune with your soul.

Living with purpose isn't about hitting a finish line; it's a constant ride. It's about adapting, growing, and shifting gears as you cruise life's highway. It's about sticking to your guns, even when the road gets rocky, and holding tight to your why, even when the world tries to shuffle your deck. Live it, own it, and let it steer you to a life that's not just full but overflowing.

In the first light of dawn's quiet fire,
I become the bonsai master of my soul,
shaping the contours of my future
with careful precision, not by chance but by choice,
like the deliberate snip of shears on tender branches,
guiding growth with an artist's touch.
Regret rustles like a breeze through fragile leaves,
touching those days when I let my mind
wander like wild vines, unchecked and unplanned,
believing life's essence lies
only in the sprawling, the untamed.

Yet, true beauty unveils itself
in the small, deliberate cuts, the quiet cultivation.
Each day, a new season, a fresh dawn,
to prune and shape, to tend and nurture,
crafting my existence twig by twig,
into a bonsai of elegant grace,
not defined by size or spectacle,
but by the touch of care and intention.

Through both storms and sunlight, I've learned
that the masterpiece of life is not in grand gestures,
but in the subtle, deliberate shaping
of each moment, each decision,
curating a living sculpture, purposefully adorned.
In each snip, a touch of intention,
each trim, a note of purpose,
leaves rustling like secrets,
roots deepening with quiet resolve.
Life, like a bonsai, thrives not in the wild,
but in the careful, considered touch,
the master's hand shaping destiny,
crafting a living ode to patience.

**"Live each day with intention, for it's in the small, deliberate choices that we craft the masterpiece of our lives."**
— March 21, 2023

It's time to peel back the layers of intentional living.

In our fast-paced lives, we often overlook the might of picking our own lane, of sculpting our fate with purposeful strides. Forget grand gestures. This isn't about big, flashy moves. Nah, it's about the quiet, daily decisions that shape us.

Kick off with your mornings. *Do you dive headfirst into the chaos, or do you hit pause, inhale, and set an aim for your day?* This choice, though tiny, sets the tone for your whole day. It's your way of saying how you plan to steer your time and your life.

Think about your interactions. Every conversation, every meeting, is a shot to spread warmth, to truly listen, to bond. In our often disconnected world, choosing to engage with sincerity is a radical act of warmth.

Your media habits speak volumes, too. What you soak up, view, and tune into sculpts your thoughts, beliefs, and perspective. Pick with care, for these pieces are the foundation of your mindset.

And let's talk about the power of saying no. In our busy badge-wearing society, choosing quiet, choosing serenity, is revolutionary. It declares your well-being as the top priority above any task list.

Living intentionally is savoring the journey, not racing to the end. It's about valuing each moment, learning from the rough patches, and finding delight in the simple things. It's a pledge to stay in the now, to be mindful of the life you're crafting with every decision.

So, as you wade through your day, ask yourself: *What intention am I setting right now? How am I carving my tale, my legacy, with this choice?*

*It's not about perfection; it's about the pursuit.*

*And within that pursuit lies the essence of a life beautifully lived.*

In the library of my soul,
shelves laden with volumes of untapped insight,
I've wandered, a stranger to my own archives,
doubting the wisdom housed within these walls.

However, I possess a wealth,
not of gold or of worldly accolades,
but of knowledge, of intuition,
a compilation of lessons learned in the silence
between one heartbeat and the next.
This journey inward, a path less traveled,
reveals the strength of my own spirit,
the depth of insight I've overlooked,
too often seeking answers in the world
when the richest counsel lay within.

With each discovery, my confidence builds,
affirming that my inner wisdom
is a reliable guide,
navigating through the darkest waters
to shores uniquely mine.
This knowledge, in both whispers and cries,
reaffirms the immense power I possess,
the profound insight I bear—
a fortune far surpassing my own understanding.

**"Have confidence in your abilities and your own inner wisdom, for you possess a wealth of knowledge and insight that far exceeds your current perception."**

— February 9, 2022

We are conditioned to crave applause and to lean heavily on what others say.

*But what if we turned the tables?*

Imagine trusting your gut, your own stories, and your own distinctive lens.

That inner voice is gold, shaped by every bump and triumph you've encountered. It's a mirror of your resilience, your growth spurt, your grasp of the world. Don't brush it off; it's crammed with insights ready to steer you clear of trouble.

*Have you ever nailed a hard decision, realizing later your gut had your back all along and ever waded through a mess armed with nothing but instinct and your history as guides?*

That's not luck.

It's your inner genius at work.

It's high time we salute our inner sage.

It's time to bank on our smarts and the wisdom we've stockpiled.

Believe it—you're sharper and more in the loop than you realize. Your inner guide is a tribute to your journey, your battles, and your wins. It's proof of your grit and your knack for bouncing back.

So, when the going gets rough, circle back to your internal compass. Listen to that quiet voice that knows the reality of your saga and insights.

Stand tall in your prowess, a byproduct of your life's trek, more potent than you've ever imagined.

In the clamor of days,
where noise silenced my inner voice,
I lost my way,
adrift in the relentless demands of the world,
a leaf caught in a relentless wind.
The silence I once avoided,
filled with constant motion and sound,
revealed itself as a sanctuary
for the soul I had neglected.

In the stillness, I hesitated,
unaccustomed to the absence of chaos,
yet in this quiet,
a discovery—
the voice of my intuition, long silenced,
began to speak.
Gentle at first, then with growing confidence,
it guided me,
through the fog of my doubts,
revealing paths overshadowed by my own noise.

This daily pilgrimage into silence
became sacred,
a nurturing ground for the wisdom within,
where my intuition found its voice,
reminding me of truths
I'd known but forgotten
in the rush of living.

**"Create quiet time for yourself each day. Silence can be a fertile ground for your intuition to surface and be noticed."**

— May 15, 2022

Carving out some hush time isn't just fancy; it's a must.

It's not about escaping reality but about rekindling that spark with your inner self.

Silence lets our intuition step up and wave hello.

This inner sage is always on standby but usually drowned out by our daily commotion. By slotting in some quiet time, we give our intuition room to pop up and step into the limelight. There is no need for big moves. Just a few quiet minutes daily can work wonders.

Scout out a serene spot, power down your phone, and just be. Let the stillness wrap around you. At first, it might feel odd. Your mind might race to fill the void. But stay with it, and the silence will start to feel like home. Your thoughts will settle, and you'll catch those subtle insights that were always there, just under the radar. This is self-care at its finest. It's a chance to reboot and declutter your mind. In the quiet, you can shrug off the world's demands and expectations. Drop the façade. You can be real, no masks. It's a moment to align with your true self, to listen to your heart, to understand your true desires.

The ripple effect of this habit is infinite.

When you make space for your intuition, you'll see your choices get sharper, you'll feel more grounded, and your life will get more precise. You'll spot patterns and chances that used to slip by unnoticed. The way forward will look brighter, and you'll feel more sure-footed as you work through life's twists and turns with confidence.

So, make it a point to sneak some quiet time into your day.

Welcome the silence and listen to the wisdom it brings.

Your intuition is a powerful ally.

When you give it the spotlight it deserves, it'll guide you to a life that's more in sync, more rewarding, and more authentic to the real you.

In the expanse of my inner cosmos,
I've navigated the starship of my soul,
each celestial body a point of introspection,
where shadows and light dance in a cosmic ballet.
This quest, a silent voyage,
reveals no grand galaxies,
only the quiet constellations of self,
stars of who I am, who I was, who I might become.

The ancient remnants of swirling stardust,
collecting in the dark matter of my memories,
reveal truths with each turn,
a cosmic portals showing hidden dimensions.
Here, the moon sings a soft tune,
and the sun's rays tell secrets
to the budding stars of discovery.
In the stillness of my voyage,
I hear the call of forgotten dreams,
feel the cool touch of cosmic dust,
savor the sweet taste of inner peace.
Each step, a silent burst of insight,
each breath, a ripple in the cosmic ocean of my being.

The real work, it turns out,
is not in the discovery of worlds unknown,
but in the mapping of the universe within,
a deep journey into the cosmos of my being.
Where answers lie hidden,
not scattered wide, but nestled,
within the nebulae of my essence.
In knowing my true self, stripped of masks and distortions,
I meet not just my spirit's light,
but also the hero within,
silent yet waiting,
eager to chart, heal, and explore.

**"Going inward. That's the real work. The solutions are not outside of us. Get to know who you really are, because as you search for the hero within, you inevitably become one."**

— August 20, 2022

The real hustle kicks in when we look inward.

Solutions aren't lurking around us but within us.

To truly grasp our essence, we've got to trek into the realm of self-discovery.

Diving into our inner world, we turn into the heroes we've been hunting for.

This inward expedition isn't about chasing external thumbs-ups or trophies. It's about digging up the truth of our being. It's in those hushed moments of self-reflection that we stumble upon the answers we've been seeking.

This path is gutsy, as it's about peeling off societal masks and personal fears.

It's about confronting our deepest shadows and owning our soft spots.

As we sift through our inner layers, we uncover our natural drives, wishes, and principles. We unearth might we never knew we had and resilience that's been our backbone through rough patches. This self-knowing boosts us, offering the clarity to make choices that vibe with our core and the guts to embrace our truth.

The journey inward is endless, a perpetual ride of growth and self-revelation.

Each day unveils fresh insights, and with every discovery, we edge closer to being the heroes of our own tales.

So, let's welcome this voyage, uncover the answers within, and step into the hero shoes we're meant to fill.

In the solitude of doubt,
I've wandered, a ghost in my own life,
haunted by the specters of could-nots and should-nots,
each step forward shackled by the chains of my own making.
A garden of possibilities left untended,
where seeds of dreams lay dormant,
unwatered by belief, unwarmed by the sun of self-assurance.

I've dwelled in the darkness of relentless night,
where each spark of possibility was extinguished
by winds of insecurity,
and every hope blown away
by the chilling breath of fear.
In the mirror, a stranger—
eyes clouded by self-doubt,
a soul crying out for recognition.

In the depths of despair,
a subtle shift began,
as if the tide itself was turning,
breathing life into the stale air.
A thought, fragile but persistent, cutting through disbelief:
*What if I hold the key to my own shackles?*
With this spark, a long-shut door creaked open,
casting a sliver of light over the darkness of doubt.
I learned, step-by-cautious-step,
to plant my feet on the ground of my own worth,
to water the garden of my potential with the belief in myself.

As faith took root, the scenery transformed,
revealing a world rich with possibilities once invisible to my eyes.
*For in the act of believing in oneself,*
*a universe of beliefs is born,*
*each one a star in the vast sky of potential,*
*lighting pathways once cloaked in the shadows of the unthinkable.*

**"The more you begin to believe in yourself, the more things you will find to believe in."**

— November 5, 2022

Confidence in yourself unlocks the door to unknown adventures.

It lights the fuse for exploration, revealing hidden treasures along the way. Nurturing this belief transforms our perspective, making distant possibilities attainable.

Dreams become realities.

This transformation isn't just about ticking off achievements. It's the journey itself—its growth, obstacles, and the wisdom we gather. Trusting ourselves lays the groundwork for a journey rich in meaning and fulfillment.

This conviction doesn't just stay within; it sends ripples outward.

It nudges others toward their own paths of self-discovery. It sparks a chain reaction that can reshape communities. Maybe even the entire world.

As we cultivate our self-trust, let's understand it's not just about finding things to believe in. It's about creating a life that's truly worth believing in. A life where every step, challenge, and victory celebrates self-belief. This isn't just for us but for everyone we inspire along the way.

By believing in ourselves, we become guides for others.

Our confidence shines, showing others that they, too, can start their own adventures.

So, let's keep nurturing this belief.

Let's build lives that celebrate and spread self-belief.

One step at a time.

**"Listen to your inner voice, for it is a deep and powerful source of wisdom, beauty, and truth, ever flowing through you."**

– Anonymous.

Your inner voice isn't just babbling—it's spilling the tea on wisdom, beauty, and truth. So, tune in and listen; it's like having your own personal guru, minus the weird beard.

# Lines in the Sand

## The Art of Saying No

**"Daring to set boundaries is about having the courage to love ourselves even when we risk disappointing others."**

– Brené Brown.

**B**OUNDARIES AND SELF-CARE: THESE messages stress the importance of setting boundaries and prioritizing self-care.

They highlight how saying no to others can be a form of saying yes to ourselves. It's strategic self-preservation.

*Welcome self-preservation.*

Let these messages remind you of the power of boundaries.

Understand that taking care of yourself is not selfish, but essential.

**As you reflect on these words, remember:** *the key to a balanced life lies in knowing when to say "that's enough" and putting yourself first. This is how you show up as your truest self, strong and genuine, ready to tackle the world.*

In the shadow of understanding,
I stood—a heart heavy, thudding like a drum,
saturated with empathy, steeped in the scent of rain,
familiar with the depths of your tempests and murmurs
that hiss through the night.
I've charted the contours of your woes,
like a cartographer mapping sorrow,
traced the origins of your fury,
a historian of your hurts, compassionate to the core.

This deep understanding does not anchor me
to the storm's center, where chaos swirls and roars,
nor does it demand my silence
in the wake of your chaos.
Understanding is not a chain,
nor is empathy an obligation to endure.
I've learned the strength in discernment,
the significance of the word 'no'.
In the space between knowing and loving,
I choose a path of self-preservation, a journey marked
not by endurance of pain, but by the wisdom to walk away.

With each step, the sound of your storm fades,
until all that remains is the rustle of wind through leaves,
and the soft, reassuring beat of my own heart,
steady and free.

**"Just because you understand someone's behavior doesn't mean you have to put up with it."**

— July 13, 2022

Getting the *"why"* behind someone's moves is one thing; enduring it is a whole different ballgame. We might grasp why a buddy's perpetually tardy or why a partner's quick to anger.

But that doesn't mean we're stuck with it.

Understanding doesn't chain you to eternal acceptance.

We've got every right to draw the line. We can say, *"I get your reasons, but it's not cool with me."*

Getting it doesn't mean giving it a thumbs up.

You can fully grasp their side of the story and still choose not to ride along with their antics. It's all about striking that sweet spot between compassion and self-worth.

Next time you catch yourself justifying someone's actions because you *"understand,"* hit the pause button. Remember, you're not under any contract to endure anything that rubs you the wrong way or dims your shine.

You're entitled to top-notch treatment and have every right to set the bar high.

In the walls I built around myself,
where yes was the only exit I saw,
I roamed, lost,
thinking kindness meant giving in,
offering my peace as a quiet sacrifice
to quench others' thirsts.
Each nod, a stone laid,
a soft sigh,
mortar in the walls of my own wishes,
veiling my true self,
its cries for liberty stifled,
silenced by my own compliance.

Then, a lightning flash—
*kindness doesn't demand my surrender,*
*and my peace deserves its own defense.*
Learning to say no,
the battle raged not against others,
but within me,
for the fortress of peace besieged
by my own trepidations—
fear of ruffling feathers, of clashes, of being shunned.

*In setting these boundaries,*
*I didn't find the end of kindness,*
*but its real beginning—*
*a kindness that honors both self and others,*
*recognizing internal peace*
*as the bedrock of external harmony.*

**"You can be a kind person and still say no to what disturbs your inner peace."**

— July 1, 2022

Being nice doesn't mean always saying yes. You can keep it kind and still drop a no.

This little gem is crucial for keeping your zen intact.

In a world that often confuses kindness with never-ending yesses, snagging that self-love is vital.

Dropping a no isn't selfish.

It's your shield.

Saying yes on repeat is a straight path to burnout, and burnout serves nobody, least of all those you're trying to assist.

Mastering the no-nod is all about knowing yourself. It demands guts and clarity on your non-negotiables.

Your time and vibe—priceless.

Turning down what doesn't echo your values is actually a big yes to your priorities.

Are you setting boundaries? Do it with grace and simplicity. Lay them down, smooth and clear. Skip the novel-length excuses—there is no need for lengthy justifications.

A simple *"Not this time"* or *"I'm focused on other things right now"* works wonders.

A no isn't a diss to the person or the request. It's you tipping your cap to your own needs.

It's about protecting your serenity.

So, wield your no when it's called for. It's a sign of self-respect and self-care, making sure you stay on top of your game, bringing your best self forward.

Beneath the canopy of care,
where protective words pattered like rain,
I trusted in the sanctity of this shield provided by others.
But, time revealed deeper truths along my path,
I saw the shadow this canopy cast—
not just shelter, but confinement,
restrictions dressed as concern,
chains forged in the guise of *"for your own good."*

This realization rolled in like a gentle tide,
quietly transforming the landscape—
those who claimed to protect me
often shielded me from my own potential,
from exploring the full scope of my abilities.
With this insight,
I learned to differentiate
between genuine protection and restrictive care,
to recognize the constraints cloaked in concern.

"Make sure that those who claim to protect you aren't the very ones enabling your limitations. Sometimes, under the guise of protection, we find the chains that hold us back."

— March 16, 2022

In many aspects of life, from family dynamics to professional environments, well-intentioned efforts to protect and guide can sometimes unintentionally hold us back.

Take families, for instance.

Parents, all heart, might clip their kid's wings to keep them safe from the boogeyman. Their hearts are in the right place, but this bubble-wrap approach can keep them from grappling with and growing from life's inevitable stumbles and tumbles.

Then there's love.

One half of a duo might grab the reins on all big decisions, waving the *"it's for the best"* flag. This move, though, can dim the other's light, robbing them of steering their own ship.

Work's no different.

A boss micro-managing every move under the guise of *"quality control"* can really kill the crew's mojo to innovate. And don't get me started on that inner voice. The one that's all *"Play it safe."* Sometimes, that's the voice keeping you from your shot to shine—blocking your path to greatness.

Spotting when safeguarding flips into stifling can be challenging. It's a game of self-checks and guts to challenge the status quo. Real growth blooms in the wild beyond our comfort zones.

The breakout begins when you voice your boundaries. Stating *"I need my space"* and drawing your lines can flip the script on relationships. It's also rooted in trust—the belief in yourself and others—to roll with the punches.

The goal here isn't to tear down the safety barriers but to fine-tune them. We're aiming for a sweet spot where caution meets courage, allowing enough room to stumble, dust off, and leap back up. That's the ticket to not just scraping by but truly crushing it.

In a place where my voice once faltered,
trapped in the thunderous demands of others,
my edges became blurred, fog on a mirror,
washed away by waves expectations I couldn't fulfill,
a self compromised by the silence
that couldn't utter one liberating word—no.
Each interaction was a rehearsal
for a role I never auditioned for,
my lines buried in a script
focused on pleasing—bending, twisting,
to fit into the molds others made for me.

The ache of this self-sacrifice,
a relentless beating in my heart,
pushed me to craft a new narrative,
a *'boundary script'*
spun from my own sense of worth.
Pen to paper, I wrote out the words
I'd choked down too often,
words that spoke of strength and serenity,
a vocabulary of boundaries
to protect my sacred self.

*"Thanks, but no,"*
*"I need my space,"*
*"This isn't right for me,"*
phrases simple but transformative,
shields for the times
my boundaries were breached.
Practicing these phrases
in the calm before conflict,
I found strength not just in words,
but in the belief behind them,
a conviction rooted in the value
of my own peace, too precious to forfeit.

> **"Create a 'boundary script.' Prepare responses for when you antic-
> ipate your boundaries might be pushed. Having a script can make
> it easier to stand firm in real-life situations."**
>
> — October 26, 2023

Setting limits isn't just about knowing what you want; it's about declaring it like a boss. It's laying out your needs, clear and strong.

Enter the boundary script.

Picture it as your go-to monologue for moments when people test your patience. Your response, polished and ready to roll, with gumption.

*Why script it out?*

Because when push comes to shove, in the heat of the moment, finding the right words can be like herding cats. Emotions surge, making it easy to falter, to give in. But with your script, you've got your dialogue locked and loaded. You've run through it, you back it, and you're all in.

*So, where do you begin when crafting this safety net?*

Reflect. Identify those instances when your boundaries blur. Maybe it's a friend who's always asking too much, a family member who doesn't know when to stop, or a coworker who thinks your time is up for grabs. Pinpoint the infringement. Next, sculpt your comeback. Keep it brief and to the point, yet polite. Suppose a friend constantly asks for favors, stretching you thin.

**Your script could be something like:** *"I value our friendship, but I need to prioritize my own tasks right now."*

Boom. You've made your stance clear without stirring the pot.

At the heart of it, a boundary script is more than words. It's a declaration of your self-worth. It's your secret weapon for steering through relationships with finesse and vigor. So, take the time to pen yours. It's a way of supporting yourself, and trust me, you're worth the effort.

After I stepped away,
you spun tales in the silence I left behind,
slithering like a serpent in the still of night,
casting shadows with words
that sought to reshape the truth of me,
a desperate attempt to regain control.
Your tales, painting me as the villain,
only revealed your refusal
to face your own reflection without distortion.

In your attempts to manipulate perceptions,
I found not pain, but the solid ground
of my own resolve,
a rock unmoved by tides,
a testament to the strength in choosing
to walk away from your toxic orbit.
*The truth of who I am*
*remains untouched by your fabrications,*
*a light that guides me forward,*
*beyond the reach of your influence,*
*illuminating the path for those still*
*wading through the darkness of manipulation,*
*helping them find their way back to themselves.*

**"When a toxic person loses control over you, they will attempt to manipulate others' perceptions of you."**
— January 12, 2022

When a toxic person starts losing their grip, expect them to play dirty and smear your name.

*What's their endgame?*

Spinning tales and bending truths to paint you black in everyone else's eyes.

It's a slick trick to corner you, stirring self-doubt.

**Here's the truth:** *their desperation to clutch at straws and mess with minds screams their frailty. It's proof you're slipping out of their clutches.*

Regaining your spirit can be challenging.

It means standing firm, even when faced with skeptical side-eyes. Cut through their fiction, and stick to your script.

Keep in mind, their trash talk doesn't determine your worth.

It's carved by your actions and how you vibe with yourself and others. Don't let their lies shake you. Hold your ground, rooted in your truth and honor. That's where your power lies.

Treading through toxic bonds is tough.

But remember, breaking free is the real win.

It's less about silencing them and more about proving to yourself that you've got more backbone than they ever gave you credit for.

In the shadows of constant compromise,
where I stood tall, stretching
to cover
the failings of those around me,
I sensed a reduction,
not in height, but in spirit.
Always bending,
shifting into shapes of understanding and forgiveness,
I turned into a bridge over endless troubled waters.

The epiphany hit, not as a beam of light,
but as an absence,
a darkness cast by the small figures
I had let surround me,
for whom I had diminished
my needs, my desires, my voice.
In the silence that followed this revelation:

*Being the bigger person*
*had shrunk my world,*
*defined by the limits of others' readiness to grow.*
*Choosing to step back*
*from the confines of narrow minds*
*was not abandonment,*
*but an act of self-preservation,*
*an acknowledgment that my breadth*
*needed room to thrive,*
*in a space not maintained by those*
*who refused to grow.*

And so, I chose a path
not lined with concessions for others' faults,
but one leading inward
to where growth
isn't about yielding,
but about one's soul stretching
towards its true infinite potential.

**"If find yourself constantly being the bigger person—maybe it's time for you to stop hanging around such little people."**

— September 21, 2021

Being perpetually the *"bigger person"* could be your cue to give your crew a stern look.

Playing the mature one means you're doling out more patience, insight, and restraint than the crowd you roll with. And if that's your every day, it's worth asking why.

Hanging with a circle that's constantly edging you to your brink is exhausting. It's like you're stuck on repeat, playing the peacemaker and letting things slide.

*But playing the perpetual good guy should be something other than your 9-to-5.*

True friendships should lift you up, not test your limits non-stop.

*Are you caught in ceaseless concessions?*

It's time to zoom out and eye the big prize.

This isn't about cutting ties left and right. It's about affirming your own worth matters.

It's about recognizing you deserve better.

Draw lines.

Set those boundaries.

Seek spaces where your generosity isn't just received but reciprocated.

If you're always the hero in your story, it's time for a squad check. Life's too short for less-than-deserving company. Look for folks who are on your wavelength and watch your world tilt towards the sunny side.

**"I encourage people to remember that 'no' is a complete sentence."**
– Gavin de Becker.

Treating yourself like the royalty you are doesn't require a press conference. Self-care isn't up for debate or a public vote. It's a monarchy, and you're wearing the crown.

# Shadow's Lessons

## Accepting the Darkness

"Until you make the unconscious conscious, it will direct your life
and you will call it fate."

– Carl Jung

**S**HADOW WORK: THESE QUOTATIONS reveal the gritty journey of shadow work. Digging deep, facing our hidden sides, finding inner peace, and growing like never before.

Shadow work pushes us to peek into our subconscious, tackle buried emotions, and bring our shadow self into the light.

This can bring deep healing, self-acceptance, and a more authentic life.

*Welcome this intense journey.*

Let these quotes nudge you to look deep inside. Self-awareness brings real fulfillment.

**Reflect on these words:** *Finding joy often means facing our shadows and uncovering hidden truths.*

In this grown-up shell,
I navigate the seas of life,
each wave a story, a scar, a lesson learned.
With every passing year, the reflection in the mirror
evolves—more lines, more shadows,
markers of battles endured,
laughter shared, tears spilled.
Within the storms and calms,
a truth breaks through the noise—
the soul within, timeless,
untouched by years,
still carries the light of childhood,
a spark of innocence, of wonder,
of a preciousness unmarred by time.

In quiet moments, I remind myself,
*You are precious,*
*not for what you've done, or what you've become,*
*but simply for being.*
In this grown-up journey,
it's easy to forget, to neglect
the child that still dreams within,
that marvels at the diamonds in the sky,
that believes in magic, in love, in hope.
To love oneself, truly,
is to honor that eternal child,
to hold it close,
to speak through the years,
*You are the most precious thing in the world.*
Because, despite the miles traveled,
the scars collected,
you are, I am, we are—forever intertwined.

**"You may have a more grown up body and more life experience but you are every bit as precious as when you were a small child. Love yourself as if you are the most precious thing in the world. Because you are."**

— November 6, 2022

Self-love, rating yourself as first-class, isn't about ego; it's a shout-out to your innate value. It's understanding that you deserve care, respect, and kindness.

Just like when you set boundaries.

Chase your dreams.

And handle yourself with a soft touch.

**But let's be real:** *hugging this self-love tight can be tough.*

Life is unpredictable, and society's got its own playbook. We might face shade, rejection, or stumbles, stirring up self-doubt.

In these moments, it's key to remind ourselves that our worth isn't about the gold stars we collect. Like a little one's natural preciousness, our value is unshakeable, regardless of the highs or lows.

Self-love means extending your kindness and understanding to a beloved child.

It's looking after your body, heart, and mind. It's about positive self-talk, forgiving your mishaps, and high-fiving your wins.

*This self-love isn't self-centered; it's crucial for a balanced and happy life.*

Each soul casts a shadow,
mine trails silently,
shape-shifting with the sun's shift.
Neglected, this shadow deepens,
spreading darkness at consciousness's edges,
its weight a constant presence,
a burden borne without light.
Ignored, it rumbles, a distant thunder,
growing, shifting, sand dunes in the wind.

The more I try to retreat from it,
the deeper its mystery grows,
a riddle wrapped in self-enigma,
unexplored, unacknowledged parts of me.
In shunning it, I've fed its strength,
letting it thicken in depth and darkness,
a testament to what lies unexamined
in my heart's and mind's corners.

This shadow holds a key,
not to suppression, but to understanding,
to accepting my full spectrum,
where light and dark dance
in the delicate balance of being.
Acknowledging this presence,
I learn not just to coexist,
but to integrate, to see the beauty
in the contrasts,
and in this acceptance,
find a path to a deeper, truer self.

**"Each soul bears the weight of a shadow, and the degree to which it is shunned from conscious awareness often determines its depth and obscurity."**

— September 10, 2021

Every heart harbors a shadow, a tucked-away slice of us we often ignore. This shadow cradles our fears, wishes, and hurts.

Neglecting it won't make it vanish; it just gets denser and burrows deeper into our core.

Our shadows are like the dirt in a garden. Just as the soil needs tending to bloom a gorgeous garden, our shadows need a nod to nurture a wholesome soul. When we dodge our shadows, they don't just poof; they thicken in depth and mystery, shaping our thoughts, deeds, and bonds.

To grasp our shadows, we've got to face them. This is no cakewalk. It takes nerves of steel to meet the bits of us we'd rather stash away. *But in this face-off lies liberation.* By recognizing our shadows, we haul them into our awareness. We begin to understand their origins, intent, and sway.

This venture into the shadow isn't about axing it but about blending it in. Our shadows aren't foes; they're mentors. They stash the lessons we need to absorb in order to evolve, heal, and become whole. Welcoming our shadows means welcoming our true selves. We become more authentic, compassionate, and in tune with our truest vibe.

The tango with our shadow is a tango of equilibrium. It's about striking a balance between our inner light and dark. It's about seeing that our shadows aren't all we are, but they're a crucial part of us.

In this tango, we learn to glide smoothly, embracing the flow of our nature and the ever-shifting terrain of our souls. In the end, the heft of our shadow isn't a drag but a boon. It reflects our complexity, our humanity, and our capacity for expansion. Every heart lugs this weight, and how much we accept it shapes the richness of our inner self.

So, let's not disregard our shadows.

Let's greet them warmly, for they clutch the keys to our most profound self-exploration and metamorphosis.

In the depths of night, where shadows loom,
I wandered like Dante in his Inferno,
tracing the winding circles of my own mind,
each turn a spiral into the abyss of denial,
where memories of forgotten hopes linger like ghosts.

A dance with unnamed shadows,
each step a confrontation with inner demons,
a ritual of unresolved torments etched into my core.
These patterns, marks of past ghosts,
speak the language of unspoken fears,
signs of sins and sorrows.
In their repetition, a message,
a call from the infernal depths to understand and heal.

Journeying inward became my pilgrimage,
a challenging passage through my soul's dark corridors,
each step a descent into new torment;
each breath, a chance for redemption.
In my personal inferno, I met shades of my past,
each specter a manifestation of deepest pains.
With every confrontation, a layer of guilt peeled away,
each exhale a whisper of absolution,
every encounter a dialogue with my innermost self,
where every pattern, every shadow,
is a call to understanding, a call to healing, a call to wholeness.

In the ninth circle, where the betrayers dwell,
I found fragments of my broken self,
frozen in the icy grip of fear and regret.
In the place where light meets dark,
I learned to listen to the stories,
to trace the roots of patterns,
discovering not just fragments, but a mosaic—
a self, beautifully complex,
crafted from the shadows once feared.
In the end, like Dante emerging from the inferno,
I found my way back to the light,
a soul no longer fragmented, but whole, radiant, and free.

**"Repetitive patterns are the voices of our unresolved shadows, calling out to us from the depths of our inner worlds, urging us to confront, heal, and integrate our fragmented selves."**
— March 30, 2023

In shadow work, those repeat patterns aren't a mere coincidence; they're our unaddressed shadows screaming from within, urging us to confront, heal, and integrate our fragmented pieces.

Our external experiences mirror our internal state.

Bumping into the same roadblocks time and again is a flare, signaling something inside needs a tune-up. These recurring themes act as a reflection. They reveal aspects of ourselves we've neglected or suppressed. They invite us to plunge into our psyche and address what we've sidestepped.

Engaging in shadow work means illuminating the concealed corners of our soul, accepting and claiming the parts we've labeled as subpar.

This journey of discovery and healing isn't easy—it demands bravery, unvarnished truthfulness. And the willingness to endure the uncomfortable.

But, oh, the payoff is grand.

Paving the way to a more unified and authentic self, liberated from past burdens and ready for new adventures.

Those repeat patterns are a wake-up call.

They are a reminder that we hold the power to shift our lives by reshaping ourselves. Welcoming our shadows lets us step into our full might and craft a life that sings with our deepest truths.

So, when you notice a recurring pattern in your life. View it as an opportunity for growth and metamorphosis.

Lean into the challenge of shadow work and watch as your world changes magnificently.

In the silent depths where shadows dwell,
I've ventured, exploring the dark seas of self,
where light seldom reaches, and hidden truths
rest like pearls in ocean's depths.
This journey, not by distance,
but depth, unveils more than eyes can see,
more than hearts dare feel,
where fear and courage clash.

Unearthing hidden treasures,
each a piece of wisdom, a fragment of awareness,
I've learned the paradox of shadows—
their obscurity brings light,
guiding me to my true essence.
The pain in this quest lies in unveiling,
confronting what was buried,
not to conceal,
but fearing what its revelation might change.

**"When we explore the depths of our shadows, we unearth the hidden treasures of wisdom and self-awareness that lay buried within."**

— November 10, 2022

Daring to confront our shadows isn't just about staring down fears.

It's granting ourselves a shot at uncovering the hidden gems—a personal treasure quest.

But, this expedition is no walk in the park.

It demands courage, resilience, and a solid vow to dive deep into our psyche. The payoff, though, is monumental. Sifting through our shadows, clarity emerges. We get us better, navigating life with newfound surefootedness.

Within our shadows lie not only our fears but our untapped might and the capacity for massive growth. By meeting our darkness, we actually stumble upon our brightness.

Shadow work merges every slice of us.

It's about wholehearted self-acceptance, embracing the good, bad, and ugly. This unity breeds internal harmony, easing that inner conflict.

Venturing into our shadows, we learn to tango with trepidations, cozying up to discomfort.

We realize our darkness isn't just a problem pit stop but also a goldmine of our finest traits. By acknowledging and understanding this, we unlock a truer self-connection and a richer bond with the world around us.

Ultimately, shadow work isn't solely about unearthing hidden truths.

It's about fully embracing our entirety.

It's about recognizing that shadows aren't external; *they're integral.*

With this realization, we don't just unearth insight and self-awareness; we also seize a profound sense of liberty and might.

In the quiet spaces between words unsaid,
anger rumbles, a storm beneath the surface,
not born of malice, but from deep, raw wounds,
a heartache cloaked in the armor of rage.

This anger, a signal flare in the night,
booms like a drum, relentless and fierce,
crackling with the heat of unspoken fire,
illuminating the pain concealed beneath,
a hurt festering in silence,
crying out for acknowledgment, for healing.
Through loud, disruptive shouts,
I've learned anger conveys a truth I've tried to mute,
a voice that rises over the noise of evasion,
insisting on being heard, seen, and healed.

In the storm's center, I find understanding—
this fury is not my foe,
but a guide, pointing to the scars
I've dressed in silence,
wounds that cry out
when I choose not to listen.
Acknowledging this pain, giving voice to the hurt,
I begin the journey of healing,
turning anger into a bridge,
a path leading back to peace,
to a self once divided, now seeking to be whole.

**"Anger is the manifestation of a hurt we've yet to heal; it speaks loudest when we choose not to listen."**
— December 15, 2021

Anger has layers and often gets a bad rap.

But within lies significant truths; *it's the voice of pain yet to be confronted.*

When we shush this voice, it amps up, screaming for recognition.

Anger isn't just a storm to be tamed; it's a spotlight, highlighting the scars begging for a little TLC.

To understand anger, we have to tune into its cries.

It talks of bruises, desires left hanging, and wrongs we've swallowed unwillingly. It nudges us to tackle the gritty stuff simmering underneath. Looking into our anger's roots, we start healing, peeling back our inner mysteries.

Healing is a twisty path.

It asks for patience, a gentle hand with ourselves, and courage to probe our soul's murky corners. Peeling away pain's layers, our life patterns emerge. We see anger not as a foe but as a navigator, steering us toward raw self-insight and a truer existence.

Welcoming anger as a push for evolution turns our sorrows into strength.

It morphs into a force for personal and external change.

Respecting our anger and its messages, we step into a more awake, connected state of being. Listening to its wisdom, we tread towards a calmer, more satisfying life.

In the dim corridors of my being,
where shadows stretch long and deep,
I've learned to move quietly,
heeding the voices of my darker selves,
long ignored, long suppressed.

Acknowledging them, like turning a key in a rusted lock,
doesn't summon hauntings, but healing,
allowing them to join the mosaic of my identity.

In this validation, a peculiar freedom,
a liberation not found in the bright expanse of day,
but in the acceptance of night,
of every hidden fear, every secret pain.

Understanding, not avoidance,
lights the way forward,
where shadows no longer lurk with menace,
but walk beside me,
integral to the dance of existence.

Here, in the welcoming of all that I am,
I find not chains, but wings,
not imprisonment, but the wide-open skies of liberation,
a soul set free by the very act of acceptance.

**"Validating our shadows is the first step to living in our light. For by acknowledging them, we set them free. Freedom comes from understanding, not avoidance. In acceptance, we find true liberation."**

— November 2, 2022

Accepting every piece of who we are, even the ones we're not thrilled about, is the pathway to our full brilliance. It's about hugging those bits of us we often sideline or shove under the rug.

When we nod to our shadows, we unlock their chains, offering us freedom. This liberty sprouts from getting it, not dodging it. By welcoming our shadows, real peace kicks in.

Those shadows are the quirks and hiccups that we're not exactly throwing high-fives about. Yet, they're also the unsung heroes of our personal saga. By giving them a nod and a solid embrace, we unlock a kind of freedom that's legit and pure. Welcoming them means we can stride forward. We can start glowing our truest glow, living as our fullest selves.

It's like saying, *"Hey, I see you, I get you, and you're part of this wild ride."*

So, let's not shush our shadows.

Let's get them, hug them tight.

Let's welcome our shadows into the party.

It's in this radical hug-fest that we find our freedom, our true light. That's where we start living out loud, in full color and without a shred of pretense.

That's how we step into our light.

**"Adopt the pace of nature: her secret is patience."**

– Ralph Waldo Emerson.

Mother Nature's not just out there throwing shade with her trees; she's schooling us on life's playlist—knowing when to hit the slow jams and when it's time to pause and actually enjoy the music instead of rushing to the next track.

# Social Fabric

## Working Through Interactions

> "People will forget what you said, people will forget what you did, but people will never forget how you made them feel."
>
> – Maya Angelou.

**R**ELATIONSHIPS AND INTERACTIONS: REFLECTIONS on connecting with others, understanding relationships, and their role in social dynamics. They prompt us to develop compassion, partake in meaningful dialogues, and acknowledge how people interact and affect one another.

By enhancing our grasp of these interactions, we grow more proficient in creating and maintaining bonds.

*Welcome the art of connection.*

Let these thoughts push you to amp up your kindness game towards others.

Realize that authentic connections are founded on empathy and open communication.

**As you read these words, keep in mind:** *the secret to a richer social life lies in valuing the complex ways we connect with each other and using that knowledge to strengthen our bonds.*

In the silence between words,
I learned to listen—not just to respond,
but to understand the unspoken sorrows
hidden beneath your laughter,
the subtle fear
in your steady voice, a river's constant flow.

With each story you share,
I see more than the story told;
I notice the shadows
in your pauses, your breaths.
No judgment from me,
no unsought advice.
Instead, I offer you my gaze,
a sanctuary for your thoughts,
a haven for your unburdening.

This practice of presence,
of giving my full attention—
it's a gift for us both,
strengthening the soul of our connection.
In truly listening,
we discover empathy, a bridge between hearts,
an understanding deeper than words,
building bonds in the silent spaces
where healing starts.

**"Practice active listening. In your next conversation, focus entirely on the other person's words, body language, and emotions. Respond with empathy and without judgment."**

— August 8, 2023

Active listening isn't just about catching words.

It's about truly engaging with the message being thrown your way. It's tuning into the speaker's words, gestures, and feelings and hitting back with empathy and openness. This knack can flip our conversations and deepen our bonds like magic.

*So, how do we get our active listening game on point?*

Kick-off with shifting your focus.

Rather than plotting your next speech, give your full attention to the other person. Watch their moves, catch the vibes in their voice, and feel the emotions they're pitching.

While you're at it, show you're all in. Nod, lock eyes, and maybe drop a *"Got it"* or *"Go on."* These are small moves, sure, but these gestures pack a punch in making the speaker feel seen and valued.

Active listening isn't just about soaking up words, though. It's about sitting back with empathy. It's saying, *"I get where you're coming from,"* without slapping on judgment. It's crafting a zone where folks feel snug and heard.

Yeah, acing active listening in our distraction-filled days is tough. But, oh boy, does it pay off. It forges stronger connections, cements trust, and spices up our conversations.

*So, next time you're face-to-face, truly listen.*

Dial into their words, catch their silent signals, and what's left hanging in the air. Answer with heart and stash your judgments in your pocket. By giving active listening a chance, we can stitch up richer connections and crack open the door to more profound understanding.

Let's ensure our exchanges really matter, leaving everyone feeling heard and valued.

In the realm of silent exchanges,
where words are unspoken yet speak volumes,
I've discovered the artistry of the unsaid—
the subtle swordplay of a samurai,
each gesture as precise as a katana's arc,
each glance a silent strike in the dance of communication.
My journey through conversation,
once focused only on spoken words,
has evolved to appreciate the depth beneath the surface—
how the tilt of a head, the posture of shoulders,
can convey as much as any spoken word,
much like the disciplined movements of a samurai
reveal honor, intent, and the unspoken code of Bushido.

I regret past conversations,
times when my words said one thing
while my body subtly suggested another,
creating a dissonance felt, though unspoken.
This realization, though quiet, is profoundly clear—
the importance of how we communicate,
not just what we communicate.
It's a call to align my gestures
with the truth of my words,
to master the silent swordplay of interaction,
where every move is deliberate,
every stance a reflection of my true self,
balancing the spoken and the unspoken
in the harmonious dance of human connection.

In this act, I am the samurai,
my gestures the katana,
slicing through misunderstandings with precision,
each movement a testament to my intent,
each silent exchange a reflection of my honor.
For in the silent exchanges,
the subtle art of the samurai
guides me to speak volumes without uttering a word,
to reveal my truest self through the unspoken,
and to find harmony in the dance of communication.

**"Be mindful of your nonverbal communication. Sometimes, how you say something can be just as important as what you say."**
— September 14, 2021

We often race through words, but it's the quiet cues, the silent talk, that really spills the tea. The nonverbal vibes.

This silent dialogue is clutch in clicking with someone or just not, and it's something we tend to miss in the daily hustle.

Take eye-locking; it's potent.

It can shout confidence, spark interest, and shout honesty, or it can hint at unease and fibs. A solid look can cement trust, while dodgy glances might stir suspicion. But here's the catch—*too intense, and it's creepy; too brief, and it screams disinterest.*

How you stand talks big, too.

Upright and open signals you're solid and inviting, while hunching or arm-crossing might broadcast you're on the defense or not quite feeling it.

And your vibe is in your moves, too.

Smooth, chilled motions say you're comfy and assured, while tense, choppy ones might show you're wired or worried.

Then there's the power of your mug. A genuine smile can warm up the whole scene, inviting folks in, whereas a scowl could have them heading for the hills. Those subtle twitches of your expression spill major tea about your mood and mindset.

Don't sleep on the little things, either.

A nod, a curious tilt of the head, or leaning in like you're absorbing every word—every silent shout adds layers to the story you're telling.

So, next time you wade into a conversation, remember your body's throwing its own chat. Hear it out, and let it amplify your words, not muddle them.

Surrounded yet isolated,
the din of the world drowned out the subtle signals
my own body tried to send,
signals I had long ignored,
leaving me adrift in shallow exchanges.

The journey back to myself was silent,
a solitary path where I learned to listen—
not the noise around me,
but the quiet cries of my soul,
the soft footsteps on a moonlit path.

There, in the stillness,
I discovered a truth long veiled:
*the key to authentic connections,*
*to relationships that truly reflect my spirit,*
*has always resided within me,*
*hidden in the language of my own body.*

**"Your nervous system is a powerful tool. It can guide you towards authentic and meaningful relationships. When you listen to its cues, you open yourself up to a world of possibilities and connections."**

— August 11, 2021

Your nervous system isn't just a bundle of wires keeping you from face-planting every time you stand up; it's your built-in radar for legit human connections.

When you tap into its subtle pings and nudges, you're not just dodging awkward encounters; you're on a mission for those authentic, soul-filled connections.

Think of your nervous system as that one friend who's always got your back, telling you, *"Hey, this feels right"* or *"Nope, something's off"* during a chat. It's like being gifted with a sixth sense, where you can sift through the blah to find the *"aha"* in relationships, leading you to those magic moments of authentic connection.

Getting in sync with these signals your body sends is a game-changer.

For instance, that stomach flutter you feel when you're around someone isn't just nerves; it's a signpost towards something awesome. Or that comfort you feel with someone isn't boredom; it's the sweet spot of a meaningful connection. By recognizing and interpreting these signals, you can navigate your relationships with more confidence and authenticity.

Welcoming this inner wisdom opens doors to a universe where relationships aren't just placeholders but life-enhancers. It's stepping into a world where you form bonds that are more than just *"adding a friend"* on social media but adding value to your life.

So, next time you're navigating the wilds of social interactions, remember: *your nervous system is the ultimate wingman in the quest for connections that matter.*

Listen to it.

Trust it.

And let it lead you to the people and places that light up your world.

Here's to tuning in, finding your tribe, and truly living in a world where connections are made and deeply felt.

My heart, filled with affection,
realized too late its unpreparedness.
Not for want of trying,
but from not knowing how to restore love's frescoes.
Love isn't just a touch or glance.
It's the careful restoration of a masterpiece,
where each crack reveals the beauty beneath.
I learned, through loss and tears,
love is like the Sistine Chapel ceiling,
a canvas of countless details, each needing attention and care.

I was an untrained restorer,
holding brushes, unsure how to begin.
Hesitant hands marred the surface,
where gentle strokes should have unveiled the colorful hues of connection.
This lesson, hard and clear,
taught me to ready my soul for when love arrives again—
to be prepared, not just to feel,
but to reveal, preserve, and cherish.
For true love is a commitment—
a choice to restore together,
a bond nurtured with precision and patience.
Every shared moment, a fleck of gold leaf,
carefully applied to highlight the intricate designs of our bond.

Neglecting our connection
is like letting dust settle on frescoes,
dulling the bright colors of our shared history.
Through patience and care,
our love, like the restored ceiling,
will stand as a testament to the beauty found in dedication.
In this chapel of the soul,
our love will shine eternal,
a masterpiece crafted by two artisans,
whose hands, though once uncertain,
have learned the delicate dance
of creating and preserving an enduring, beautiful work of art.

**"A person can experience the depths of love and yet be ill-equipped to nurture and tend to that love. Love, like any other emotion, requires care and attention, and it is essential to be aware of one's own emotional and mental readiness before committing to the responsibilities of caring for another person."**

— January 3, 2023

Love is powerful, but it needs care. Like a garden, it requires attention and nurturing.

You can't give from an empty cup. You can feel love's intensity and passion but still be unprepared to truly care for and sustain it. It's not enough to feel love; you must also be ready to tend to it through its highs and lows.

Check your emotional toolbox.

*Are you ready to handle the responsibilities that come with loving someone?*

This means understanding your own emotional and mental state. It's important to be aware of your capacity to give, to support, and to grow with someone else. Love isn't just about joy and happiness; *it's about weathering storms together and maintaining a strong connection even in tough times.*

Be ready before you commit. Emotional readiness matters.

Before taking on the responsibility of caring for another person, make sure you have the tools and mindset to do so. This involves self-reflection, understanding your own needs and limits, and ensuring that you can give love as well as receive it.

Nurture yourself, then nurture love.

Your ability to care for someone else is directly linked to how well you take care of yourself. Self-care, emotional health, and personal growth are foundational. When you are balanced and whole, you are better equipped to share that stability with someone else.

Remember, love is not just an emotion; it's a commitment and a journey that requires both partners to be fully engaged and prepared. By ensuring you are emotionally and mentally ready, you set the stage for a deeper, more fulfilling relationship.

*So, tend to your own garden first, and you'll be ready to help love grow.*

We collided not as healed beings
but as warriors with battle scars,
drawn together by the magnetic force
of shadows crying and light singing.
Our bond, forged in the crucible of pain,
imperfect yet striving towards a horizon
where every wound becomes a bridge.

Together, we navigate these city streets,
A Dark Knight on a hero's journey,
embracing the shadows and alleyways,
turning pain into a source of strength,
each wound a lesson in resilience,
each scar a symbol to our resolve.

In the darkness of our struggles,
we become our own Gotham,
where fears and doubts loom,
a Joker in the night,
challenging our every step.
Yet, within this chaos,
we ignite the Bat-Signal of hope,
casting a light that pierces through our night,
a symbol of our unyielding spirit.

The beauty of us lies not in perfection
but in our shared commitment
to face the darkness,
side by side,
each step a promise,
each setback a lesson.
In our shared vulnerabilities,
we find strength,
healing not just as individuals,
but together,
undaunted by imperfections,
in the name of love,
we become our own caped crusaders.

"**A conscious relationship isn't about two people who have already solved all their problems coming together. Instead, it's about two imperfect individuals dedicated to dealing with their traumas and unhealthy attachment behaviors as a team. They each take full responsibility for their healing and support and love each other through the process.**"

— April 5, 2023

When it comes **to** conscious coupling, forget about flawlessness.

It's about two souls, each with their own bundle of peculiarities, banding together to heal old scars and break less-than-stellar habits. They're in it together, buoyed by a deep, nurturing love.

*Being transparent and authentic is non-negotiable.*

It's about owning your imperfections and squaring up to them. It calls for the courage to expose your vulnerabilities, trusting your partner to handle them with tenderness.

Communication is the linchpin.

It means hashing things out, even when the going gets rough. It's genuinely hearing your partner, getting where they're coming from, and brainstorming solutions that honor both parties.

Setting healthy limits is key.

It's about knowing where you stand and clearly articulating these boundaries. It ensures both partners can flourish in their individuality without the pressure to conform or control.

Growth is the heartbeat of it all.

It's gently pushing each other towards your peak selves. It's about celebrating the victories, learning from the stumbles, and emerging stronger, both individually and as a pair.

It's about two souls coming together not just to fill voids but to enrich each other's lives.

In the aftermath of pain,
I stood among the shattered shards of self,
a landscape irrevocably scarred by the storm.
Each piece, a fragment of a life once lived
in the comforting arms of routine and expectation.
But healing, an uninvited architect,
sketched new blueprints across the terrain of my being,
demanding reconstruction, not mere restoration.

With each layer of hurt peeled back,
a light, dim at first, flickered, reshaping shadows.
This process, though cloaked in the guise of destruction,
held the promise of renewal,
urging me to reassess my values,
what truly matters in the grand scheme of life.
Priorities, once fixed, now flowed like water,
shaping to the new contours of a landscape
forged by recovery's scorching fire.

I learned to welcome this fluidity,
to see the uncertainty of change as an ally,
not an adversary.
For in the heart of transformation lies freedom—
the liberty to choose, to redefine, to emerge
not merely unscathed but reborn,
with eyes open to the beauty of evolution,
and a soul attuned to the shifting sands
of a life rebuilt on the bedrock of newfound wisdom.

**"Healing will cause your priorities to shift. Remain open to change."**

— August 17, 2023

Healing changes us. It reshuffles our perspective, our reactions, even our favorites.

As we heal, yesterday's big deals might not cut it anymore. Our priorities pivot, urging us to be flexible with change. This healing process is way more than just slapping band-aids on old hurts. It's a total refresh. It's seeing life through a new lens. The stuff we used to chase might lose its shine. Now, it's the simple joys, genuine connections, and soaking in the now that matter.

*Adapting to change is challenging.*

It means bidding farewell to the comfy old ways and wading into the murky waters of the unknown. But it's in this fog of uncertainty that we find our true colors. We uncover what truly matters, what gives us peace, and what pushes us forward.

Change puts us on the spot.

It asks us if we're truly vibing with our chosen path. It's tempting to stick to the same old, but healing dares us to trust and believe in a life that's in sync with our deepest truths.

As our priorities shift, our circles might change, too. We might connect with different people who reflect our new outlook. Some bonds might grow, others might fade. It's a bittersweet part of evolving, of finding our tribe. In this process, cut yourself some slack. Healing's not a straight line. There'll be moments that feel like regressions. But every twist, every turn, inches us closer to who we're meant to be. It's about the climb, not perfection.

Healing opens us to a fresh way of living.

It schools us to cherish the now, to relish the little things, to chase what truly fills us up. As we heal, we learn that change isn't a boogeyman. It's a friend. It's the road to a life that's genuine, a life that's ours.

So, let's stay open and welcome it, knowing it's guiding us to where we need to be.

Healing is not just about bouncing back. It's about stepping up to what's next. And in that step, we find our true selves, our true priorities, and our true path.

**"We can improve our relationships with others by leaps and bounds if we become encouragers instead of critics."**

– Joyce Meyer.

Let's make lifting others the new trend. Forget squats; boosting spirits is where the real gains are. Time to flex those kindness muscles!

# Olive Branches

## Paths to Forgiveness and Peace

**"Forgiveness does not change the past, but it does enlarge the future."**

– Paul Boese.

**F**ORGIVENESS AND RECONCILIATION: REFLECTIONS on the importance of forgiveness, whether it's forgiving ourselves or others.

These thoughts stress the need to let go of resentments and self-criticism, as this act frees the soul from the chains of past hurts.

*Welcome the power of forgiveness.*

Let these reflections guide you in shedding the weight of grudges and self-blame.

Realize that forgiveness is a gift to both the giver and the receiver.

**As you contemplate these words, remember:** *the path to a harmonious and compassionate future is paved with the stones of forgiveness and the willingness to move beyond past wrongs.*

In darkness deep, I once walked,
clutching regrets like stones in my pockets.
Each step, a swirl of a tornado,
paths twisted in dim light,
mirroring my inner chaos.
But time, the gentlest teacher,
words of grace through the storm,
each gust a reminder of Oz,
where past selves fumbled, reaching for a spark of light.

I extend my hand back through the years,
offering forgiveness to that younger self,
who had to walk the Yellow Brick Road with nothing
but a gut full of doubt, and a heart full of hope.
To the Scarecrow seeking wisdom,
who taught me that missteps are questions,
leading to hidden answers in my mind.
To the Tin Man yearning for heart,
revealing that even a rusted heart can beat anew with compassion.
To the Lion searching for courage,
showing us that true bravery is found in the embrace of fear.
Each brick beneath my feet, a marker of a moment,
where I stumbled and rose again,
the road's twists a map of growth and understanding.
We did our best, under skies not yet clear,
with twisters swirling.
Now, in reflection, I lay down the burdens,
and watch the clicking of red shoes carry them away.
Leading me to the Emerald City within,
a place of gentle understanding:
*Every past self deserves my grace, for they were me, doing their best.*

Like Dorothy, I realize now,
there's no place like home,
a home within myself,
where every storm and journey
has led me back to the start,
to find the wisdom, heart, and courage
always within me, under the rainbow's arc.

**"Every past version of you was doing the best you could with what you knew. Show your past self some grace and kindness."**
— July 26, 2022

Each version of you, with its own brand of cool, was just doing its thing as best as it could. They were winging it through life with the tools they had on hand.

Cut your former self some slack instead of throwing shade.

Those old-school moves, whether you now see them as slick or kind of cringe, were crucial steps on your path. They led you here, schooling you in priceless life lessons along the way.

Life's all about leveling up and getting wiser.

Every version of you was just a chapter in this never-ending story. Give a nod to the strides you've made since. Treasure the moments that molded you into the champ you are today.

Show your old self some love, just like you would for a good buddy.

Remember, you were giving it your all with the cards you were dealt. Every challenge tackled, every laugh or tear, it all added depth to your present self.

Marching forward, keep this mindset.

Applaud the bravery in your past plays. Hug the evolution they sparked.

By showering your former self with kindness, you're laying down a path for a future filled with self-love and rock-solid faith in your own journey.

I've stood, a spectator,
as words sharp as daggers were thrown,
whistling through the air, slicing silence,
clinking with each impact, aimed with precision,
revealing a truth not about me, but the hand that wields them.
It's a curious insight, how unkindness clinks and clatters,
reflecting the soul of its bearer,
a window into troubled hearts, restless spirits,
casting shadows not on their targets,
but back upon themselves like dark clouds over a still pond.

In this realization, I find a clever shield,
not to deflect, but to observe,
understanding that their rudeness
is not a measure of my value,
but a confession of their own strife.
*Now, I choose not to absorb,*
*not to carry the burden of others' discontent.*
Instead, I step back,
a knowing smile shaping my response,
reminding myself:
their words define them, not me,
and in this knowledge,
I stand a little taller,
a little more immune to the barbs of the world.

**"It's not your fault. It's not about you. Their behavior has more to do with their own internal battles than it will ever have to do with you."**

— November 11, 2022

Everyone has baggage, their own little monsters.

When someone throws shade or stings us, it's usually their inner demons doing the talking, not a scoreboard of our worth. Realizing this can be like a breath of fresh air. It lets us see things with a softer lens and not take it all to heart.

Now, don't get it twisted.

This doesn't mean we roll out the red carpet for negativity.

Nope.

Far from it.

We can offer a hand, set boundaries, and choose our vibe, all while knowing their drama isn't about us. It's about their own battles, their own scars.

So, next time you're wondering if you're the reason for someone's sour mood, remember it's not your fault.

It's not about you.

Their actions are just reflections of their own story, not a rating of your worth. By accepting this truth, you can glide through relationships with a sense of cool and clarity, knowing you're not the keeper of the chaos others are fighting inside.

In the still early hours,
silence fills the room,
and I sit with the shadows of old arguments
echoing in the heart's vacant corridors.
Words, once thrown sharply, left hidden scars,
and misunderstandings clouded our connection like dense fog.
The lost art of listening now offers a path to healing—
to see through another's eyes,
to hear with another's ears,
softening the remnants of old wounds.
Understanding quietly unfolds,
a hallway leading us deeper into the mansion,
beyond mere words to the fears unspoken.
In this space of empathy,
forgiveness begins its gentle work,
repairing the broken walls with panels of compassion.

Each step toward understanding the other
is a move toward the peace we seek,
turning conflict into connection.
Our hearts, once like an abandoned mansion,
now filled with the warmth of renewed belonging,
where forgiveness clears the dust of neglect,
and understanding opens long-sealed windows.
In these restored rooms,
new understanding finds its place.

**"Seek to understand the other person's perspective. Often, conflicts arise from misunderstandings or differing viewpoints. Truly listening can pave the way for forgiveness and reconciliation."**

— February 7, 2023

Disagreements are as common as morning coffee.

Yet, lending an ear holds a magic key to patching up and moving past beefs. When we genuinely listen, we absorb more than just words; we catch the entire scene—feelings, viewpoints, the works.

**Picture this:** you and a pal are at odds, each clinging to your stance like it's sacred. But hit pause and actually listen. I mean, soak in the entire saga, not just the spoken parts but the silent screams, too.

*Suddenly, the plot thickens.*

You might see the whole drama in a new light. Maybe your buddy's got a point, or there's more to the story than you realized.

Listening isn't just about agreeing with every word.

It's about offering the floor with respect. It's about walking a mile in their kicks, trying to get their angle. Sure, it's tough, especially when you're steamed or hurt. But often, the bridge to mutual ground is built here.

Forgiveness tends to flow from understanding the whole story.

It's easier to drop old grievances when you view the other person as, well, a person juggling their own chaos, not just your rival. It doesn't mean you ignore the pain or brush it off. But you do toss out the resentment eating at you.

Next time you're butting heads, really listen.

It could flip your whole perspective, edging you closer to understanding and, who knows, maybe even peace.

Forgiveness, they say, is a path to peace,
but the road is uneven,
littered with the debris of past hurts
and the sharp stones of regret that crunch underfoot.
It's a journey through a thicket,
where thorns of guilt snag at my skin.

I've learned, slowly,
that to forgive is not to forget,
but to walk forward,
with the lessons etched into my heart.
Patience, my steady companion,
sharing that healing takes time,
a slow drip of rain carving canyons.

So, I tread softly,
knowing that each step
is a gentle act of defiance
against the chains that bind me to the past.
With kindness as my guide,
I explore the complexity of my emotions,
accepting the slow bloom of forgiveness
as it unfolds within,
a delicate flower reaching for the light.

**"Understand that forgiveness is a process. It doesn't happen overnight and often requires you to work through complex emotions. Be patient and kind with yourself as you navigate this journey."**

— June 1, 2023

When we're hurt, our instinct is to curl up in that pain, using it as a kind of armor against more blows. But carrying all that bitterness is like hauling a giant rock—it just drags you down. Dropping that load is what forgiveness is all about.

Kickstarting this trek involves facing our feelings head-on.

Mad.

Hurt.

Betrayed.

It's all totally valid.

These feelings are real, and they're yours. Your feelings are genuine. But clinging to them won't turn back the clock. Moving on is the real play here.

Forgiveness isn't about hitting *"forget"* or saying *"all's well."*

Nope.

It's not handing out get-out-of-jail-free cards. It's about cutting loose from resentment's grip. Think of it as your personal wellness kit, your path to peace and healing.

Strolling down forgiveness lane means going easy on yourself. Trips and stumbles are part of the scenery. Each tiny step forward is a leap towards a lighter heart and a spirit unchained.

Keep in mind that forgiveness is your solo voyage.

It's not about matching anyone else's pace or expectations. It's about charting your own course towards release and renewal. And though the road may be long, the destination—a place of serenity and self-acceptance—is the ultimate prize.

Alone with the past's shadows,
I grappled with memories—each a painful reminder.
Unspoken words, hurried actions,
weighed heavily on my heart,
a burden I feared was mine forever.
My unresolved regrets were like the hidden soldiers
within the Trojan Horse, wreaking havoc from within,
each silent betrayal, a warrior with a spear,
each unspoken word, a shield of sorrow.
They lay in wait, within the fortress of my mind,
striking at moments of weakness,
turning my heart into a battlefield where no respite could be found.

Yet, in solitude,
a truth emerged from the chaos:
*Forgiveness was the realization*
*that dismantling this deceit, piece by piece,*
*was the only way to reclaim my inner Troy,*
*fortifying my heart against further invasions of sorrow.*
With each act of forgiveness, I dismantled the wooden façade,
revealing the hidden soldiers one by one.
Some were stubborn, entrenched in their positions
like battle-hardened warriors within the wooden belly,
clinging to their posts with grim determination.
But I launched a relentless assault,
dragging them from their shadowy hideouts,
into the blinding light of day,
where their power crumbled and disintegrated,
their once formidable presence reduced to ashes.

*Forgiveness doesn't erase the past*
*but frees me from its relentless hold.*
Slowly, like the morning's first light
creeping over the horizon after a long bloody battle,
I realized peace was mine to shape,
not a gift dependent on another's regret.
*Forgiving didn't mean forgetting,*
*nor did it heal all wounds instantly,*
*but it was my declaration of strength, my reclaiming of Troy.*

**"Forgiveness doesn't mean you're completely at peace with what happened, it means your peace isn't in someone else's hands."**
— July 29, 2023

Forgiveness is not about turning foes into besties.

It's about taking back your chill from someone else's drama. It's about realizing that clinging to grudges is like tying yourself down while letting go is your ticket to freedom.

This journey is neither easy nor quick.

It demands the courage to face the hurt head-on, really feel it, and then let it fly. It's about accepting that your past is just that—the past. It doesn't get to dictate your tomorrow.

Forgiving is a boss move, not a sign you're soft.

It's choosing to cut loose from bitterness, deciding to unshackle yourself from sour vibes. Forgiving doesn't mean you're rolling out the welcome mat again. It's about living in the present, not being chained to old news, and unburdening your spirit.

It's key to remember that forgiving doesn't mean you have to trust or keep them close.

It's about lightening your heart's load. It's choosing your peace over the chaos others stirred up.

Forgiveness is your gift to you.

It's a power play in your journey of healing and growing. It's about owning your joy, not letting it be puppeteered by someone else's actions.

So, go ahead, forgive—but on your terms. Drop the weight and reclaim your zen.

In the tangled thicket of relationships,
I've wandered, lost, like a lone wolf's howl
through the night, seeking
the distant moon's understanding,
trying to shape each encounter to fit my expectations,
a fruitless effort that left a trail of pain
from forced connections.

Each attempt to train another,
to mold them into a figure suited for my pack,
only brought the sting of disillusionment,
a heartache from reality clashing with desire,
like thunder against a clear sky.

The lesson, learned in sorrow,
was that people are not clay to be shaped,
but lone wolves, star-bright and wild,
howling at an indifferent moon,
their cries a testament to their untamed souls.

With this painful liberation came the realization:
the need to control, to change, must be let go.
Some stars, like the lone wolf's solitary path,
were never meant to orbit my sky.
*"Let people be who they are,"*
a mantra that bore both the weight of loss
and the gift of freedom,
urging me to adjust my own space,
not that of others.

In this adjustment, a bittersweet peace—
redefining my landscape to include only
those whose light complements my own,
leaving behind the void of trying to hold
what was never meant to stay,
finding solace in the cosmos of my own creation,
much like the lone wolf, finding peace in his solitary howl to the moon,
understanding that not all howls will be answered,
and not all moons will share their light.

**"Let people be who they are and *adjust your space* accordingly."**
— December 1, 2022

Each soul marches to the beat of its own drum, flashing a dazzling array of quirks and qualities.

Attempting to nudge, nuzzle, or nip them to fit into our tailored boxes of preferences is like trying to put a square-peg into a round-hole.

**Spoiler alert:** *that's a no-go from the get-go.*

*How about we change things up?*

Just let folks be. Celebrate their raw, unfiltered selves.

Got a loudmouth in the crew—maybe they're just overflowing with zest. And the quiet ones—they could be the thinkers, the visionaries, silently cooking up revolutions in their noggin. Each unique vibe adds another hue to our world's vast palette.

Consider your circle as your personal sanctuary. You're the curator of this space.

When a flower doesn't mesh with your sanctuary's aura, you don't scramble to change its hue; you scout a new nook for it to flourish. It's about aligning your zone with souls that resonate, not about exiling those who don't fit the bill. This practice isn't about exclusion; it's a process that ensures every plant gets its moment in the sun.

This adjustment spree is grounded in respect—respect for the essence of others and the tranquility of your space. It's a recognition that not everyone is destined to be your cup of tea, and that's totally okay. The real charm unfurls when we stop trying to alter others and instead adjust our stance. In doing so, we plant the seeds for a garden rich with understanding and calm.

Letting folks be themselves and adjusting our circles isn't just about keeping the peace.

It's about celebrating diversity and creating room for connections that truly resonate. Here's to nurturing an ambiance where authenticity thrives and our collective voyage sparkles just a bit brighter.

**"To forgive is to set a prisoner free and discover that the prisoner was you."**

– Lewis B. Smedes.

Forgiving is like tidying up your mental space. It's not about making the place nice for visitors; it's about not living in a dumpster fire of grudges. Clean up, live large!

# Action Avenues

## The Path to Making Things Happen

**"The only way to start is to start."**

– Mark Zuckerberg.

**A** CTION AND INITIATIVE: WORDS of encouragement urging us to take the initiative to enact transformations. Seizing control of our lives acts as a motivating invitation to move away from passivity and assume control over our fate.

They prompt us to recognize that the future is not merely a predetermined event but a result of our efforts.

*Welcome the call to action.*

Let these words inspire you to take the reins of your life.

Understand that your future is shaped by your choices and actions.

**As you ponder these thoughts, remember:** *the key to a fulfilling destiny lies in your hands, and it's your proactive steps that carve the path to a brighter tomorrow.*

Lost, not physically but in my mind's deserted amusement park,
I found solace in the sound of unchosen steps.
The shock, raw like a fresh wound,
opened doors to unknown rooms within me.
Each hesitant step carried the weight of old dreams—
carefully planned, yet dissolving like morning mist.
Where rides of ambition rust under the weather of time,
the ferris wheel of aspirations, now a ghostly silhouette,
its carriages creaking, sharing secrets in the wind.
Haunted house of hopes, groaning with each gust,
windows like hollow eyes, staring into nothingness.

Navigating these forsaken attractions,
I passed the carousel of memories, its horses frozen mid-gallop,
paint peeling, colors fading, a silent tune in the air.
Yet, in the broken funhouse mirrors,
I glimpsed fragments of resilience,
distorted reflections of strength,
waiting to be pieced together.
With each unplanned turn,
I became an accidental acrobat,
performing on tightropes of uncertainty,
crafted from remnants of past desires.

Creak, clang, the sounds of disrepair,
rumbled through the forgotten grounds,
reminding me of the thrill of the unknown.
The park, once eerie,
revealed its secret: the thrill
of wandering without a guide.
In despair's depths,
I discovered a peculiar freedom—
the liberating truth:
Sometimes, the best paths
are those we never planned.

**"Sometimes, the best paths are those we didn't initially plan."**
— December 22, 2021

We plot and plan, yet it's those off-the-map detours that lead us to wild, off-grid side treks where the real treasures lie.

**Picture this:** You're cruising on a path you know, like the back of your hand.

Then, bam!

A curve, a detour, a wrench in your master plan.

It shakes you up, sure, but it sparks a bit of thrill, too. This unforeseen twist might just be your ticket to an epic saga you never saw coming.

There's a certain magic in the unexpected.

It pushes us to adapt and transform. We learn to roll with the punches, to dance in the rain.

These trials mold us, etching layers into our being we never glimpsed before.

Digging in your heels, resisting the shift is an option, but sometimes, just sometimes, going with the flow, diving into that detour, unveils passions unknown, talents buried, lands uncharted. It's in these unscripted chapters that we often stumble upon our authentic selves.

So, next time life yanks the rug out from under you, don't fret.

Hug that detour tight. The highlight reel of your journey might just be the bits you never penciled in.

I am, a player marked by setbacks,
holding my failures like pawns sacrificed,
their cold weight pressing in my palm.
Plans once strategic, now shattered,
a brittle glass underfoot, sharp reminders
of moves not taken, tactics misjudged.
The chessboard lay, life's complexity reflected,
its black and white squares stark under dim light,
each space a choice, a battlefield.
In this arena of paused games, I listened—
not to mourn, but to truly hear
the silent chants of those shadows,
urging not retreat, but a battle
with uncertainty, a move, a counter-move,
in pace with the unpredictable.

Each misstep and fall became not a defeat,
but a pivot, a knight's leap to forge a new offensive,
to shape a journey not with rigidity,
but with the grace of a queen's glide,
flowing, ever shaping the board
not through force, but persistence.
Pawns moved bravely, their small steps
marking the start of greater plans.

The king, my core values, steadfast and sure,
bishops, advisors with diagonal wisdom pure.
Knights leaping, opportunities bright,
rooks standing strong, my stability and support's light.
The queen, symbolizing strength and adaptability,
moved with grace and power, ever vigilant.
With hands unclenched, I learned to hold my plans lightly,
to walk unburdened by inflexibility.
Each move, a calculated dance,
in rhythm with the unpredictable,
a tribute to the power of change,
the courage to adapt,
and the wisdom to accept
the evolution of self.

**"Stay flexible and adapt as you take action. Initiative often requires adjustments and changes to your initial plan. Be open to learning and evolving as you go."**

— November 24, 2022

Flexibility is your ace in this fast-paced game.

When you leap into action, stay limber, ready to tweak your game plan. Rolling with the punches, growing on the fly—that's the ticket. Expect the unexpected, and let those moments guide your journey.

Dreams on the horizon keep your perspective broad. Be ready to shift directions with new insights.

This adaptability is your medal of valor. It shows you're fully committed, scouting for the best path, based on fresh insights.

This agility is a badge of honor.

It proves you're all in, hunting for the smartest route, even if it's a detour from your planned course. Remember, every detour is an adventure waiting to be explored.

Being quick on your feet, open to evolving with change—that's your edge.

Remain pliable.

Welcome the journey's sculpting hands, and watch as you smoothly sail to victory.

In the hush of night, I grasped
that forever was a mirage,
a trick of light and longing.
The ground beneath me crumbled,
like old foundations giving way, and down I tumbled,
a freefall into an abyss where light dared not tread,
the cold air rushing past my ears,
my fingers scraping against rough, unyielding walls.

But even in this descent, a spark—
not of light, but of fierce determination,
igniting the draftsman's lamp,
casting a warm, golden glow amid the cold, desolate ruins.
In the darkest moments, I found parchment,
smooth and crisp against my fingertips,
the scent of fresh ink filling the air,
and I began blueprinting dreams anew,
with compasses marking precise arcs,
and rulers drawing straight, unwavering lines.

Each small victory, a step toward reclaiming myself,
a brick laid carefully in the foundation of my soul.
The scratch of the pencil on crisp parchment,
each stroke a sign of resilience.
The smell of sawdust mingled with ink,
the cool touch of metal tools and blueprints,
in the careful recalibration of hopes,
in the shattering and the rebuilding,
I discovered strength in the minute,
in the power of one stroke, one measurement.

For in the end, it's the smallest lines
that initiate the grand architecture of change,
the rustle of paper plans unrolling,
the faint scent of fresh cement and stone.
Who knew that in the careful crafting,
in the detailed blueprint of progress—*I'd find the path back to myself?*
Each fragment, a reminder of past aspirations,
each line, a step toward a reimagined future.

> **"Break your goals into small, manageable steps. Taking action often becomes more manageable when you can focus on one small task at a time."**
>
> — August 14, 2021

Slicing your goals into digestible chunks is like turning a scary mountain into a bunch of friendly molehills. Each one ready for a leisurely stroll, one step at a time. This game plan shifts the daunting into the doable.

Starting with the big picture might have you gawking at a mountain, its summit lost in clouds. But chop it up, zero in on one tiny task, and voilà, you've got a hill, a chill incline you can conquer with a pep in your step. This method lights up your path and sprinkles mini victories along your way, sparking your momentum.

Picture your goal as a jigsaw puzzle.

Trying to snap it all together in one fell swoop is a fast track to a headache. But sort those pieces, group them by color or shape, and tackle sections bit by bit, and suddenly, it's not a chore; it's a game. Each piece in its proper place is a mini win, revving up your engine and stoking your belief that, yeah, you've got this.

This mindset brings a key player to the table: *control.*

In a world that sometimes feels like a rollercoaster, honing in on small, actionable steps hands you the reins. It's your shout-out that while the endgame might be up in the air, your moves and choices are all you. This sense of command is a turbo boost, egging you on to push ahead.

Sure, adopting this stance doesn't guarantee a breezy journey. Snags will appear, and surprises will challenge you.

But remember, these bumps are part of the gig. They dish out priceless insights and chances to level up. Each tiny stride is a lesson, toughening you up and priming you for whatever's next.

The road ahead might be a long one, but it's paved with opportunities for growth, learning, and, ultimately, success.

The day news came, a shout roaring through my veins,
my colorful world turned gray,
a silent film with me, the unsmiling lead.
Dreams, fragile as glass, shattered in my grasp,
leaving shards of what might have been.

In this absurd theater, audience and actor both,
I watched my life's scenes unfold with detached curiosity.
*"What now?"* the shadows asked at despair's crossroads.
Tiny actions, seemingly insignificant,
accumulated like clouds before a storm.

I began to move, a puppet cutting its strings,
each step a word in the story I told myself.
With each new day, a page turned, a habit formed,
a silent rebellion against the inertia of sorrow.

Like water shaping stone,
my resolve, persistent, relentless, began carving a new path.
In the quiet aftermath, as dust settled on my ruined plans,
a new landscape emerged, shaped by tiny, consistent acts of defiance.

In the end, it wasn't grand gestures but quiet persistence,
water on stone,
reminding me, in its subtle strength, that even in despair,
there lies the potential for greatness.

**"Like drops of water shaping stone, tiny actions repeated consis-
tently, carve the path to greatness."**

— October 5, 2022

Life's epic voyage is not about those blockbuster leaps.

Nah, it's the hush-hush grind of the every day that sculpts our greatness. Like a relentless drip of water carving rock, it's those mini, steady moves that shape our fate.

Every sunrise brings a blank slate, a chance to sprinkle a few more dots onto your life's canvas. Maybe it's rising a tad earlier to soak in the quiet, scribbling in your diary, or choosing an apple instead of a cookie. These seem small, but oh, they stack up. They're the silent builders of tomorrow.

This perspective levels the playing field of greatness.

It's accessible not only to the gifted few but to all who commit to the daily grind of minor tasks. It's knowing that epic feats don't just happen in a leap but from a pile of small steps.

So, let's not underestimate the power of the small.

The force of the everyday.

Each humble choice. Every little hustle.

Plays a pivotal role in the masterpiece of greatness.

Lean into the daily grind, the small wins, and watch as they gradually pave the road to your wildest dreams, just like those relentless drops of water shaping the stone.

I found myself lost, spirit splintered, shards scattered,
A vessel shattered by missteps, fractured with doubt.
There was no melody in my despair,
just a silent scream festering in a once hopeful heart.
But, in this silence,
a spark—timid yet insistent—flickered to life.
Not a blazing inferno, but a hint of warmth,
a gentle ember glowing softly,
reminding me that broken glass is merely potential
for future masterpieces to be forged, tenderly, persistently.

In the glassblower's studio, the furnace roars—
hiss and pop of flames,
the heartbeat of creation.
Heat pulses, a molten glow of orange and red,
reflecting off shards scattered like fallen stars.
The air thick with the scent of molten silica,
a chorus of crackling embers and rhythmic hammering.
For in this moment, I am like shattered glass,
once whole, now broken, scattered in pieces.
But in the hands of a master glassblower,
each fragment is gathered, not discarded,
melted down in the crucible of determination.

With breath and precision, a new form begins to take shape,
the glassblower's breath a gentle caress,
transforming chaos into coherence.
More intricate, more resilient, more profound
than the original could ever hope to be.
The shards of my past—
painful memories and broken dreams—
are not just remnants of what was lost
but raw material for what can be.
Each piece, a story, each flaw, a record
of trials endured, resilience found.

In the heat of the forge,
my spirit is not merely repaired, but transformed,
into something rare and exquisite.

**"The power for creating a better future is contained in the present moment: You create a good future by creating a good present."**
— May 8, 2022

Crafting an awesome now isn't about seismic leaps.

It's hidden in the everyday choices.

Like the pep talk, we give ourselves after a slip, the smile shared with a stranger, or the tuning into our breathing when chaos cranks up.

These moments, these snapshots, are the building blocks for a tomorrow we're pumped for.

Here is the catch, though—the now is a slippery fish, always darting away.

Drowning in yesterday's mess-ups or tomorrow's what-ifs makes the present a blur. The solution is found when we plant our feet firm in the current beat. This means dialing up mindfulness, really soaking in the moment, minus the judgment or zone-outs.

This isn't about giving the cold shoulder to our history or flinging future goals out the window.

It's finding that sweet balance. Learn from the bygones without getting stuck. Eye the horizon without drowning in it. That way, our now isn't just great; it's a springboard for what comes next.

The secret sauce for a dazzling future isn't tucked in a time loop.

It's chilling in the now, in our choices and the steps we take. Let's hug the present tight—it's got the mojo to not just shape our future but also to sprinkle some color on the world's broader picture.

Beneath silent stars, I've roamed,
a collector of quantum scars, each a story untold,
etched in the wells of my eyes, a reservoir of wave functions.
Misunderstood, I journey alone,
to the rhythm of a particle heart,
resonating waves of lost tomorrows, entangled yesterdays.

Life is a quantum mirror, reflecting endless possibilities.
Each scar, a particle collision,
creating ripples in the fabric of existence.
Through the night, I stumble,
over unobserved states and unchased probabilities,
a traveler in a multiverse of potentialities.
Misunderstood, I navigate these dimensions,
where unspoken words are quantum entanglements,
linking lost tomorrows, entangled yesterdays.

In the aftermath of collapsed states,
a soft revelation emerges like a particle wave,
illuminating quantum pathways through the fractures.
Life is not a prewritten equation,
nor chapters determined by fate's constants.
It is an open sky, vast and awaiting,
the quill of my existence in hand.
With each heartbeat, I collapse a wave function,
crystallizing moments of resilience in infinite probabilities,
of tomorrow's unbound manuscript.
In this quantum reality, I am both scribe and hero,
writing in the margins of the infinite.

The scent of fresh ink fills the air,
each breath a crisp, new word,
each moment a captivating sentence,
each day a textured page,
in the poetry of the living.

**"Life is not a series of chapters to be read, but an unwritten manuscript, where every heartbeat pens its own poetic verse."**
— February 4, 2022

Life is not a pre-written novel destined by fate.

It's a blank page begging for our signature touch.

Each moment is a chance to pen our saga, to sprinkle our days with the poetry of our adventures.

The beats we hear are more than just biology—they're the beat of our own drum, the vibe of our creative soul.

In this unwritten book of life, there's no backspace, no erasing. Every action, every choice carves a permanent line in our story.

But that doesn't doom us to a dreary or repetitive narrative.

On the contrary, our life can be a work of art, a story that moves, that digs deep into the essence of what it means to be alive.

The chapters behind us may shape us, but they don't cage us. We can kick off a fresh chapter anytime, shaping our futures with the decisions of today.

Our destiny isn't written in the stars but in our steps, in the love we share, and in the bonds we build.

Let's grab this unwritten book of life. With courage and curiosity, optimism and humility, let's draft our own epic.

Let's fill our pages with laughter and tears, victories and challenges, in a tale that's purely us.

Let's pen a life story that's worth the read, a poem that's worth reciting.

A life that's worth every moment.

**"Be not afraid of going slowly; be afraid only of standing still."**
— Chinese Proverb.

Progress, regardless of its velocity, still counts. It's like a universal law of motion for self-improvement: An object headed towards its goals, however leisurely, is infinitely preferable to one parked on the couch.

_ele_

# MIRROR MAZE

## The Quest for Inner Clarity

**"The unexamined life is not worth living."**

– Socrates.

**R**EFLECTION AND INTROSPECTION: THESE quotes inspire us to think deeply, reflect, and contemplate, urging us to explore beyond the surface and into the vast world within.

Through this journey of self-exploration, we uncover insights about ourselves and the world around us, gaining wisdom and perspective that enrich our lives.

*Welcome the journey of introspection.*

Let these quotes motivate you to plunge into your soul's depths.

Realize that true understanding comes from within.

**As you begin on this voyage, remember:** *the secret to a richer life is nestled in the nuggets of knowledge and understanding hidden within, just waiting to be unearthed and welcomed.*

In a moment of self-reflection,
where shadows shake hands with light,
I set forth,
a lone traveler on an inward path,
guided by the distant sounds of my own voice.
Each step, a layer peeled,
revealed truths long buried
under the debris of pretense and façade,
a landscape both foreign and intimately known.

This journey, silent and fraught,
demanded courage I wasn't sure I possessed,
a face-off not with mythical dragons,
but with the dragon within—
its breath reflecting my fears,
its scales the armor guarding my vulnerabilities.

In the depths of this inner sanctum,
where light filtered through cracks of my own making,
I found not the beast but the beauty,
the strength not in walls built,
but in walls torn down,
the power of facing the wholeness of my being
with eyes wide open.
This quest, the bravest of all,
not for glory or gold,
but for the treasure of understanding,
of peace with the person at the core,
revealed in the quiet confrontation
with the self,
where true strength lies not in the sword,
but in the heart,
and the greatest victory
is the journey home.

"The journey of inner work is the bravest quest one can venture on. It's in the quiet confrontation with our true selves that we find our deepest strength."

— December 21, 2023

Quietly squaring off with who we really are, that's where we hit the goldmine of grit.

This isn't your everyday stroll. It's a deep dive into the heart of who we are, armed with guts, brutal honesty, and an unwavering thirst for authenticity.

*Forget chasing applause or momentary highs.*

This expedition is all about spelunking into our soul's caverns, stripping away layers accumulated from years of playing it safe, dodging judgment, and living up to everyone else's expectations. It's about ditching the masks to meet the genuine, unairbrushed version of ourselves.

*The beauty is in the simplicity of the quest.*

No need for fanfare or earth-shaking upheavals. It's in the hush, those moments of raw dialogue with ourselves, listening to the words of our heart, and honoring the truths that surface.

This soulful tête-à-tête is where we find our treasure—acknowledging our vulnerabilities, owning our peculiarities, and reveling in our one-of-a-kind flair. Realizing our mojo doesn't come from hitting some mythical mark of perfection but from rocking out in our own, unadulterated skin. Navigating these inner parts is complex, filled with obstacles, missteps, and bouts of self-doubt. Yet, it's also where we blossom, heal, and discover ourselves anew. Every step peels away the old, drawing us nearer to our authentic selves.

*So, gear up for this bold voyage.*

Venture into your soul's unexplored territories.

Confront your true self with gentleness and curiosity.

*And in the silence, you'll uncover the powerhouse that's been waiting to shine.*

I sat with myself, a meeting long overdue,
across the table of my own making,
laden with the debris of denial, the trappings of self-deceit.
I've played the roles—the hero, the victim,
in stories spun from half-truths and full lies.
This self-examination, a mirror long avoided,
shows not just the face I wish to see,
but all aspects I've dodged—
the blemishes, the scars, the unvarnished truths.
In my journey for betterment,
I've adorned myself with achievements,
a façade shimmering with success,
but fragile under the faintest touch of scrutiny.

Honesty, a blade sharp and precise,
slices through the stories I've crafted,
revealing a core raw and radiant with potential.
*For true growth, I've learned,*
*is not in the tally of triumphs,*
*but in the acknowledgment of flaws,*
*the acceptance of imperfections,*
*and the relentless pursuit of self-awareness.*
In this honest reflection,
I discover not frailty, but strength—
the strength of being true to every part of me,
both light and dark.
And in this acceptance, a path forward,
paved not with the gold of false glories,
but with the substance of real self-reflection,
a journey not just toward improvement,
but toward wholeness, toward truth.

**"Be honest with yourself. True introspection requires looking at both your strengths and weaknesses, your successes and areas where you fall short."**

— December 11, 2022

At times, we might balk at facing our whole truth, spooked by what it might spill.

However, it's when we dare to dig deeper that we hit on the core insights sparking actual change.

Acknowledging our flaws isn't waving the white flag; *it's pinpointing where we can level up and refine.*

See your achievements as more than just trophies; they're proof of your grit, ability to shine, and your skill in riding life's rollercoaster. And don't just brush off your missteps. They're not just hiccups; they're rich with lessons, chances to adjust, toughen up, and progress.

Genuine introspection strikes a balance.

It's valuing your strengths without arrogance and accepting your faults without self-reproach. It's understanding that self-betterment is a perpetual path, one that requires perseverance, courage, and, above all else, stark honesty with yourself.

Remember, every piece of you, from your zeniths to your pitfalls, crafts the unique individual you are.

Welcome your whole self.

*For it's in acknowledging your imperfections you unlock your genuine power and potential.*

In a kiln all too familiar,
I stood as a silhouette against dim light,
surrounded by choices unmade, of clay shaped by my own defiance.
Soft clay, unformed yet full of promise,
waited for purpose, for the shaping hands of intention.
I built barriers, not vessels,
from fears and doubts—a fortress masking as self-preservation.
In the skilled hands of the potter, my form took shape,
each movement molding my essence, each touch a decision made.

I've spun on the potter's wheel,
mistaking each turn for progress, not hesitation, a cycle of avoidance,
where each rotation led further from truth.
Upon the wheel, I spun endlessly,
each turn a cycle of self-discovery, each rotation a step closer to truth.
In my crafted vase, I saw not reality,
but a self distorted by denial.
After the fire of self-reckoning,
a murmur, faint yet firm, cut through the glaze
I had layered around my essence.
It spoke of awareness, not blame—the ghost of self-sabotage,
masked as routine and comfort, was my own reflection,
in choices unchallenged, in paths feared to walk.

With each revelation, I stepped forward
into the light of understanding,
where shadows instruct, and reflections guide.
It is in facing these vessels—
those we avoid, and those we confront—
that we forge a path of evolution,
marked not by past fractures, but by the potential within.
In the kiln of life's trials,
I became pottery, fragile yet resilient,
each crack a testament to survival.
Fears and doubts once sealed within
now filled with gold,
transforming fractures into lines of strength.
I am a vessel mended through kintsugi,
my flaws illuminated, my essence whole.

**"Every path to self-improvement is marked by the signs we often ignore; self-sabotage is not a mysterious enemy, but an ignored reflection in life's mirror."**

— September 9, 2021

This trek to betterment zigzags, littered with signals we're quick to ignore. Those moments of hesitation, procrastination patterns, and self-limiting moves are not roadblocks set by the universe, but by us—showcasing our inner trembles and unfinished business.

Catching these hints calls for unfiltered truthfulness. It means looking inward, really grilling our hesitations.

*Fear of failing or shining? Or feeling like we don't measure up?*

It's all a reflection of our deeper selves, the parts we often tiptoe around.

Self-sabotage is a guard mechanism that backfires, keeping us comfy but stunted. Authentic growth prods us into unknown waters to square off with our apprehensions face-to-face.

Stopping this self-defeat starts with spotting its shadows in our actions. It's unpacking these clues and drilling down to their roots. It involves plunging into our psyche and wrestling with tough realities.

Getting the hang of our self-sabotage storylines allows us to rewrite them. It's challenging our self-limiting tales and seeding thoughts that uplift. This pivot—from viewing ourselves as extras to the lead in our saga—is crucial.

The path to polishing ourselves isn't marked by flamboyant gestures or overnight revolutions but by steady, intentional steps across our self-made hurdles. It's a saga of unveiling, of celebrating our idiosyncrasies and applauding our leaps.

In short, self-sabotage isn't some cloaked adversary but a mirror reflecting our internal battles.

By confronting this mirror and working through our fears, we unlock our highest capacity and step into authentic growth.

In an old attic, hidden away,
a dusty trunk creaks in the corner,
its hinges groaning like old bones.
Inside, hundreds of sealed letters rest,
each an unspoken word
or a suppressed emotion, the paper brittle,
the ink faded, each envelope marked with the date of its silence.

Nights stretch into endless expanse,
painted with regret and haunting what-ifs.
The quiet before sleep a battlefield,
wars waged with the ghosts of my own making.
As I open each letter, moths
flutter out, aged and frail words
transforming into vivid memories and long-buried truths.

In the dark, I face my deepest fears,
mirroring my insecurities,
their shadows elongated by silence.
Through restless nights, I learn
the power of pause, the grace of reflection—
a simple act, yet profoundly healing.

I make time, not as an afterthought but as ritual,
to unravel the day's complexities,
illuminating lingering doubts.
Reading and acknowledging these letters
becomes a cathartic journey, each one a relic
from moments when fear stilled my voice.

This journey through the attic of my past,
with paths still unexplored,
reveals strength in stillness,
resilience in self-examination,
and the liberation found in the art of reflection.

**"Set aside regular time for reflection. This could be a daily journaling session, a weekly meditation, or simply a few moments each night to contemplate your day."**

— June 13, 2022

Life zips by, and we often skip the simple step of just pausing to ponder.

*Reflection packs a punch.*

It's carving out regular time, be it daily scribbles, weekly zen sessions, or nightly recaps. This isn't just sugar-coated talk; it's a plunge into the essence of who we are.

Journaling is like chatting with your soul, a window into your inner self. Forget about fancy words; it's about raw honesty.

Meditation is your clarity in the calm, an opportunity to sync with your inner voice, to find serenity within.

And those evening reflections help you spot your wins and lessons. It's not about stewing over the past but marching forward wiser.

Incorporating these practices isn't just another item on your list.

It's about making room for growth and change. It's a commitment to live with intent.

So, let's anchor our lives in reflection.

In those silent moments, we unearth the strength to tackle life's challenges, coming out tougher and savvier.

In the silence of a room too still,
I've replayed scenes of stubborn pasts,
a private cinema of regrets, each moment frozen.
The past, a looped reel, brings no comfort,
only the sting of what was,
reflecting what might have been.
I've held moments, a curator of pain,
clinging to shards as if they were precious.
But these pieces did not strengthen; they split further,
a self-mosaic, pieced with grief's glue.

Then, a voice of wisdom, soft yet clear,
pierced my reverie.
It spoke of transformation,
turning past pain into paths of healing.
I learned to sift through ashes, not to keep them,
but to find buried lessons,
to replay not to hold on,
but to understand, heal, and grow.

In this new practice, the past is not a jail
but a classroom, where I am both learner and teacher,
mastering the art of holding memories lightly,
letting them inform but not confine.
In healing replay, we find the power
to open our hands,
to let go of the weight,
and embrace what may come.

**"If you find yourself replaying the events of the past, make sure it is for healing, and not holding."**

— January 25, 2023

Stuck in a rerun of yesterdays, is like being stuck on replay, playing the same old episodes over and over.

The critical question here is whether we're flipping through these memories to heal or just to keep the pain alive. Healing is all about sifting through our backstory, not for a pity party but to get it. It's like tidying up a closet. You haul everything out, give it a once-over, and then pick what stays and what goes.

Healing is about holding onto the lessons and ditching the hurt. It's viewing the tough times not just as agony but as steps that brought you here.

But if we're just hoarding our yesterdays, it's like we're too scared to release our grip. This just traps us in yesteryear, blocking our now. It's like trying to drive while glued to the rearview mirror. You're asking for a crash.

Letting go is tough, no doubt.

It's not about erasing what went down. It's more like saying, *"Yep, that happened, but it's not going to hold me back."* It's realizing you're the one holding the pen to your story, and you can kick off a fresh chapter whenever.

And you don't have to go solo.

Sharing your saga, whether with friends, family, or a therapist, can cast new light on old shadows.

Sometimes, just talking it out makes everything a bit clearer and a bit easier to handle.

Choosing to heal is just that—a choice. It's deciding to take your bumps and bruises and spin them into lessons. So, when you glance back, make sure it's with the intent to heal, not just to linger.

Let your history guide you, not chain you, leading you toward sunnier days.

I lost the sound of my own voice,
a forgotten username buried under static login attempts,
drowned under the weight of expectations—others' and mine,
a silent scream, like a password in a void,
wondering, always wondering,
why peace seemed always in view, yet always out of reach.
I've felt like a stranger in my own account,
a visitor in the archives of my thoughts,
where folders stayed locked and betrayal floated like ghostly emails,
haunting the inbox of my soul.
I sought answers in security questions from without,
a user with no remembered credentials.

In a moment of despair during another fruitless search,
I paused—found a reset link, a still moment—
and in that space, a faint hint emerged: my own username,
long ignored, quickly forgotten.
It was weak, yet held immense power,
a key to access myself once more.
Listening—really hearing—became my recovery,
a cure not found in external noise,
but in the stillness within.
Each heartbeat sent a verification code; each breath wrote a new password;
a conversation with parts of me
I'd avoided, neglected, needed to heal.

In this meeting of self with self,
I found healing in attention,
the remedy of being present,
a kind of listening that heals slowly,
like finally finding the forgotten password
that unlocks the shadows of the night's doubts.
For it's in hearing my own username,
in holding my deepest truths,
that healing begins—a meandering path,
leading back to an account I thought lost,
rediscovered in the sacred act of truly listening
to the one username that always mattered—my own.

**"When you finally take the time to truly listen to yourself, you will begin to be able to heal yourself."**

— October 19, 2023

Our days are swamped with noise from every corner, making it a chore to eavesdrop on our own inner guidance. But it's in those scarce quiet moments that the treasure of self-discovery lies.

Listening in is like casting a spotlight into the dark corners of our psyche.

It's facing the hurts, hugging our wants, and tending to our long-ignored needs.

This act, recognizing our true selves, is the bedrock of healing. By listening, we unearth what our soul is starving for—be it forgiveness, self-affection, or a drastic change of scenery.

*The adventure begins and ends with us.*

Through listening, we uncover what our spirit's needs for healing—be it pardon, self-love, or a total life flip.

So, hit the brakes. Throw it in park.

Seek out silence.

Explore your thoughts, your feelings, your body's signals.

*What's the message? What's needed for your healing?*

The clues are in there; just waiting for you to tune in.

**"Knowing yourself is the beginning of all wisdom."**

– Aristotle.

Turns out, the more you play detective with your own personality, the better you get at selecting choices that don't make you facepalm later.

# DAWN'S PROMISE

## Illuminating the Path of Possibility

**"Hope is being able to see that there is light despite all of the darkness."**

– Desmond Tutu.

**H**OPE AND **O**PTIMISM: THESE messages stir the spirit, provoke thought, and ignite hope during tough times. Signaling that difficult moments are temporary and darkness eventually yields to light.

They cultivate a sense of possibility and belief in the future, encouraging us to hold onto the vision of a tomorrow filled with joy and fulfillment.

*Welcome the power of hope.*

Let these messages guide you through the challenges, reminding you that brighter days are ahead.

Realize that hope is the seed from which the future blossoms.

**As you reflect on these words, remember:** *the blueprint for a sunnier future is watering the hope within you today, and trusting in the promise of a better future.*

In the silent aftermath of unseen battles,
I've walked, bearing wounds only I can see,
my victories muted, my progress unnoticed.
A solitary warrior, my struggles masked by a brave façade,
I've overlooked the peaks I've scaled,
the sheer resilience it took to climb from the abyss of despair.
In the dust-choked arena of my inner conflicts,
each breath a struggle, each heartbeat a defiant roar,
my scars, though invisible, sear like fire upon my soul.
With the weight of unseen armor, I trudged through the sands,
each grain a memory of pain, each step a mark of survival.

The scent of iron and sweat clings to my skin,
remnants of past skirmishes linger in the silence,
the taste of victory, bittersweet on my tongue,
each drop of blood shed, a sacrifice unseen, uncelebrated.
The roar of an invisible crowd fills my ears,
a haunting reminder of battles fought and won in solitude.
My sword, a symbol of my inner power,
gleams with the light of hard-fought victories,
cutting through the darkness of despair,
wielded with the precision of honed skill.
In the grand amphitheater of my own making,
I am the gladiator who rises, undefeated,
each fight a step towards reclaiming my destiny,
each roar, a silent acknowledgment of my worth.

The wheat fields call to me with their golden waves,
a balm to my weary eyes, a longing for the calm of home,
a sanctuary within the chaos of strife,
where my heart finds solace and strength.
Now, in this pause, I turn inward,
not with critique, but with kindness,
acknowledging the resilience I've built,
the courage forged in the fires of my trials.
I celebrate not just survival, but the capacity to thrive,
recognizing in myself a conqueror, a soul enriched by its journey,
a warrior of the heart, stronger than I ever believed.

**"Unfortunately, most people don't give themselves enough credit for overcoming things and getting better. You have made it this far. Begin to recognize and celebrate your strength. You are capable of so much."**

— February 5, 2023

It's common—most of us don't give ourselves enough credit for the mountains we've climbed and the storms we've weathered.

We tend to focus on what's ahead or what we haven't achieved, forgetting to acknowledge how far we've come. But here's a little reminder for you: you've made it this far. That's not just luck; it's solid proof of your grit, your perseverance, and your knack for battling through.

Pause a second.

Give a shout-out to your wins, no matter how small they may seem.

Celebrate the challenges you've faced and the growth you've experienced. You're a powerhouse of potential, and it's high time you owned up to it.

Think about the hurdles you've jumped, the fears you've conquered, and the progress you've made. Each step, each triumph, is a piece of your unique story. It's what makes you who you are—tenacious, resilient, and unstoppable.

As you move forward, carry this knowledge with you. Let it fuel your confidence and drive. Remember, you have a track record of weathering the rough and coming out stronger on the other side.

Here's to you and your incredible journey.

Keep believing in your strength, keep pushing forward, and keep shining. You are capable of amazing things, and I can't wait to see all that you will achieve.

*Take this to heart, and never sideline the fact that you're downright astounding.*

In the darkness of the night, I sit,
counting the milestones not reached,
the aspirations that hang, like stars, too high to grasp.
Each day a reminder of the gap
between where I am and where I wish to be.
The chasm feels wide, insurmountable,
a landscape littered with the debris of failed attempts
and half-starts that fizzled into nothingness.

In this moment of introspection,
a truth gently comes to the surface—
*I am not where I once was.*
*This place, though not the peak of my dreams,*
*is no longer the valley of my fears.*
Each step taken, no matter how small,
has moved me from the shadows of my past.
The failures, the setbacks,
they are but stepping-stones,
marks of a journey that is uniquely mine.

So, as I sit amidst the unfinished,
the yet-to-be,
I hold onto this fragile seed of realization:
*Progress, no matter how slight,*
*is a victory in its own right.*
*I may not be where I want to be,*
*but I am not where I used to be.*
*And that, indeed, must count for something.*

**"You may not be quite where you want to be yet. But you're also not where you used to be. That has to count for something."**
— May 13, 2023

Growth should be seen as the ride, not the final stop.

It's in the strides we make, every barrier we leap over, and every nugget of wisdom we pocket along the way. It's realizing that even if we haven't hit our mark yet, we've definitely outpaced our former selves.

And that's no small feat.

You've hit snags, goofed up, and maybe felt glued in place at times.

But look at you now, a bit further along, even if just a smidge.

You've picked up lessons from the trenches—*that's growth in its purest form.*

It's easy to fixate on where we want to end up and simmer in frustration at our current situation. But remember, every inch forward is a win. Each day, every interaction, every challenge is a golden chance to soak in knowledge and up your game.

Pause and give yourself some kudos for the distance covered.

Tip your hat to the gains, no matter their size.

Toast to the triumphs, draw wisdom from the slip-ups and keep on trucking. Because even if you're not exactly where you aim to be, you're definitely en route.

And that, my friend, is priceless.

They speak of growth as a journey, glossing over the pains—
the discomfort of shedding old ways,
the awkwardness of stepping into shoes that don't yet fit,
their leather stiff and unyielding, creaking with resistance.
Every day, new challenges surface,
tests of bravery I didn't choose.
I'm in unknown waters, the waves crash, splash,
charting who I'm meant to become,
a path not yet drawn, a blank map awaiting ink.
The unknown terrifies, each step a leap into void,
the only sure thing is the shifting ground, loose and unstable.

Then, in this chaos, a soft voice cries out,
reminding me this discomfort, this fear,
are the prices paid for venturing into new territories.
I've never been here,
never been this raw, unrefined, this authentic.
This daunting unknown is also a canvas ripe with potential,
a space where new versions of me can take shape,
free from past confines.

So here I stand, on the edge of expansion,
enduring the discomfort,
offering myself patience,
and the gentle grace of gradual growth.
It's okay to be scared,
okay to feel adrift in this new expanse of self.
Here I am, persevering,
standing strong,
a tribute to the power of vulnerability.
Let me remember to breathe through this,
to allow myself the grace to falter,
to learn, and to eventually,
boldly walk into the unknown.

**"Growth is uncomfortable. You have never been here before. You have never been this version of yourself. Unknown territory is scary and causes most to retreat. Yet here you are, still pushing on. Please give yourself a little grace, and breathe through it."**

— June 17, 2023

You know, growth is a tricky thing.

It pushes us out of our comfort zones into territories we've never explored before.

It's like we're constantly evolving, becoming new versions of ourselves that we've never been. And while that's exciting, it can also be pretty daunting. The unknown is always a bit scary, and it's natural to feel like retreating to safer, more familiar ground.

Yet here you are—despite all the uncertainty and the urge to pull back, you're still here. You're still pushing forward, still striving to grow.

That's a pretty big deal.

It takes courage to keep going when everything inside you is screaming for the comfort of the known.

So, as you continue on this journey, I encourage you to give yourself a little grace. Shower yourself with kindness during those moments of doubt and fear.

And remember to breathe through it all.

Each breath is a reminder that you're alive, you're capable, and you're moving forward, one step at a time.

Growth might be uncomfortable, but it's also incredibly rewarding. It's in these stretches of discomfort we uncover just how resilient and adaptable we can be.

So, lean into the discomfort, knowing that it's a sign of your continued evolution.

Cheers to you and your journey of growth. May you find strength in the unknown and beauty in the process of becoming.

I often wrestle with restless shadows—
thoughts that twist through the corridors of my mind,
fears that chant doubts, insecurities that cling like cobwebs,
cold and sticky against the corners of my consciousness.

Each morning's battle is unseen,
fought within the intricate confines of my own soul.
The world sees smiles, not struggles,
hears laughter, not my silent screams.
Unknown are the wars waged within,
of the effort it takes to simply be,
to stand within the chaos,
resisting the urge to fall apart,
a crumbling statue beneath the weight of the world.

But with each dawn, I choose to rise,
to face the day with all its potential for pain and promise,
as the sun's first light pierces the heavy shroud of night.
This act, though small, is a defiance,
a statement of strength in the face of relentless doubts.
For each morning I emerge from the night,
each step taken in spite of the weight I carry,
is a victory, modest yet mighty,
a single blossom breaking through a crack in the cement.

Battles within are indeed the fiercest—
they demand courage of a different kind,
the bravery to confront one's own darkness,
to fight a foe that knows all too well
the secrets and sins we hide from the world,
shadows lurking in the depths of a still, dark lake.

**"Battles within are the fiercest, yet each day we rise, we claim victory, one heartbeat at a time."**

— February 16, 2023

Inner battles can be the most grueling, yet with every sunrise, we clock in victories, moment by moment.

Each new day is a confirmation of our resilience, a shout-out to our strength. It's not just about the hurdles we face but how we stand up to them. It's about finding the courage to keep going, even when every part of you is shouting for an exit.

Life tosses us into countless conflicts, big and small.

Yet, what truly defines us isn't the size of these battles but our approach to them.

It's in the subtle wins, the silent fist-pumps that often slip under the radar. It's in the pulses that fuel our perseverance when giving up looks all too easy.

*We are warriors, each one of us.*

We navigate unseen battlegrounds, conquering covert fears. With every minor win, we're shaped a little more. We discover our capacities stretch far beyond our imaginations.

So, let's face our challenges head-on. Let's meet them with valor and resolve. Let's celebrate every victory, each heartbeat that drives us.

Because, at the end of the day, it's these struggles that carve us, revealing who we truly are.

And it's by rising, time and again, that our victories are genuinely savored.

In the marrow of my bones, a chill seeps in—
a relentless, unwelcome cold takes hold.
This ache, ever-present, mocks the lost warmth
that once filled my heart.
I've danced with shadows,
held hands with my laughter,
now a stranger.
Joy, once vibrant within me, now lies dormant,
entombed beneath my skin, inaccessible.
My own reflection, a ghost of my past self,
taunts me with a twisted smile,
haunting me with memories of sun-soaked days
now overshadowed by endless night.

However, in this storm of despair, a spark—not of hope,
but of sheer defiance.
A rebellion against the tyranny of pain.
I am not the sum of my sorrows,
nor am I bound by what has been.
One day, I'll step out from under this cloud,
not just to seek the light, but to hold it,
to live fully in every moment,
not just enduring, but celebrating each breath.
And on that day, I will not just survive;
I will thrive.

**"For those who are struggling right now, I know it seems hard to believe in this moment of time, but one day you'll be able to live each day and enjoy them, not just wait for them to be over."**
— November 30, 2022

If you're feeling stuck in a rough patch right now, I totally get it.

It might seem like you're just trudging through each day, waiting for the sun to set so you can hit the reset button and start over. But hold on tight because I've got something to tell you.

One day, and I promise this day will come, you'll wake up and feel a different kind of energy.

You'll start living each day, not just surviving it. You'll find joy in the small moments—the first taste of your morning brew, a burst of laughter, the sunlight kissing your cheeks. You'll start to appreciate the beauty in the every day, and you won't just be waiting for the days to be over.

I know it's hard to believe when you're in the thick of it. But trust me, change is coming, even if it's just a tiny shift each day. You're forging determination, stockpiling strength, and pocketing life lessons that'll guide your way forward.

For now, tackle it day-by-day.

Show yourself some love—*toast to the small wins.*

And remember, you're not alone in this. You've got a whole community cheering you on, believing in you, eager to watch you flourish.

Hang in there. Stay the course.

The best chapters are yet to come.

Cheers to the brighter days on the horizon and to you, greeting each one with open arms and a heart full of joy.

In the dim light of dusk, I find myself
tracing the contours of lost days,
years slipping through fingers
too weary to hold fleeting moments of joy.
I've borne the weight of despair,
a constant companion on this journey,
telling tales of chances missed
and paths too daunting to tread.

Loneliness, a cloak I've worn too well,
covering the warmth I once held inside.
Regrets pile up like unread letters,
secrets of a heart too afraid to reveal its desires.
In the mirror, I've seen the reflection of a soul
battered by storms, yet still standing,
a testament to resilience I never claimed as my own.

But as night surrenders to dawn,
a voice pierces the silence of resignation:
*"It's not too late."*
This life, with all its scars and unshed tears,
still holds the promise of unexplored beauty.
A canvas awaiting the brushstroke of hope,
for hands willing to shape chaos into art.

So to the weary spirit reading these lines,
know this:
*The road ahead, though marked by shadows of the past,*
*is yours to illuminate.*
*Please, don't give up on the masterpiece*
*that is your life.*
*For in the heart of every ending lies the seed of a new beginning,*
*a chance to create a beautiful life for yourself.*
*It's never too late for that.*

**"It's not too late to make a beautiful life for yourself. Please don't give up on that."**
— August 21, 2021

Some moments in life feel like crashing into a brick wall. Hope appears as ancient history, and that famed happiness you always hear about seems more like a mean joke. Giving up starts to look pretty cozy, luring you toward the edge.

**But you should know:** *it's always the right time to craft a stellar existence.*

Life's not a dead-end road plastered with a *"too late"* billboard. It's a collage of evolving perspectives. Every sunrise is a chance to sketch your route, to mold the bits into a masterpiece reflecting your true desires and ambitions.

*"Too late"* is a mind-forged myth that shackles you to what-ifs and might-have-beens.

It's that sneaky voice hissing failure, saying your ship's sailed.

*But really, who's the timekeeper? Who says when the window for joy or chasing what you want snaps shut?*

Only you can do that.

This journey isn't a race against time; it's an expedition of finding and flourishing. Every step, regardless of its scale, inches you closer to your dream scenario. The trick is to never throw in the towel, to not let yesterday's stumbles outline tomorrow's can-dos.

*Are you teetering on the brink of calling it quits?*

Pause, inhale, and preach to yourself that it's never too late.

*Your saga's ongoing, and guess what?*

You're holding the pen.

You've got the juice to flip the script, to turn over from the used-to-bes and embrace the blank page brimming with maybes and what-ifs.

Ultimately, life's charm isn't in its predictability but in its infinite paths. Crafting a beautiful life for yourself—there's no expiry date on that. Hang tight to that truth.

**"Once you choose hope, anything's possible."**

– Christopher Reeve.

Opting for hope is like choosing the VIP pass in the concert of life. Suddenly, you're not just in the crowd; you're backstage, discovering doors you didn't even know existed.

# TRUE NORTH

## The Journey to Authenticity

**"To be yourself in a world that is constantly trying to make you something else is the greatest accomplishment."**
—Ralph Waldo Emerson.

**A**UTHENTICITY AND TRUTH: THOUGHTS that encourage us to embrace our authenticity and lead a life of integrity prompt us to shed the masks we wear for others and fully accept ourselves.

By doing so, we create a life grounded in honesty and authenticity, where our words and actions reflect our core values and beliefs.

*Welcome your true self.*

Let these ideas inspire you to live authentically, without pretense.

Realize that authenticity is the foundation of a meaningful life.

**As you ponder these thoughts, remember:** *the key to a fulfilling existence lies in being true to yourself, aligning your actions with your beliefs, and courageously presenting your genuine self to the world.*

In the everyday routine of life,
I've walked, weighed down by days that blend into each other,
a spirit tired not from effort,
but from the missing spark, the absent blaze.
I've felt a weariness no sleep can ease,
drained not by work, but by voids within,
a shell moving without meaning, without aim.
Drowned in the noise of expectations,
I've lost my own desires,
the soft calls of passion silenced
by demands, by the ceaseless, gray rhythm of the everyday.
In this desert of disengagement,
I've yearned not for rest, but for connection,
for the refreshing touch of purpose,
for an oasis of inspiration.

Slowly, a realization sharpens—
exhaustion can be a guide, not just to stop,
but to begin anew, to venture within
to where my genuine interests lie hidden,
buried under *"shoulds"* and *"musts."*
Digging deep into my spirit's soil,
I unearth the seeds of dormant dreams,
desires awaiting the light, the air.
Here, in this inner realm,
I find the cure for my fatigue—
immersing in activities filled with personal meaning,
pursuits that ignite the spark of enthusiasm,
that breathe life into my being.
This tiredness then transforms not into defeat,
but into a call to action, a cue to align
with my true passions,
to rekindle the fires of purpose and passion.

*For in pursuing what truly moves us,*
*we discover not just energy but a cosmic force,*
*propelling us, lighting our way*
*with the brilliance of a life inspired.*

**"The feeling of exhaustion is not always a result of over-exertion; rather, it can be a symptom of a lack of engagement in the things that truly inspire and ignite our passions."**

— July 11, 2022

Feeling drained may not be from a constant state of overdrive. It could be that you're just running in circles, missing the sparks that truly make you come alive.

It's like being a hamster on a wheel, going through the motions but not really getting anywhere. The real juice of life comes from chasing what sets your soul ablaze, not just ticking boxes and crossing off to-dos.

Think about it.

*This exhaustion isn't from an overload but from a shortage of what sets your soul on fire.*

It's like a gentle prod, a soft voice from within saying, *"Psst, it's time to mix things up and chase those dreams that get us up in the morning buzzing with energy."*

If you're feeling toastier than a marshmallow at a bonfire, perhaps it's time to strike a different match—a match dipped in passion, thrill, and just the right amount of boldness. Find that thing that makes you lose track of time that makes you feel like you're not just existing but living vividly.

*Don't just stay busy; stay passionate.*

Use that weariness as a guide back to your passions, to pursuits that breathe life into your days.

It's about swapping *"I'm tired"* for *"I'm wired."*

Because, when it comes down to it, recharging might not just be about taking a break—it's about rekindling your passions and fully immersing in the marvels around you.

In the clamor of many voices, my own was lost—a faint cry,
drowned out by overwhelming expectations,
a chameleon's call stifled by a jungle of societal norms.
I walked paths not my own,
each step heavy with the weight
of dreams that belonged to others,
in a landscape foreign and unforgiving.

I shifted to my environment, changing hues,
a camouflage artist, blending to survive,
my colors shifting to match the expectations of onlookers,
a mirror reflecting desires not my own,
a chameleon's skin patterned with the hopes and aspirations of others,
emptied of essence, devoid of self.
The joy I sought always seemed just beyond reach,
a fleeting mirage over someone else's landscape.

But in the quiet of solitude,
my true colors began to emerge—
softly at first, like the tentative rays of dawn
chasing away the shadows of night.
My voice spoke in a language only I understood,
a chameleon's secret dialect of dreams and untold desires,
of passions smoldered under the weight of conformity.
Listening, truly listening, I discovered the map of my own making,
not charted in the ink of external validation,
but in the glow of internal recognition.

For no one knows the contours of my soul as I do,
no one can navigate the depths of my desires,
decipher the cryptic language of my joy.
This realization illuminated my return to myself,
to the passions that pulse with my life,
to the joys that reflect my deepest truths.
In welcoming what truly ignites my spirit
and fills my life with authentic joy,
I discovered that I alone hold the key
to unlocking the full richness of my happiness.

**"No one knows you like you do. Your inner voice speaks uniquely to you. Only you can recognize the things that ignite your passion and bring true joy to your life."**

— May 17, 2023

When it comes to understanding who you are, no one holds the key quite like you do.

Your inner voice, that faint cry or roaring shout inside your head, speaks a language crafted just for you.

It's a dialect of dreams, fears, hopes, and desires that only you can fully comprehend.

In this loud world, it's easy to lose sight of that voice, to let the opinions and expectations of others drown it out. But remember, you're the sole keeper of the flame that lights up your passion and brings true joy to your life. These aren't just fleeting pleasures or momentary delights. They're the deep, soul-stirring experiences that make your heart sing and give your life meaning.

So, take the time to listen to that inner voice.

It might take some quiet reflection or a bold leap into the unknown, but it's worth it. Because when you start living in alignment with your true self, life becomes richer, more colorful, and infinitely more fulfilling.

Own the uniqueness of your journey.

Celebrate the eccentricities and traits that make you, well, you.

And never lose sight of the fact that your story is unparalleled, brilliant, and utterly vital.

*Cheers to you, to your voice, and to the extraordinary adventure of being fiercely, unabashedly you.*

I wandered, aimless,
searching for signs in the cosmos,
for maps in the moonlight,
under a canopy of twinkling stars,
their cold, silver light acting as a guide in the darkness,
overlooking the north star I carried within.

Then, in a tranquil, fleeting moment,
I paused, listened—
and in the silence, my heart spoke,
its rhythm a deep, resonant drum,
pulsing warmth through my veins, undeniable.
With each beat, a direction,
a path shaped not by logic, but by the truth of desire,
of dreams long silenced now stirring to life.
Clarity dawned like the first light of morning,
the sky blushing with the hues of the heavens',
brightening the path ahead,
a purpose sparked not from the mind's cold calculations,
but from the fiery passion of a heart unleashed,
its warmth radiating like a sunburst,
a north star,
guiding my steps through the darkness of night.

"When we listen to our hearts, the path becomes clearer. And with clarity, comes purpose. A purpose that ignites passion and drive. Follow your heart, it knows the rhythm of your dreams."

— April 9, 2023

Tuning into our hearts clears the fog, unveiling a trail ablaze with purpose. This purpose isn't just a goal; it's the fire that ignites our passion and drives us onward. It's not about marching down a path laid out by others; it's about moving to the beat of our own aspirations.

This voyage transcends simple choice-making; it's about sculpting a life that reflects our deepest truths. It's aligning our actions with our core values, making every step a mirror of our inner selves.

The clarity from this alignment is life-changing.

It cuts through the chaos, unveiling a vision so clear, so compelling, we're drawn to follow it. With this clarity comes purpose—a purpose that bubbles up from within, infusing our lives with meaning that transcends the mundane. It's a purpose that lights up our eyes and sets our souls ablaze. It's what pulls us out of bed each morning, eager to seize the day, leave our mark, and live our truth. Heeding our hearts is more than a lofty notion; it's a potent act of self-belief. It's acknowledging that we hold the blueprint to our joy, that we possess the keys to our happiness. It's a vow to cherish our desires and nurture their growth. When we embrace this, when we let our hearts lead, we tap into a reservoir of passion and drive. We find ourselves propelled by purpose, with an energy that's both exhilarating and infectious.

So, pause and listen to your heart.

Truly listen.

It's not about being swept off your feet by momentary passions or whims. It's about tuning into the deep, steady rhythm that guides you.

Let it lead. Let it illuminate your path.

Your heart knows the cadence of your dreams. Follow it, and witness as your path unfolds, rich and full of vitality.

Caught in the blur of days and nights,
I became a stranger to myself,
masks worn so long
I no longer recognized my own face,
living life by others' scripts,
detached from the dreams I once held dear.

Lost, I paused, confronted by the reflection
of a life lived out of tune with my inner values.
This dissonance, a wake-up call,
proposed a question through the chambers of my soul:
*Are my actions a true reflection of my beliefs?*

In moments of quiet introspection,
I sought to bridge the gap between doing and being,
to realign my daily rituals with the heartbeat of my own values.
Each self-check, a step towards authenticity,
a practice in tuning my life to resonate with the core of my being.

This journey back to myself,
a path of deliberate living,
taught me the power of living with intention,
crafting a life that mirrors my deepest truths.
For only in the congruence of actions and values
does the soul find peace,
and life, its most authentic expression.

"**Regularly check in with your feelings and thoughts. Are your actions aligned with your personal values and beliefs? Adjust accordingly to ensure you're living authentically.**"

— September 4, 2021

Sailing through life's twirls and tumbles, its ups and downs can sometimes blur out who we really are. Yet, hitting the sweet spot of living—authenticity—means making sure our actions and core selves are in harmony.

*Beginning with self-reflection is non-negotiable.*

Regular check-ins with our feelings and thoughts clarify our priorities.

It's about asking the big questions: *"What values guide me?" "What sets my soul on fire?" "What battles am I willing to fight?"*

But getting those aha moments is just the beginning. The real challenge lies in translating those insights into real-world moves. *Knowing what you stand for is one thing; living it out, especially when the going gets tough, is where the true test lies.*

Our convictions and values aren't set in stone.

Growing means being open to change, ready to mold our actions to reflect our evolving selves. Authenticity means continually adjusting our sails, so our deeds reflect our deep-seated values.

*Being authentic doesn't mean being perfect.*

It's about striving for consistency between our inner world and our outward actions. When we walk our talk, we find peace within and inspire others to find and follow their own truth.

In the depths of my unraveling,
I've stood, raw and exposed,
a soul stripped of its armors,
each layer peeled back, not gently, but with the harshness of truth.
I've felt the sting of vulnerability,
a chill wind on the bare skin of my psyche,
leaving me shivering, shelter-seeking,
in the barren landscape of my fears.
This exposure, a crucible,
where the flames of judgment, both from within and without,
threaten to consume what little strength I claim as my own.
I've mistaken this openness for fragility,
this honesty for a fault line threatening to fracture
the precarious balance of my existence.

It was in this space of apparent weakness,
a revelation, quiet as the first light after the longest night:
Vulnerability, this openness, is not the enemy.
It is the path to authenticity, a bridge built from the very essence of self,
connecting me to the world with cords stronger than any armor could provide.
Through this lens, each crack, each perceived flaw,
transforms from a chasm of weakness
to a doorway of possibility,
an invitation to explore the depths of my true nature,
to welcome the beauty of my raw, unvarnished self.

*Acknowledging my vulnerabilities,*
*I discover strength not in invincibility,*
*but in the bravery to be seen, to be known—*
*as I am,*
*not a fortress closed off,*
*but a garden open to the heavens,*
*where authenticity flourishes,*
*nurtured by the very vulnerabilities I once dreaded.*

**"Your vulnerabilities are not weaknesses; they're the doorways to authenticity."**

— March 14, 2022

Your soft spots aren't flaws; *they're the secret passages to your realness.*

This sounds topsy-turvy in a world that often mistakes being open for being breakable. But, it's when we bare our souls, showcasing our fears and blemishes, that we truly connect with others.

Welcoming your vulnerable side means nodding to your imperfections, and that's totally fine. It's about owning up to who you are and your feelings.

It's about daring to declare, *"Here I am, flaws and all,"* without flinching at the thought of side-eyes or pushbacks that might follow.

Think back to a time when someone dropped their armor around you, revealing they're not always on top of their game.

*Didn't that bond you tighter?*

That's vulnerability's magic. It demolishes walls and cultivates a bond of common humanity.

But hey, being open doesn't mean laying your soul bare to every random Joe. It's about staying true to you and letting that genuineness color your exchanges. It's understanding those tender spots aren't shortcomings but signs of your unique path.

It's time to rethink vulnerability.

Let's hail it as a forte, a route to richer ties and a truer existence.

Here's to owning our vulnerabilities, for they're the portals to our most unfiltered selves.

In the story of my life,
pain has been a persistent presence,
a deep and enduring shadow.
However, in this darkness,
an unexpected alchemy occurs—
my deepest sorrows become the guide
toward my true purpose,
turning wounds into wisdom,
suffering into strength.

*From the depths of my pain,*
*emerges a clearer sense of self,*
*a purpose born not in spite of the ache,*
*but because of it.*
*In this paradox, I find comfort,*
*and a quiet recognition that often,*
*my toughest challenges direct me*
*to my most significant destinies.*

**"Sometimes it's your pain, that leads you to your greatest purpose."**
— February 24, 2023

The path to our purpose isn't always a stroll through the park. It's the stumbles, the face-plants, and the tears that nudge us closer to our true calling. Pain, raw and uncut, schools us. It strips away the façade, spotlighting what genuinely deserves our hours and what's mere window dressing. In our lowest lows, we stumble upon a kind of clarity that's elusive in our high-flying moments. This clarity lights the way, nudging us toward our purpose. Now, this isn't about putting pain on a pedestal, claiming you've got to hurt to find meaning. It's more about recognizing that pain, a sure bet in life, can be a catalyst for deep self-discovery and growth. It's about spotting the silver lining in storm clouds, the learnings in letdowns.

*Everyone's story is different.*

For some, pain shows up as loss—a gut-wrenching goodbye that, despite its sting, carves out a deep sense gratitude for life and love. For others, it's the burn of failure which teaches toughness and the courage to persist. Think about all the people who've spun their struggles into their life's work. Artists channel their deepest aches into their art, entrepreneurs cook up solutions to problems they've faced, and advocates are often spurred by injustices that have hit close to home.

This transformation doesn't happen overnight.

It calls for some serious soul-searching, the courage to confront what's eating us, and the bravery to step into the unknown. It's about asking the tough questions: *What's the takeaway here? How can this rough patch help me grow? How do I leverage my story to uplift others?*

By turning our pain into purpose, we don't just patch ourselves up; we throw a lifeline to others riding out their own storms. Our biggest battles become our loudest anthems, showing us and those around us that it's possible to rise from the ashes and be reborn with a clearer sense of purpose.

So, if you're wading through a rough patch, remember it might just be the groundwork for something epic. Your pain, as impossible as it might seem now, could be the key to unlocking your greatest purpose. Lean into it, learn from it, and let it steer you toward the person you're destined to be.

**"Authenticity is not something we have or don't have. It's a practice - a conscious choice of how we want to live."**

– Brené Brown.

Authenticity isn't a one-and-done deal; it's like choosing your outfit every day. Some days you're all glam, and others, it's pajamas at noon. Either way, you're rocking 'you'.

*Change, life's only constant,*
*bears not just fear but the promise of new beginnings—*
*a cycle of birth, death, rebirth,*
*coloring the world with endless hope.*

# Final Thoughts

## Dawn is Coming

THE MOST CHALLENGING TIMES often come before the breakthrough, and a new beginning is on the horizon. Have faith in your path and believe in your strength.

Cling to hope no matter how dim its light may appear.

Don't quit.

Keep recovering. Keep evolving.

**You serve as an inspiration to all of us.**

I appreciate you being a part of my journey.

Here's to the chapters, the untold stories, and the unexplored paths ahead. Here's to healing, progress and change. Here's to you—to your voyage towards self-discovery and recovery.

*Cheers to Healing Thoughts. The community we're creating together.*

One step towards healing at a time.

**Remember this:** You're not on your own. We are a community united in healing.

**Onwards, to a brighter tomorrow.**

**"The privilege of a lifetime is to become who you truly are."**
– Carl Jung.

And the challenge of a lifetime is trying to figure out who that is while at the same time, pretending to have it all together.

# ACKNOWLEDGEMENTS

"We have a calling. We are the people who know what we need. What we need surrounds us. What we need is each other. And when we act together, we will find Our Way."

- John McKnight

## Reflecting on the journey of this book fills me with gratitude.

**T**HIS IS A HEARTFELT shout-out to my daily text crew! Your constant engagement has been instrumental in shaping this work.

"Ryan, you truly have no idea how your words have saved me during my divorce. Thank you."

## This chapter is all about you.

Your insights, willingness to connect, and words of encouragement have been my guiding lights. Real talk, you are the heroes of this story.

"Ryan... you are an amazing incredible person too. Thank you for helping me get thru one of the most difficult times of my life."

"I know everyone heals differently, and has different ways of dealing with things, but I am always here if you need someone to vent to or even just need someone to listen. You're not alone."

"You deserve a break too! Big heart hug!"

"That's right—we need to be gentle with ourselves, show ourselves compassion. You need to take care of you. Please remember how loved you are."

"We don't quit. And it is perfectly alright to have an off day. Thank you for the blessings!"

"I'm so sorry you're struggling right now. I hope things get better for you soon. I can definitely relate though. You are so important and very much appreciated!"

"No don't thank me. I thank you from the bottom of my heart for starting and sharing your journey and allowing me to come with you. You have given me more courage since I've ever had before. You help me battle my demons on a daily basis. i am honored I got to meet you and spend some time with you."

"I haven't messaged you in awhile... but I wanted you to know your daily messages remind me why I should always keep moving forward and never give up. I don't tell you often enough but your messages have made the difference on several days... thank you. It means so much to me."

Every message, every shared experience, and every word of support has fueled this book's creation. Your bravery in sharing reflections and supporting one another has been key.

"May I say how much I appreciate that you have stayed the course here! You have been the catalyst for so much healing in our world and this little community that you have built. You are so deeply appreciated!"

You've not only influenced the making of this book; you've also been my source of resilience and motivation.

Every day... know u may not understand... but most the time they come at the perfect timed."

I want to express my gratitude to all of you who have been a part of this community since the start. You trusted in the impact of coming through words and finding healing as a collective.

"Shine bright my friend, you shine a light on everyone you text and those in your daily life. Thank you for being you!"

Your dedication and active participation have truly been the foundation that has supported this community.

"So I know we are here to spread positivity and I may not participate some times but I thought about you twice today and it reminded me to smile and not sweat the small stuff. So with that said it make me wonder if in all the positive things you spread if you get checked in on and how you are?"

To all the folks in our group, your unique viewpoints and genuine eagerness to learn have brought a breath of air to our discussions. You've demonstrated that the path to self-discovery and healing is a changing journey, and your excitement serves as a constant inspiration for the limitless possibilities that reside in every one of us.

"I really needed this right now. Thank you. You just saved my life I'm serious."

Cheers to you my friend! I may not be where I am today if it wasn't for you. I've had some of biggest life struggles this year and don't know how i would have coped without you!"

A big thank you to all those who have courageously shared their challenges and victories, allowing us to learn from and alongside you. Your stories have yet to deepen our understanding. They have also served as a source of hope and unity, showing us that we are not alone in our paths.

"Yep. Opened a whole ass business with that hope. I'm a hairdresser and the amount of clients I've helped get started in healing is just the best thing."

"My mood and spirit needed this so badly today, and I took your advice! I've been enjoying the benefits of it this afternoon. Thank you!"

"Some days... it's like you see into my soul and know exactly what to say. Thank you Ryan from the bottom of my heart."

To those who have taken the time to respond to my prompts, your answers have been truly inspiring.

You've taken each question, like ***"What is one thing you wish people better understood about you?"*** and turned them into something personal and deeply meaningful.

"I wish they understood that although I seem strong, I need support too. I may have lived a life that would make me what one would call resilient but I still need a person to lean on too. Sometimes its lonely being the strong friend."

"That I'm not mad at them when it seems like I am, I'm either mad at me, or them not understanding me makes me feel dumb. It's always a reflection of how I look—never the other person (usually hah)"

"The fact that you can want to die but still want to live."

"That my enthusiasm is real and not weird."

"I wish people didn't believe everything they heard from other people, wish they would take time to understand and learn more about me. Nobody knows who I truly am, not even my parents. They haven't tried to sit down and talk to me or even ask me about what's going on in my life. They just see me leave, hear stuff and assume everything. I just hope I will find the people right for me and the people who truly care for who I am."

"That I process things differently than most and I might seem harsh at times but deep down I have the biggest heart and would honestly do ANYTHING for anyone even said enemies."

"I wish that people understood that I am a survivor and not always perfect but because I don't want others to feel the way I do so I do my best to hide it."

"When you see me laughing and smiling doesn't mean I'm not falling apart inside."

"That social interaction is exhausting for me."

"That I have a good heart and I am a good person I have changed from the person I was in active addiction quit judging me on my past mistakes and allow me to be the new person I am stop holding me captive in my past."


"That I have a complicated mind... I ask ALOT of questions and tend to overthink."


"My anxiety. That I know they love me but I need reassurance, because I feel people just put up with me to be nice."


"That I do not just speak in metaphors or exaggerations. What I am experiencing is very real. You don't need to understand. Just BELIEVE that I am a whole human being having a very messy human experience and it is messy and painful and beautiful all at once."


"I wish people understood that I may look and act ok but inside I'm healing and I need time to do so."


"I'm not faking how hard it is to live and fight everyday with this mental illness. If I could choose to work like I use to instead of relying on other ppl for my basic needs I wouldn't be begging for disability. It's soooo hard to "prove" mental disability to a judge."


"That my need to care for others comes from a need to be cared for myself. I work in social services because I enjoy helping others. I enjoy helping others because I know the pain and trauma of not being helped myself."

"That I am not a toy. I'm human. That I don't need a knight in shining armor. I need real and raw. I don't love for what can be done for me. I love for who they are at their core no matter how ugly or dark parts of them can be. I wish people would understand that I'm real."

"That even though I am over weight I am worthy. that I am smart, kind, loving and empathetic. That I am beautiful just as I am. Not 'so pretty of you lose weight.'"

"That even though I have a physical disability I'm normal person just like everyone else. I just do things a little differently."

"What I wish people understood is how hard it can be for me to get through each day. To be living in the emotionality inside my head even though things look functional on the outside. Thank you for asking! Bless you!"

"I wish people understood eating disorders aren't a choice or about vanity."

"I have thought about your question and keep coming back to I want people to understand that as much as I like to be there for them they need to show and do the same for me because the last few days I been feeling alone but I can hide it pretty well."

**I also want to recognize the members of our community who engage by reading and reflecting without posting.**

*Your presence is valuable and felt.*

You remind us that there are ways to contribute to a community, with listening and reflecting being forms of participation in themselves.

"Just want to take a moment and let you know that I am very grateful for your messages. They seriously always come when I am needing it. You are an incredible young man who is wise, strong, caring and so much more. TY for taking me step by step on the journey. Keep shining."

Lastly, I offer my appreciation for the sense of community we have built together.

This book proves what can be accomplished when we unite to support the exchange of ideas and grow together. It honors the wisdom, empathy, and resilience embodied by each one of you.

"I love all of the messages you send. I even send them to my family to encourage them from time to time. They really appreciate them just as much as I do. Thank you."

As we continue our journeys together as a community, this book may serve as a reminder of the strength, wisdom, and camaraderie surrounding us.

"Honestly, some days it's nice to just hear that little ding and read your kind words. I am sure there are plenty of ppl who you are the only txt they get in a day. That alone is worth so much, Ryan. ty"

**Cheers to our progress, recovery and bond.**

# Afterword

S O HERE WE ARE the closing pages of this book. During these moments, I sense a tranquil atmosphere enveloping me. The gentle embrace of the chair, the subtle sounds of the creaking wood, and the rhythmic clicks of the keyboard all form a soothing backdrop for my thoughts.

I truly appreciate your presence as you read these words. You are not an observer but an integral part of this narrative. Your role is fundamental in this journey of self-discovery, growth, and transformation. Your engagement brings warmth to these pages quietly yet powerfully.

Your contributions breathe life into these written words. Your empathy, understanding, and shared perspectives transformed my monologue into a dialogue. By experiencing the highs and lows of this story, you make its teachings your own.

Our bond grows stronger through this shared exploration. It enriches our path toward healing and comprehension. This warmth lingers with us, fostering a lasting sensation of togetherness and connection.

At this moment, the room gently blurs into softness. The surroundings fade into shadows around me, creating a sense of tranquility. Outside, the world's buzz quiets down as if absorbed by contemplation.

The air feels calm and charged with anticipation and insight. It seems to hang, listening intently to the weight of my thoughts. The pages before me transform into a connection, bridging the distance between us.

I imagine you, the reader, in your setting. Perhaps you're nestled in an armchair among the comforting scent of books – new. Maybe you find yourself in a café where the background noise fades into a distant murmur as you delve into these words. The aroma of your coffee wafts up with warmth and richness.

Our separate thoughts and emotions begin to intertwine despite our distance. It's like a dance of shared experiences unfolding between us. I can almost sense your breath, hear the gentle rustle of pages turning, and feel your movements as you absorb each word on the page. This fragile, profound connection is forged through words and empathy – to a delicate thread woven through our lives.

This bond guides our self-discovery paths – cutting through uncertainty, like a beacon of understanding.

Acknowledging, we recognize that our journeys diverge; our quest for understanding and authenticity aligns. Within this realm of connection, the tangible reality diminishes. What remains is the tie of mutual encounters and compassion.

As I take a moment to pause, the gentle rhythm of my breath reminds me of the passage of time. Each inhale feels like a caress, while each exhale allows me to release the past. I am truly grateful for your presence on this journey. A warmth begins to fill me, spreading like the light of dawn.

Your involvement and insights illuminate the way for others to tread paths. For this and more, my gratitude knows no bounds.

Remember, your remarkable chapters are still ahead of you. They eagerly await you to take up the pen and craft a tale of achievement, growth and happiness. Your story is an evolving masterpiece. Each day adds layers to it. The scent of ink and paper beckons you to continue creating.

So, gaze forward with hope and anticipation.

The future is yours to mold.

May the excitement of what lies ahead be as enticing as a fragrance, promising marvels.

As we part ways through these words, remember this.

Every step you take paints the canvas of your life. Feel the brush in your hand painting over the canvas with ease. Each stroke mirrors your decisions and encounters.

The future is a book waiting to be written. You are its author, crafting its chapters.

Allow the pages to invigorate you with their possibilities. They serve as a symbol of the canvas awaiting your creativity.

# About the Author

## Author, Mentor, and Guide in Personal Transformation

MEET **Ryan Puusaari**, AN author and creative alchemist dedicated to igniting sparks within others. Ryan is an architect of possibilities, crafting eloquence, creativity, and inspiration into the foundation that bridges the ordinary with the extraordinary.

## Crafting Pathways to Growth

Ryan's work, including his acclaimed *Healing Thoughts Newsletter*, is a testament to his mastery in storytelling and personal development.

His daily messages of hope, delivered through text messages, offer wisdom and comfort, assuring readers of their seen and heard presence in this world.

## Deepening Self-Awareness

Ryan's *365-Day Shadow Work Series* dives into the realms of shadow work, self-awareness, and personal growth. His journal prompts draw from mythological archetypes, ancient wisdom, and his own lived experiences, guiding users through the depths of their unconscious minds.

**To Learn More Visit: WoodIslandBooks.com**

## Digital Media and Mental Health Advocacy

Utilizing platforms like TikTok, Instagram, and YouTube, Ryan transforms digital media into tools for mindfulness and personal growth. His commitment extends to mental health advocacy, drawing from his own experiences to cultivate awareness and unity.

## An Invitation to Transformative Journeys

Ryan's work is an open invitation to welcome life's rhythm, celebrating each step towards self-fulfillment and joy. He envisions a world of empowered individuals united in awakening their latent potential.

**Discover more about Ryan and his mission at RyanPuusaari.com, and join his journey towards healing and self-discovery.**

## Explore Ryan's Literary Contributions

Ryan's books, including the *Trigger Warning Collection* and *My Daily Gratitude Series*, offer guided pathways for shadow work, emotional healing, and gratitude practice. Each book is crafted to facilitate personal growth, self-care, and mindfulness.

**To Learn More Visit: WoodIslandBooks.com**

**Thank you for exploring this journey with Ryan.**
**To explore more please visit: www.RyanPuusaari.com**

# Your Opinion Matters

Y OU MIGHT NOT THINK twice about the importance of leaving a review or comment. It's easy to dismiss them as minor, perhaps even insignificant gestures in the vast ocean of online content.

But for us writers, your feedback is the heartbeat of our creative lives. We pour our hearts into crafting narratives that captivate, inspire, and entertain.

What truly sustains our spirit and fuels our pens?

**Your feedback.**

—ell—

Let me share a personal story.

I remember one chilly autumn evening, I was sitting in my small, dimly-lit study, surrounded by stacks of notebooks and the faint aroma of vanilla from a candle I had lit in an attempt to soothe my frayed nerves.

I had been wrestling with a particularly stubborn chapter for weeks; nothing I wrote seemed to convey the emotion I felt so deeply. Discouragement crept in, making me feel that perhaps my story wasn't worth telling after all.

That's when I noticed a notification for a new email—a notification that seemed as innocuous as any other but it had caught my eye.

It was a reader's review, posted late into the night. The reader wrote about how a scene in my book had mirrored their own life experience, bringing them both comfort and a sense of companionship during a tough time. They thanked me for sharing my world with them, for giving them a place to escape when reality became too heavy.

As I read those words, something shifted within me. The loneliness of the writer's path dissipated slightly, replaced by a warm, invigorating rush of connection. This wasn't just polite applause—it was a lifeline thrown across the digital divide, a reminder of why I had started writing in the first place.

When you take the time to write a review for a book, it's not merely a courteous gesture—it's a powerful surge of motivation for us. It propels us to refine our craft and continue delivering stories that deeply resonate with you.

Your comments are like a lifeline, guiding us through the often-murky waters of creativity. They push us forward, illuminate our strengths, and pinpoint where we can improve.

Every piece of feedback is a reminder of our journey's purpose.

Therefore, the next time you turn the final page of a book that has moved you, stirred your thoughts, or sparked your imagination, I urge you to share your reflections in a review.

Your support is not just appreciated; it's crucial.

It shapes the very essence of our storytelling future.

Let's solidify this partnership between reader and writer.

Your involvement doesn't just help us craft stories—it inspires tales that enchant, uplift, and linger in your memory long after the reading is over.

Below is a review from my latest book that had inspired me to keep creating.

It's a beautiful cycle: we create, you enjoy, and together we enhance this journey, making it richer and more fulfilling for both readers and writers alike.

Let's keep this cycle going, transforming every story into an adventure we embark on together.

**Trigger Warning: A Guided Shadow Work Journal & Workbook for Reparenting Your Emotional Triggers**

"Because the author shares his own struggles throughout the book, the content is very relatable to the reader. You learn quite a bit about WHY we are the way we are, but equally important, you're informed early on that you have the power to change the things that tend to "steamroll over you" without warning.

The process that's outlined (which involves identifying and assessing your own triggers and traumas) is well organized, insightful, and presented in manageable bite-sized sections. The reader is prompted to answer thought-provoking questions and is guided to write about his/her own thoughts and experiences. Every exercise keeps the reader engaged.

I'm only halfway through it, but I already recommended this effective, introspective workbook to a close friend. I am ALREADY enjoying the benefits of the self-healing I've done so far; I'm sure many others will, as well."

-Pam E.

Continuing from that moment, it's not only the writers who benefit from your reviews—other readers do as well.

**Consider this:** as readers explore the vast array of books available online, many rely heavily on reviews to make their reading choices. It's like having a trusted friend guiding them through a crowded bookstore, pointing out hidden gems or cautioning against less engaging reads.

For example, I recall a moment when a reader mentioned in their review how my journal on shadow work and healing trauma helped them uncover hidden aspects of their past.

This comment sparked a wave of interest from others who were on similar healing journeys but might have otherwise overlooked my journal. That single review not only lifted my spirits but also connected my work with an audience that truly appreciated the depth and care I had put into those healing exercises.

Reviews can also create a community around a journal or an author. They start conversations and build connections among readers who share similar passions. When someone writes that a journal's prompts resonated with their own struggles or triumphs, it invites others to reflect on their experiences and share them. This shared connection can be incredibly powerful, turning individual reflection into a communal experience.

Also, honest reviews help paint a fuller picture of a book. They highlight aspects that may resonate differently with various readers, helping potential readers gauge whether a book might be right for them. Whether it's praising the depth of character development or offering a critical view on the pacing of the plot, each review contributes to a richer, more nuanced understanding of the book.

So, the next time you close a book that has moved you or provoked thought, remember that your review does more than support the author. It becomes a roadmap for other readers, guiding them in their choices and cultivating a community of shared insights and experiences.

In sharing our thoughts and reflections, we not only support the creators of these works but also help each other as readers work their way through the expansive and ever-changing landscape of literature.

Let's continue to support this ecosystem of reading and writing with our honest and thoughtful feedback. Together, we create a world where every story finds its audience, and every reader finds their next great adventure.

**Please take a moment to leave a review of this book, *Healing Thoughts*, on your preferred retailer's website. Your feedback means the world to me and helps others discover the healing journey this book offers.**

In the quiet, I stand,
heart heavy, words trapped.
Every breath a struggle,
every thought a storm.

She moves through shadows,
a ghost in the dark,
unseen, unheard,
lost where light never reaches.

My cries go unnoticed,
a plea drowned in silence,
her presence a haunting,
my loneliness, a prison.

In this darkness,
I see her,
a soul yearning,
a heart crying out.

My heart aches,
trapped in silence,
every beat a burden,
every breath a wound.

Behind her smile,
a hidden world of pain,
silent screams,
tears that never fall.

Laughter masks her cries,
joy a fragile façade,
inside, she fights demons,
invisible to all.

I see her struggle,
her unseen wounds,
and in her shadows,
I find my own.

My spirit is torn,
broken and battered,
each day a struggle,
each breath a fight.

I see her,
a mirror of pain,
scars telling stories,
battles endured,
hope slipping away.

In her eyes,
a world cold and distant,
love misplaced,
warmth forgotten.

We share this silent grief,
a bond of unseen wounds,
both seeking solace,
both longing for peace.

I tried to call out to her,
but trauma stole my voice,
invisible chains grip my throat,
words suffocated, cries unheard.

Behind a mask of calm, I hide,
a façade to shield my shattered self.
My words, a sea of stars,
unreachable,
caught in the orbit of an untamed heart,
yearning for escape.

She is near, yet so far,
blind to the storm within me,
oblivious to the silent screams
of a heart desperate
to bridge the divide.

But the words suffocate,
unborn,
the chasm between us a universe,
my love, a ghost,
watching over depths too vast to navigate.

I was dying for someone to say
that I didn't need to try so hard
to be perfect,
to say the right thing,
that I was enough,
that it was okay.

In a world that demands perfection,
I longed for reassurance,
for validation that I was worthy
just as I am.

And eventually, I stopped trying,
stopped hoping,
stopped believing
that things will ever be better.

I surrendered to the bleakness,
to the darkness that swallowed me,
and I accepted it as my reality.

The flicker of hope that once burned bright
was extinguished, leaving only ashes in its wake.
I resigned myself to the idea that this is all there is,
that I am destined to languish in this endless night.

Little did I know she was in the same boat,
at times, feeling the urge to vanish.
Yet deep down, she craved to be acknowledged,
to be valued,
to be accepted,
to be held.

She longed to be noticed for who she truly was.
As she looked up into the moonlight, she wondered,
*"Does anyone see me?*
*Will anyone ever get me?"*

As I drove through the night,
the urge to look up at the setting moon strikes.
As if I can hear her calls,
crying out in the cool night air.

In the stillness,
two hearts beat in silent symphony,
each unaware of the other's presence,
yet bound by this invisible connection.

A single star flickers,
a shimmer of hope in the night sky,
and maybe, just maybe,
our paths will converge,
and we will find comfort
in the shared understanding
of our silent suffering.

For in the quiet, we stand,
hearts heavy, words trapped,
but together, perhaps,
we can find the strength
to shatter the silence,
to let our voices be heard,
and to heal.

I remember the darkness, the weight of loneliness,
walls built high around my heart, impenetrable,
every attempt to reach out, stifled,
every gesture of kindness, met with suspicion.

Then she came, a gentle presence,
her touch, a feeling of hope,
her smile, a flicker of warmth,
slowly, patiently, she broke through my defenses.

She saw me, really saw me,
beyond the pain and the silence,
her eyes, a reflection of understanding,
her kindness, a bridge to a world I had forgotten.

She reached into the shadows,
pulled me into the light,
not with force, but with unwavering compassion,
each act, a step toward freedom.

In her presence, I found my voice,
my heart, once heavy, began to lighten,
the walls crumbled,
the chains fell away.

Through her, I learned to trust,
to let go of the fear that bound me,
to believe that I could be seen,
and that it was enough.

I used to think I had to be perfect,
every flaw hidden, every wound healed.
But then you took my hand,
showed me that it wasn't true.

We walk together now,
imperfect, healing, but always moving forward.
You don't need me to be whole,
just willing to try, to understand.

Hand in hand, we face the world,
our steps sometimes faltering, yet always in sync.
In your eyes, I see acceptance,
in your heart, I find peace.

We don't need to be flawless,
just committed to the journey,
welcoming each moment of growth,
cherishing the connection we share.

Together, we stand, unguarded and true,
our voices, a testament to our bond,
a reminder that perfection is a myth,
and understanding is our strength.

# Don't Miss Out

## Subscribe to the Newsletter

Be sure to subscribe to our free weekly newsletter to stay up to date on future releases. **Visit HealingThoughts.com to sign up now.**

Don't miss out! Hook yourself up with our free weekly newsletter and stay in the loop on all the upcoming goodies.